V
S
Y

FitzGerald
to his Friends

Selected letters of Edward FitzGerald

Edited with an introduction by
Alethea Hayter

London: Scolar Press 1979

197707

Published by Scolar Press,
39 Great Russell Street, London WC1B 3PH

Printed in Great Britain by
The Scolar Press, Ilkley, West Yorkshire

Hardback ISBN 0 85967 400 2
Paperback ISBN 0 85967 499 1

Contents

List of Illustrations

Endpapers
Edward FitzGerald as an undergraduate. Pencil drawing
by James Spedding. (*Fitzwilliam Museum, Cambridge*)

Edward FitzGerald in old age. Watercolour, artist unknown. (*National Portrait Gallery*)

Introduction

'I am astonished to find myself writing a very long letter once a week to you: but it is next to talking to you: and after having seen you so much this summer, I cannot break off suddenly,' wrote Edward FitzGerald to his friend John Allen. His letters are continued conversations. Some letters read like diaries – they are not really communications at all, but overheard soliloquies. Others read like manifestos or company reports, addressed to a general audience, not to any individual. But the best letters are neither too private nor too public; they imply a response, but from one particular person.

FitzGerald said that writing a letter was 'next to talking to you', but in his case it was really better than talking to his friends. Some men, even if they are professional writers, are – like Coleridge, for example – far more interesting in conversation than in their letters. But FitzGerald's letters are what he would have liked to have said in conversation. He suffered from *l'esprit de l'escalier*; it was only when he was alone, and had had time to reflect, that he really knew what he thought and felt and wanted to say.

The writing and receiving of letters was the peak of his emotional experience. 'I suppose that people who are engaged in serious ways of life, and are of well filled minds, don't think much about the interchange of letters with any anxiety: but I am an idle fellow, of a very ladylike turn of sentiment: and my friendships are more like loves, I think.' He felt most alive, most himself, when writing letters, more than when he was with other people. The act of writing letters provided just enough communication with other human beings to enliven and freshen his own solitary intellectual life, it stimulated him to a 'gathering up of feelings', it tossed and aerated his thoughts as hay-makers tossed hay. But it still protected him from the fullness of human contact which he feared. He was afraid of giving himself away, of proving inadequate, of disappointing people, afraid also of being disappointed or bored or chilled; and he was unable to summon up the presence of mind for the *bons mots*, the 'ceaseless collision of beaux esprits', that the life of society demanded. So he constructed for himself a strange protective way of life, an increasing withdrawal from the company of his intellectual equals, even when they were loved and loving friends. Instead he satisfied his need – never very strong – for human company by consorting with the intellectually undemanding: with convivial commonplace country neighbours, with his unsophisticated sister and her children, with Lowestoft fishermen, with the boy readers-aloud whom he paid to stumble through his favourite books. With such company he shared none of the intellectual preoccupations which were at the centre of his life and found expression in his letters. Company of this kind suited him best precisely because it was undemanding; he recognized early in life and with complete clear-sightedness that he had a 'talent for dullness'. He did not justify his way of life; he called it idle, irresponsible, childish; but it suited him best, and at least did no harm to anyone else, whereas his rare attempts to accept responsibility for others ended in disaster.

All the vitality, the warmth, the wit, the tact and sympathy, the taste and discrimination, the deep thoughts, which FitzGerald kept bottled up from most of his daily life, he poured into his letters. This was his real self, this was what made his friends devoted to him, what made both Tennyson and Thackeray, when they had hardly seen him for decades, still put him at the top of the list of friends they loved and trusted most. He was choicely equipped for friendship, since he was never boring, never pompous, never clumsy, never demanding. All his friends wanted to see more of him than he would concede. Most of them treasured his letters; thousands are extant, many of them still unpublished.

Edward FitzGerald was the seventh child of John Purcell, who changed his name when he married an heiress, Mary Frances FitzGerald. The family owned many properties in England and Ireland, but lived mainly in Suffolk; at the time of Edward's birth, on 31 March 1809, they were living in a rented house, a substantial Jacobean mansion, at Bredfield, near Woodbridge. His father was a sanguine un-businesslike man, fond of sport; his mother was proud, handsome, rather cold-hearted, preferring London life and society; neither took much notice of their children. FitzGerald's relations with his two elder brothers, John and Peter, were rather detached, though they never lost touch altogether, and he was fond of John's wife Augusta. Of his four surviving sisters he loved best the second, Eleanor, who married John Kerrich, but the strangely named Andalusia, the eldest sister, nicknamed Lusia, also appears fairly often in his letters.

In 1816 the FitzGerald family went to France, and spent two years at Saint-Germain-en-Laye and then Paris. When they returned to England in 1818, FitzGerald was sent to the King Edward VI Grammar School at Bury St. Edmunds, an excellent school where he was happy on the whole but only erratically industrious, and where he made two lifelong friends, William Bodham Donne and James Spedding. In 1824 his family moved to Wherstead Lodge, near Ipswich, and in 1826 he went to Cambridge. He was at Trinity, but lived in digs in King's Parade throughout his pleasant Cambridge career, during which he made more friends for life: John Allen, W. H. Thompson, and above all, Thackeray. Friendship, not love, was to be the strongest emotional experience of his life. He did contemplate marriage a few years later in 1836, but his very tepid descriptions of the lady make it clear that no passion was involved, and nothing came of it. He had a low opinion of women's intellectual powers; he could not be quite fair to the achievements of contemporary women writers such as Jane Austen, Charlotte Brontë, George Eliot and Elizabeth Barrett Browning, and his letters are sprinkled with anti-feminist sentiments; he appreciated only submissive home-keeping women.

FitzGerald never took up – never even contemplated taking up – any profession. He had a sufficient income on which to live in the way that suited him best, and no ambition or sedulity. He spent the first seven years after he left Cambridge in moving around staying with his relations and friends in English country houses, occasionally helping his father over estate business or escorting his mother and sisters to theatres and visits. Constantly on the move, he never travelled far; he detested the actual business of journeys, the packing and timetables and general upset, he mistrusted picturesque sites beloved of tourists, and he was rather jingoistic about the inferiority of countries other than his own. The sum-total of his lifetime travel was a few visits to Paris and brief sorties to the Low Countries and Germany.

But in these years, and to some extent throughout his life, he would come up to London at least once a year, live in lodgings, see Thackeray and Spedding and three new friends who became important to him – Alfred Tennyson, his brother Frederick, and Thomas Carlyle – and have an orgy of art exhibitions, theatres and operas. His taste in painting was for the serenely grand – Raphael, Titian,

Claude, Poussin – and for Rembrandt; he could not abide what seemed to him strained and over-emphatic – Rubens and Veronese, for instance – or nigglingly detailed, like his contemporaries Holman Hunt and Frith. He was a collector of pictures, a haunter of dealers, a friend of several painters, and himself a sketcher. He loved the theatre, too, and had an acute ear and memory for individual actors' interpretations of his favourite Shakespearean roles. But of all the arts music was, next to literature, the one that meant most to him. He himself sang and composed songs, played the piano and the organ, and in his letters he often described operas and concerts he had just attended, and subtly compared the qualities of Handel, Mozart and Beethoven, whom he loved, as he did 'the old God save the King style: the common chords, those truisms of music, like other truisms so little understood in the full'. He was curious but critical about contemporary composers; only Mendelssohn won occasional praise.

After such a spell in London, FitzGerald would return to the country with his intellect stimulated and re-charged by what he had seen and heard and by the conversation of his brilliant friends, but with a feeling that he was being left behind in the race; he felt, though, that he really preferred not to run it at all, but to go on strolling about before the starting-point. So he would make long visits to the Kerrich family at Geldestone, to watch his sister knitting, to hear his Tory brother-in-law snoring over an agricultural treatise, and to romp with the children in the sandpit. He would spend long lazy weeks, too, fishing and sitting in pubs with William Kenworthy Browne, a cheerful unintellectual young man whom he had met in 1833 and of whom for the next twenty years he saw more than of any other friend. In 1837 he sent down deeper roots into the country by moving into a cottage of his own outside the park gates of Boulge Hall, near Woodbridge, to which his family had moved a year earlier. He had little interest in comfort, and his cottage was damp, ill-equipped and desperately untidy. The few old neighbours whom he invited there to smoke and drink grog were given rather comfortless and disorganized meals. FitzGerald himself had been a vegetarian since 1833; he lived on bread and butter, cheese, fruit, tea, radishes, and an occasional milk-pudding, though his guests were given meat.

FitzGerald was not yet thirty, but he had already begun the habits and the complete disregard of convention and public opinion which were to make him notorious for eccentricity in his later life. His natural appearance was prepossessing – he was six feet tall, with bright blue eyes, a sunburnt complexion, rather rugged features, a dimpled chin, and bushy eyebrows. But he went partly bald and his hair turned grey in his early thirties, he put on weight and began to stoop, and he was most peculiar in his dress – not unfastidious or dirty, he had his clothes well made out of good cloth, but he wore them for a long time, and oddly combined. At home he would be found sitting in a dressing-gown, with slippered feet in the fender and a top hat on his head; out of doors he might be seen in a baggy blue suit, a flowered satin waistcoat, a green and black plaid shawl, a hat tied on with a handkerchief, and bare feet. Loose-fitting ease was his only criterion for clothes – sometimes not even that; once when he fell overboard into Lowestoft harbour, he refused to change his clothes after being fished out, but lay down in the scuppers and let the sea wash over him because he 'couldn't get any wetter'.

He could be silent, uncomfortable, and even haughty and repressive with strangers; he sometimes maddened his friends by his elusiveness, his failure to keep appointments; he hardly ever attended any formal ceremony or event, not even the funerals of his own family and close friends; but he was not a recluse, cut off from human contacts. If some of his neighbours found him odd, brusque, even slightly mad, others were devoted to him and visited him often, and all his servants liked him. 'So kind he was, not never one to make no obstacles. Such a joky gentleman he was too,' was the verdict of his last housekeeper, Mrs. Howe. He was a generous alms-giver, in thoughtful individual ways such as paying for seaside holidays for a young man tied to uncongenial London work. Concerned at the privations of agricultural labourers in the hungry forties, he gave small weekly allowances to many of the surrounding cottagers. He disclaimed any interest in politics, but there are quite a lot of comments on current affairs in his letters. He was not in sympathy with the popular ideals of his day; he regretted the industrialization, the imperial expansion, and the population explosion of nineteenth-century England. 'Would that we were a little, peaceful, unambitious, trading Nation, like – the Dutch!' was his prayer. He combined a fervent admiration for England's past achievements and essential character with pessimism about her immediate future, but he still felt an insular conviction that all other nations were not so blest. His comments on foreign affairs, quirky and sometimes superficial – as in his contempt for French political achievements, and his comment on the Austrian domination of Italy, that 'Only people who deserve despotism are forced to suffer it' – show that international affairs did not really impinge on his inner mind where true judgements were formed.

If politics remained on the periphery of his attention, religion penetrated his inmost consciousness. He thought much about theological and liturgical matters, and studied the works of the great Anglican divines. He longed for full belief, but he did not achieve it; he was really an agnostic, though for much of his life he was a regular church-goer, preferring Evangelical forms of worship and deploring what he regarded as the ritualistic excesses of the Tractarian Movement. He seems to have felt a kind of devotion to Christ as a person, but he enjoyed none of the consolations of religion. His agnosticism made him a sympathetic interpreter of Omar Khayyam, but his 'doubts' increased his isolation from his country neighbours.

FitzGerald had his periods of gloom about the human condition and destiny, his 'blue devils' of depression and melancholy, but he was not a generally unhappy man, or his letters would not make such genial reading as they do. For every 'blue devil' passage in the letters, there are half a dozen which exhale contentment and even joy. He captures a moment of sunshine and birdsong in a garden with a lively book, or a meal of bread and cheese and beer with rough companionable sailors as his yacht skims along the Suffolk coast, or the shiver of anticipation as the curtain goes up on a splendid stage set to the sound of a stately Handel overture. Next to friendship and to literature, his keenest and most limpid enjoyment was of natural beauty. The landscape he preferred was not the picturesquely wild beauty-spot – Loch Lomond and the Rhine Valley left him cold – but a smiling inhabited countryside with a farm or a church spire beyond the fields, small streams, clumps of oaks or poplars, hedges skirted with violets, the smell of gorse blowing across an open heath, an inquisitive robin watching from an ivy stump; a range of hills on the horizon, perhaps, but more important to him were the wide skies and piled clouds of East Anglia, and the ever-present sense of the neighbouring sea, on which he was to spend so much of his later years. His letters were so full of the flowers coming out in his garden and the birds he had heard on his long daily walks that one of his correspondents, Frederick Tennyson, forbade him to mention his garden again; but his impressionistic sketches of light and weather and growth in the country around him give a freshness and sheen to his letters.

The main business of FitzGerald's life, though, was reading. He read even in the garden or on the deck of his yacht, all through the summer; and when the damp and frigid East Anglian winter set in, he sat with his feet in the fender and read all day long. Sometimes he accused himself of being an unsystematic reader, who could not concentrate properly and found his thoughts always wandering. But if he was vain of anything, it was of his taste in literature; he was convinced that his taste was true, adult, perspicacious, uninfluenced by fashion; he felt that he could speak for the best part of the permanent general public. His comments on the books he was reading, of which his letters are full, are not quite as judicial and objective as this claim suggests, or they would not make such good reading, they would become literary criticism instead of letters. They are warmly personal; he was apt to be involved and carried away by what he read, and to enjoy and write about the company of characters in books – above all of his much-loved Don Quixote – as though they were living friends actually with him as he wrote. His very wide reading – of Greek, Latin, Persian, French and Spanish classics, as well as of English poetry, history, theology, biography, letters – cannot be fully represented in a selection of his own letters, but these will be seen to be concerned, more often than with any other subject, with his devotions and dislikes in the literature of the past, and his watchful and sometimes disapproving attention to the works of his contemporaries, Wordsworth, Tennyson, Thackeray, Dickens, Trollope and Carlyle, about whom he relates anecdotes which have been the prize of biographers ever since. His critical insights on Blake, on Keats, on Jeremy Taylor, on Samuel Richardson, were much ahead of his time. His judgements were sometimes cranky and perverse, but never boring; his delight and indignation, his keen observation of his own reactions, have a quite individual intonation, whether he is extolling his favourite Montaigne and Madame de Sévigné, or comparing Aeschylus and Sophocles.

It will seem strange to have said so much about Fitz-Gerald's life and opinions without yet mentioning what made his name known to the world, and alone caused his letters to be published: his own writings. But these make so slight a show in his own letters that if all mention of them were omitted, the letters would not be much the poorer. If his own writings were closest of all to his heart, he did not reveal this in his letters to his friends or his publisher, not even to Edward Cowell, the friend whom he made in middle life and who inspired him to undertake the Persian and Spanish studies which led to the translations on which his fame rests. He was a late starter; he was forty before his first piece of prose, a memoir of Bernard Barton, was published. In the next few years his *Euphranor: a Dialogue on Youth*, an anthology called *Polonius*, and translations of six Calderón plays and of the Persian allegorical poem *Salaman and Absal* followed. His only celebrated work, his translation of the *Rubaiyat* of Omar Khayyam, appeared in 1859, but at first attracted almost no attention; it was not till late in his life that it began to be widely read and admired in England and America. His later translations from Aeschylus and Sophocles, and his selection from Crabbe's poetry, also passed almost unobserved, and his fine translation of the Persian poem *The Bird Parliament* remained unpublished at his death. The literary output of this supposedly indolent man was thus considerable, and involved hard study of hard languages. But in his letters he always made light of his own literary powers and achievements; the references to them are rueful, deprecating, and rare.

When FitzGerald was nearly fifty, he made the great mistake of his life – his only attempt to behave by conventional standards utterly alien to the strange but well-fitting way of life he had formed for himself. He had enjoyed a ten-year friendship with a man much older than himself, the Quaker poet Bernard Barton, who lived at Woodbridge and often visited FitzGerald at Boulge. When Barton was dying, he asked FitzGerald to look after his daughter Lucy, to whom he had almost nothing to leave. FitzGerald interpreted this as meaning he was to make financial provision for Miss Barton, which he duly offered her after her father's death. Her propriety was affronted by this, and FitzGerald was so appalled at having offended her delicacy that he thought he was bound to make the only reparation in his power by offering her marriage, which to his horror she accepted; she had in fact understood the death-bed promise to her father as implying this.

At this time the fortunes of FitzGerald and his family were endangered by his father's mining speculations, which ended in bankruptcy in 1848. FitzGerald had to retrench his expenses, and to spend much time in distasteful business interviews on his own and his family's behalf, but his income, which came mainly from his mother's fortune, was not permanently impaired; however, the temporary financial uncertainty made it reasonable to postpone the unpromising marriage for some years.

By 1856 he felt that he could no longer delay honouring his promise, and he and Lucy Barton were married in November of that year. FitzGerald is reported to have been visibly wrapped in gloom throughout the ceremony, and to have made only one remark: when he was offered blancmange at the wedding breakfast, he waved it away with the exclamation, 'Ugh! congealed bridesmaid!'.

Lucy Barton was a few months older than her husband, who after their marriage tended to refer to her as 'The Elder'. She was a tall robust heavy-featured woman with a striding walk. She was sociable and popular, a good though fussy housekeeper who liked her meat underdone, which revolted the vegetarian FitzGerald. She was a good-tempered and well-meaning woman; but she had resolved to tidy up FitzGerald's appearance and habits, and turn him into a respectable householder (he had given up Boulge Cottage three years earlier, and had no settled home at this time) and a genial host at conventional dinner-parties. FitzGerald however had no intention of changing his chosen way of life. His wife's attempts to remodel him had the power to make him miserable, but not the power to make him change. They had an unhappy honeymoon at Brighton, lived in London lodgings for a few months, parted for a little and then took lodgings at Yarmouth; but by August 1857 it had become clear that the marriage was a total failure, and they separated for good, FitzGerald making his wife a generous allowance.

Little of all this appears in the letters. To a few close friends FitzGerald admitted, both before and after the marriage, that it was unworkable, a doomed experiment, but to most people he baldly announced that he was getting married, and nine months later and equally baldly, that he and his wife had separated. Thereafter he rarely referred to the marriage, and when he did, it was to put most of the blame on himself.

The late 1850s were years of unhappiness for FitzGerald. His marriage had been a catastrophe, and though it was now over, he reproached himself (and was regarded with disfavour by some of his Suffolk neighbours) for his share in its failure and termination. He had no home, but shifted about staying with friends or in lodgings. His friends the Cowells were far away in India; he missed them greatly, and was worried about their safety during the Mutiny. He lost his old friend George Crabbe, son of the poet and Rector of Bredfield. A much worse loss came in 1859 when William Browne, still quite a young man, died from injuries in a riding accident. Lonely and miserable, FitzGerald wandered about the beaches at Yarmouth and Lowestoft, watching the fishermen and their boats, and from these wanderings grew a new interest and a new friendship which were to shape the next ten years of his life.

The interest was sailing. He began with a little boat to sail on the river Deben; two years later, in 1863, he had a sea-going yacht, the *Scandal*, built for him; by 1867 he was part-owner of a Lowestoft herring-lugger. More and more of every summer was spent at sea, mostly off the Suffolk coast, though he occasionally took his yacht to France or Holland. His company was now mainly that of the crew of his yacht, and of the master of the herring-lugger which he had built and part-owned. This man, Joseph Fletcher, known as Posh, was at the centre of FitzGerald's emotional life for years after their first meeting in 1864.

The question of whether FitzGerald was homosexual cannot be simply ignored, but if he had such tendencies, he himself was quite unaware of them – his letters make that clear. The naïveté with which he praised the noble character, and even the manly beauty, of Posh Fletcher and William Browne, in letters to other friends of both sexes (including Browne's wife), shows that he can have had no idea he was revealing anything unusual, let alone anything dangerous to be told. Equally innocent was his description of himself as ladylike in his sentiments, with friendships that were more like loves. His more sophisticated friends may have regretted such expressions, and have wished to rescue him from Posh Fletcher; some of the inhabitants of Lowestoft seem to have mocked his infatuation with the fisherman; but he himself was perfectly open and guileless about it. Posh himself seems to have been embarrassed, fond of FitzGerald but also impatient and contemptuous, and very ready to profit financially from the friendship. FitzGerald was perhaps duped, certainly in the end disillusioned, but his years with Posh gave him a great deal of consolation and fun.

Three years after parting from his wife, FitzGerald had settled in lodgings in the centre of the Suffolk town of Woodbridge, and these remained his home for fourteen years. He terminated his lugger partnership with Posh Fletcher in 1870, and in the last decade of his life his restlessness and anxiety subsided into a more tranquil melancholy, faintly spangled with small habitual pleasures. He bought, and began building onto, a cottage on the outskirts of Woodbridge. His taste in architecture was for the gables and clustered chimneys of seventeenth-century manor houses, not for the great Palladian palaces of the eighteenth century; houses like Hampton Court, or Helmingham, or Wimpole, or his own childhood home at Bredfield, appealed to him most, and his own modest house, Little Grange, was in this style. He did not actually move into it till 1874, but it had been finished long before, and he had gradually filled it with the quaint intricate furniture and bric-à-brac that he liked – oriental tables and boxes, old-fashioned chairs, statuettes, pictures of doubtful attribution in heavy gold frames. In every room there were shelves and cupboards full of books – some with five-pound notes slipped between their pages and forgotten – mostly bound in green with bright red labels, for he loved bright colours: the red and gold splendours of a cock's plumage, the red dress and cloak which he made his house-keeper Mrs. Howe wear, above all the gay colours of his flower-garden. Orange was his favourite colour, so he loved nasturtiums and marigolds best; but he also loved the jewelled brightness of poppies and anemones and morning glory, and sweet-smelling wallflowers and pinks and mignonette, and his garden at Little Grange blazed with close-packed colours. Along one side was an elm hedge, with a walk beside it which he called his 'quarter-deck' – he could step onto it from the French window of his study, and halfway along it there was a summerhouse where he sometimes sat and regaled his friends with whisky.

He was now in his sixties, and his circle was contracting; he lost his parents in the 1850s, his best-loved sister, Eleanor Kerrich, and Thackeray in 1863, and later Carlyle, Spedding and Donne. But he made new and younger friends – the painters Edwin Edwards and Charles Keene, Aldis Wright the Librarian of Trinity; he acquired some stimulating new correspondents, the American writers Charles Eliot Norton and James Russell Lowell and the actress and author Fanny Kemble; he kept in touch with the children of old friends, with the Browne children and Mowbray Donne and the younger George Crabbe, and his Kerrich nieces stayed at Little Grange for months every summer; old friends like Cowell and Thompson – once even Tennyson – came to visit him, and he still sometimes went to London, though more often to Aldeburgh or Lowestoft.

Perhaps the old friends with whom he now spent most time, though, were friends in books; Walter Scott's characters were more than ever delightful to him, and letters and memoirs of all kinds from Madame de Sévigné to Carlyle. His eyesight was now failing, and he had to employ schoolboys to read aloud to him, and to put up with the weird blunders they made. In the last years of his life he was still doing translations from the Greek, and planning abridgements to interest the public in his favourites Richardson and Crabbe. Himself a lifelong commonplace-book-keeper, selector and abridger of other men's works, he would not have disapproved of a selection being made from his own letters. He did not like them to be shown round in his lifetime, and he condemned over-hasty publications containing references to men still alive, but his comments on memoirs and letters of his contemporaries, from Keats to Carlyle, show that he approved of even the most intimate records being published eventually, so long as it was not done in malice.

By the 1870s his *Rubaiyat* translation had achieved some celebrity (even to the extent of being pirated in India, as he boasted with amusement), and had gone into a third edition, though it was not widely known that he was the author.

The letters of his last years sound mellow and almost contented, but he was ready to die, hoping only for a quick and merciful death. This hope was fulfilled; he died in his sleep on 13 June 1883, when he had just arrived on a visit to congenial old friends.

Thackeray called FitzGerald his 'best and oldest friend'. Tennyson said: 'I had no truer friend: he was one of the kindliest of men, and I have never known one of so fine and delicate a wit.' Spedding called him 'the Prince of Quietists . . . his tranquillity is like a pirated copy of the peace of God. Truly he is a most comfortable companion'; but to Donne he was 'Diogenes without the dirt'. His was not a transparent or homogeneous character. Many readers will never have heard of him except as the translator of Omar Khayyam, and their idea of him, if they have any, will be identified with the sceptical all-too-quotable Persian under the bough with his jug of wine and his singing mistress. FitzGerald was a much more complex and less blatant personality than that, and a much more likeable one, with all his crotchets and withdrawals. In his letters, with their idiosyncratic punctuation and capital letters, their spontaneities of syntax, a voice is audible – like his own speaking voice which sounded 'like a cricket-ball, with a break on it, or like his own favourite image of the wave falling over' – which, once heard, is unforgettable.

Note on Sources and Text

The letters which follow are quoted from the following published collections of FitzGerald's letters or biographies of him. The abbreviations are those used at the head of each letter to indicate its source.

Blyth = *Edward FitzGerald and 'Posh', 'Herring Merchants'*, James Blyth, John Long, London, 1908.

F.F. = *A FitzGerald Friendship, Being Hitherto Unpublished Letters from Edward FitzGerald to William Bodham Donne*, ed. N. C. Hannay, Faber & Faber, London, 1932.

F.K. = *Letters of Edward FitzGerald to Fanny Kemble, 1871–1883*, ed. W. A. Wright, Bentley, London, 1895.

Glyde = *The Life of Edward FitzGerald*, John Glyde, C. A. Pearson, London, 1900.

Groome = *Edward FitzGerald, an Aftermath*, F. H. Groome, T. B. Mosher, Portland, Maine, 1902.

L.F. = *Letters of Edward FitzGerald*, 2 vols., ed. W. A. Wright, Macmillan, London, 1894.

M.L. = *More Letters of Edward FitzGerald*, ed. W. A. Wright, Macmillan, London, 1901.

N.L. = *Some New Letters of Edward FitzGerald*, ed. F. R. Barton, Williams and Norgate, London, 1923.

Quaritch = *Edward FitzGerald. Letters to Bernard Quaritch, 1853–1883*, ed. C. Q. Wrentmore, Bernard Quaritch, London, 1926.

H. Tennyson = *Tennyson and His Friends*, Hallam Tennyson, Macmillan, London, 1911.

Terhune = *The Life of Edward FitzGerald, Translator of the Rubaiyat of Omar Khayyam*, A. M. Terhune, Oxford University Press, Oxford, 1947.

W.B.D.F. = *William Bodham Donne and His Friends*, ed.

Catherine Johnson, Methuen, London, 1905.
Wright = *The Life of Edward FitzGerald*, 2 vols., Thomas
Wright, Grant Richards, London, 1904.

The most authoritative biography of FitzGerald is Alfred
McKinley Terhune's 1947 volume (see above). Other
books on FitzGerald include:
Benson, A. C., *Edward FitzGerald*, Macmillan, London,
1905.
Blyth, James, *Edward FitzGerald and 'Posh'* (see above).
Glyde, John, *The Life of Edward FitzGerald* (see above).
Richardson, Joanna, *Edward FitzGerald*, Longmans Green,
London, 1960.
Wright, Thomas, *The Life of Edward FitzGerald* (see above).

In the following selection of FitzGerald's letters, brief
biographies of his main correspondents are given in the
headnote to the first letter to each correspondent; heavy
type in the index indicates the page-number of such
biographical notes. The main outline and dates of Fitz-
Gerald's life are given in the Introduction; the headnotes
to each letter explain topical references to persons or events.
Passages omitted from letters are indicated by the usual
row of dots. FitzGerald's unusual punctuation, and
occasional archaisms of spelling such as 'eat' for 'ate',
'staid' for 'stayed', have been preserved.

Acknowledgements

Permission to quote from nine otherwise unpublished letters by Edward FitzGerald which were included in *The Life of Edward FitzGerald: Translator of Omar Khayyam* by the late Alfred McKinley Terhune has kindly been given by Mrs A. M. Terhune, to whom I am most grateful.

I am also most grateful to Folcroft Library Editions for permission to quote from the texts of seven letters first published in *A FitzGerald Friendship*, edited by N. C. Hannay.

Letters of Edward FitzGerald

1 To John Allen
L.F., I, 4–5   Paris. May, 1830

After taking his degree at Cambridge early in 1830, FitzGerald went to Paris with Thackeray; before his return he gave a prophetic sketch of his future way of life to John Allen, who had been at Cambridge with him and remained a lifelong friend. Allen became a clergyman; after a period of lecturing in mathematics at King's College London, he held a living near Shrewsbury and eventually became Archdeacon of Salop.

I start for England in a week, as I purpose now: I shall go by Havre de Grace and Southampton, and stay for a month or two perhaps at Dartmouth, a place on the Devonshire coast. Tell Thackeray that he is never to invite me to his house, as I intend never to go: not that I would not go out there rather than any place perhaps, but I cannot stand seeing new faces in the polite circles. You must know that I am going to become a great bear: and have got all sorts of Utopian ideas into my head about society: these may all be very absurd, but I try the experiment on myself, so I can do no great hurt. Where I shall go in the summer I know not.

2 To William Bodham Donne
F.F., 1–3   Geldestone. October 6, 1830(?)

Geldestone Hall, Norfolk, was the home of FitzGerald's favourite sister, Eleanor, who was married to John Kerrich and had two sons and eight daughters. FitzGerald stayed there for long periods every year. W. B. Donne and FitzGerald became friends during their schooldays at King Edward VI School, Bury St Edmunds. At this time Donne was living at Mattishall, in Norfolk, where FitzGerald often stayed with him. The friendship lasted till Donne's death. Donne later became Librarian of the London Library, and then Examiner and Licenser of Plays in the Lord Chamberlain's Office. He was also a reviewer and editor, and a notable letter-writer.

I have been intending to write to you for some days past: & now I am vexed that I have not, seeing that the days slip away so, and that I am so soon about to leave this place. For I wanted to ask you to come over here & see me for a day or two: and I do heartily ask you to do so now. We don't leave here till the 14th of this month: surely you can come for a day. I should be sorry to leave the country without seeing you again, as I dont know when I may be back. Present my compliments to Mrs Donne & beg her in my name, and I hope with your own desire to back it, to spare you for a very little time. I know you are somewhat shy of strangers: but you need be in no fear here: for we are homely people; and don't put ourselves out of the way: and so if you can put up with dining off a joint of meat at ½ past one with us and the Children, and can stand an occasional din of the same Children romping in the passage, I think you have no excuse at all. I dont speak of entertaining you, or shewing you sights, which I think is a poor compliment to a man: here are books, & you may do as you please . . . You must come up to London this winter, Donne: we will get abroad in that sinful place, & be very profane indeed. But it is the first part of my letter which you are now to think of: and yet I wish you would think but once, & slap your thigh, & say 'Damme, if I wont'.

3 To William Makepeace Thackeray

Terhune, 57–8, 68–9   Geldestone. October 11, 1831

FitzGerald and Thackeray became friends when they were at Trinity College, Cambridge, which they both left in 1830. What follows is part of a very long journal letter of four foolscap pages, some of it written late at night after drinking port. It is a spontaneous outpouring of religious speculation, poetic stanzas, literary criticism, self-scrutiny, wild high spirits, affection, and sheer nonsense. In later life FitzGerald, finding some of these 'old foolscap letters' between himself and Thackeray, felt ashamed of their 'kindness' and burnt many of them. This one began by saying that he had got over all his doubts about Christianity except that he could not find the evidence for Christ's miracles convincing. The fear which he expressed later in the letter that his friends would find him less impressive in person than in correspondence partly explains his later reluctance to meet even those he loved best and wrote to most faithfully. The final paragraph is the first of many revelations of his scorn of any feminist pretension to equality with men.

. . . Religious people are very angry with one for doubting: and say, 'You come to the question determined to doubt, not to be convinced'. Certainly we do: having seen how many follow and have followed false religions, and having our reason utterly against many of the principal points of the Bible, we require the most perfect evidence of facts, before we can believe. If you can prove to me that one miracle took place, I will believe that he is a just God who damned us all because a woman eat an apple; and you can't expect greater complaisance than that, to be sure.

You are wrong, my dear Thackeray, in fancying that Christ does not call himself God. Every page of the Bible will show you he did. There is one thing that goes some way with me: if Christ was not really God, he was either a fanatic, or an impostor: now his morals and advice are too consistent, and too simple and mild, for a fanatic; and an impostor, one fancies, would not have persevered in such a blameless life, nor held in his heart at once the blasphemous design of calling himself the Son of God and a code of principles which the best and wisest of men never preached before. What do you say to this point? Think of it. I am in a quandary of doubts.

. . . Now, Thackeray, I lay you ten thousand pounds that you will be thoroughly disappointed when we come together – our letters have been so warm, that we shall expect each minute to contain a sentence like those in our letters. But in letters we are not always together: there are no blue devilish moments: one of us isn't kept waiting for the other: and above all in letters there is Expectation! I am thus foreboding because I have felt it – and put you on your guard very seriously about it, for the disappointment of such hopes has caused a flatness, then a disgust, and then a coldness betwixt many friends, I'll be bound. So think of meeting me not as I am in my letters (for they being written when in a good humour, and read when you have nothing better to do, make all seem alert and agreeable) but as you used to see me in London, Cambridge etc. If you come to think, you will see there is a great difference. Do not think I speak this in a light-hearted way about the tenacity of our friendship, but with a very serious heart anxious lest we should disappoint each other, and so lessen our love a little – I hate this subject and to the devil with it . . .

I am angry with Hume for admiring the French so: and standing up so for polite manners to the ladies – a practice which turns Nature topsy turvy. I have got the character of being rather a brute in society – can't help it; I am worth more, I believe, than any young lady that ever was made, so I am more inclined to tell them to open the door for me, than for me to get up and do it for them. This is a most horrid sentence, on second thoughts – for millions of girls have existed a million times more virtuous than I am; and I am ashamed of having said it. I ought to scratch out the sentence – but why should you not see that I can say a silly thing? . . .

4 To Allen
L.F., I, 10–11   Southampton. July 31, 1832

FitzGerald was waiting at Southampton to meet Thackeray for a trip to France, but they missed each other, and FitzGerald never got to France that year. While he was waiting, he did some sightseeing.

. . . And now I will tell you of a pilgrimage I made that put me in mind of you much. I went to Salisbury to see the Cathedral, but more to walk to Bemerton, George Herbert's village. It is about a mile and a half from Salisbury alongside a pleasant stream with old-fashioned watermills beside: through fields very fertile. When I got to Bemerton I scarcely knew what to do with myself. It is a very pretty village with the Church and Parsonage much as Herbert must have left it. But there is no memorial of him either in or outside the walls of the church: though there have been Bishops and Deans and I know not what all so close at hand at Salisbury. This is a great shame indeed. I would gladly put up a plain stone if I could get the Rector's leave. I was very sorry to see no tablet of any kind. The people in the Cottages had heard of a very pious man named Herbert, and had read his books – but they don't know where he lies. I have drawn the church and village: the little woodcut of it in Walton's Lives is very like. I thought I must have passed along the spot in the road where he assisted the man with the fallen horse: and to show the benefit of good examples, I was serviceable that very evening in the town to some people coming in a cart: for the driver was drunk and driving furiously home from the races, and I believe would have fallen out, but that some folks, amongst whom I was one, stopped the cart. This long history is now at an end. I wanted John Allen much to be with me. I noticed the little window into which Herbert's friend looked, and saw him kneeling so long before the altar, when he was first ordained.

5 To Allen

Terhune, 56-7   London. November 21, 1832

After failing to meet Thackeray, FitzGerald went to Tenby, Pembroke-shire, to see Allen, a happy visit which left FitzGerald lifelong memories of talks with Allen and his pleasant family in picturesque surroundings. But in these years FitzGerald was often depressed by his religious doubts, from which the devout Allen tried to extricate him. He wrote frequently from London that autumn to Allen about his 'blue devils'.

. . . I was unhappy and in low spirits on account of the same turmoil in my head that I once had at Seaford. The other night when I lay in bed feeling my head get warmer and warmer, I felt that if I should pray to some protector for relief, I should be relieved: but I have not yet learned the certainty of there being any. It is a melancholy thing that the want of happiness and security caused by scepticism is no proof of the truth of religion: for if a man is miserable because he has not a guinea, it may make him happy to believe he has a guinea, but still he has it not. So if one can delude oneself into a belief, it is a happiness; but some cannot help feeling all the time that it is a delusion . . .

6 To Allen

L.F., I, 13–14   London. November 27, 1832

*'My Paradise', mentioned at the end of this letter, was FitzGerald's
name for his commonplace book. All his life he assiduously extracted,
copied, abridged, his favourite passages in literature. He carried one of
his 'paradises' – long thin books with marbled covers – about with him
wherever he went so that he could make insertions at any time.*

The first thing I do in answering your letter is to tell you
that I am angry at your saying that your conscience pricks
you for not having written to me before. I am of that
superior race of men, that are quite content to hear themselves talk, and read their own writing. But, in seriousness,
I have such love of you, and of myself, that once every
week, at least, I feel spurred on by a sort of gathering up of
feelings to vent myself in a letter upon you: but if once I
hear you say that it makes your conscience thus uneasy till
you answer, I shall give it up. You, who do not love writing, cannot think that anyone else does: but I am sorry to
say that I have a very young-lady-like partiality to writing
to those that I love . . .

   I have been reading Shakespeare's Sonnets: and I believe
I am unprejudiced when I say, I had but half an idea of him,
Demigod as he seemed before, till I read them carefully.
How can Hazlitt call Warton's the finest sonnets? There is
the air of pedantry and labour in his. But Shakespeare's are
perfectly simple, and have the very essence of tenderness
that is only to be found in the best parts of Romeo and
Juliet besides. I have truly been lapped in these Sonnets for
some time: they seem all stuck about my heart, like the
ballads that used to be on the walls of London. I have put a
great many into my Paradise, giving each a fair white sheet
for himself: there being nothing worthy to be in the same

page. I could talk for an hour about them: but it is not fit in a letter . . .

7 To Allen
L.F., I, 17, 18, 20   London. December 7, 1832

Though FitzGerald and Tennyson were at Cambridge at the same time, they were not actually to meet till 1835. Tennyson's forthcoming volume referred to here is his 1833 Poems, *which included 'The Lady of Shalott' which FitzGerald had already seen in MS; in 1832 he described how as he dozed on a night journey by mail-coach, 'the sights of the pages in crimson and the funerals which the Lady of Shalott saw and wove, floated before me: really, the poem has taken lodging in my poor head'.*

. . . The news this week is that Thackeray has come to London, but is going to leave it again for Devonshire directly. He came very opportunely to divert my Blue Devils: notwithstanding, we do not see very much of each other: and he has now so many friends (especially the Bullers) that he has no such wish for my society. He is as full of good humour and kindness as ever. The next news is that a new volume of Tennyson is out: containing nothing more than you have in MS except one or two things not worth having . . .

I have been poring over Wordsworth lately: which has had much effect in bettering my Blue Devils: for his philosophy does not abjure melancholy, but puts a pleasant countenance upon it, and connects it with humanity. It is very well, if the sensibility that makes us fearful of ourselves is diverted to become a cause of sympathy and interest with Nature and mankind: and this I think Wordsworth tends to do . . .

My sister is far better. We walk very much and see such sights as the town affords. Today I have bought a little terrier to keep me company. You will think this is from my reading of Wordsworth: but if that were my cue, I should go no further than keeping a primrose in a pot for society. Farewell, dear Allen. I am astonished to find myself writing a very long letter once a week to you: but it is next to talking to you: and after having seen you so much this summer, I cannot break off suddenly . . .

8 To Allen

L.F., I, 21–2 Castle Irwell. February 24, 1833

FitzGerald's parents at this time were living at Wherstead Lodge, near Ipswich, but they had several estates elsewhere – in Ireland, Suffolk, Northamptonshire, Staffordshire, and at Castle Irwell, near Manchester, where FitzGerald was staying when he wrote this letter; he sometimes helped his father by inspection visits to the family estates.

. . . I am fearful to boast, lest I should lose what I boast of: but I think I have achieved a victory over my evil spirits here: for they have full opportunity to come, and I often observe their approaches, but hitherto I have managed to keep them off. Lord Bacon's Essay on Friendship is wonderful for its truth: and I often feel its truth. He says that with a Friend 'a man *tosseth* his thoughts', an admirable saying, which one can understand, but not express otherwise. But I feel that, being alone, one's thoughts and feelings, from want of communication, become heaped up and clotted together, as it were: and so lie like undigested food heavy upon the mind: but with a friend one *tosseth* them about, so that the air gets between them, and keeps them fresh and sweet. I know not from what metaphor Bacon took his 'tosseth', but it seems to me as if it was from the way haymakers toss hay, so that it does not press into a heavy lump, but is tossed about in the air, and separated, and thus kept sweet . . .

9

9 To Allen

Terhune, 65   Cambridge. March 14, 1833

FitzGerald spent the spring and early summer of 1833 in Cambridge. De la Motte Fouqué's Undine *appeared in English translation in 1818 and 1830.*

. . . I am filled with this kindness just now by having read Undine at breakfast. I think I must be a very great fool, and it must look like vile affectation to talk of being moved by books, and childish books, in this manner: but I swear it is so (as to me). Nor is there anything to affect in it, because it shews that one has a mind which lies ready to be swayed either way by good or bad: which is truly the case with me. So it happens that whenever I open Undine, I become very tender and loving: and in such a humour, I do not like to think that perhaps if I were to read a page of Voltaire I should feel inclined to scoff. When I am in these humours I cannot believe that I should so soon change into their opposites. It is a great vanity to tell other folks of one's feelings, as if one were a great man: but I speak of them because I suppose you feel the same kind of thing. After having read Herbert or Jeremy Taylor, and become suffused with their spirit, do you not wonder that you ever go back to coldness and wordliness? Our good feelings are so entrancing while they last: but that is the reason they last so short a time: but our more paltry propensities are cold and rational, and so stay by us, and become part of our natures. When I came from Leicester the other day on the Coach, I am sure I felt like an Angel: it was a fine morning, the country richly tilled and full of promise, and here and there spires of churches, and little villages, over the face of the country. I felt tears in my eyes often, I could not tell why. Now I was not ashamed of feeling this: but I am ashamed now I tell you of it: it looks like foolish romance but it is not: however it requires an indulgent friend to confide it to.

10 To Donne
L.F., I, 25–6   London. October 25, 1833

After a second visit to Tenby, during which he first met William Kenworthy Browne, whose friendship was to be so important to the next twenty-six years of FitzGerald's life, FitzGerald spent the autumn of this year in London. He was one of the earliest discoverers and admirers of the genius of Blake, who had died six years earlier.

. . . Tennyson has been in town for some time: he has been making fresh poems, which are finer, they say, than any he has done. But I believe he is chiefly meditating on the purging and subliming of what he has already done: and repents that he has published at all yet. It is fine to see how in each succeeding poem the smaller ornaments and fancies drop away, and leave the grand ideas single . . .

I have lately bought a little pamphlet which is very difficult to be got, called the Songs of Innocence, written and adorned with drawings by W. Blake (if you know his name) who was quite mad, but of a madness that was really the elements of great genius ill-assorted: in fact, a genius with a screw loose, as we used to say. I shall show you this book when I see you: to me there is particular interest in this man's writing and drawing, from the strangeness of the constitution of his mind. He was a man that used to see visions: and make drawings and paintings of Alexander the Great, Caesar, etc., who, he declared, stood before him while he drew . . .

11 **To Allen**
L.F., I, 29–30   Geldestone. September 9, 1834

FitzGerald spent the year 1834 with his parents at Wherstead and on visits to Cambridge, London and his sister at Geldestone. He had been experimenting with a vegetarian diet for the past year, and believed that it improved his spirits, but he was oppressed by the contrast between his aimless existence and the 'serious ways of life' of his friends.

I have really nothing to say, and I am ashamed to be sending this third letter all the way from here to Pembrokeshire for no earthly purpose: but I have just received yours: and you will know how very welcome all your letters are to me when you see how the perusal of this one has excited me to such an instant reply. It has indeed been a long time in coming: but it is all the more delicious. Perhaps you can't imagine how wistfully I have looked for it: how, after a walk, my eyes have turned to the table, on coming into the room, to see it. Sometimes I have been tempted to be angry with you: but then I have thought that I was sure you would come a hundred miles to serve me, though you were too lazy to sit down to a letter. I suppose that people who are engaged in serious ways of life, and are of well filled minds, don't think much about the interchange of letters with any anxiety: but I am an idle fellow, of a very ladylike turn of sentiment: and my friendships are more like loves, I think. Your letter found me reading the Merry Wives of Windsor too: I had been laughing aloud to myself: think of what another coat of happiness came over my former good mood. You are a dear good fellow, and I love you with all my heart and soul. The truth is I was anxious about this letter, as I really didn't know whether you were married or not – or ill – I fancied you might be anything, or anywhere . . .

As to reading I have not done much. I am going through the Spectator: which people nowadays think a poor book: but I honour it much. What a noble kind of Journal it was! There is certainly a good deal of what may be called '*pill*', but there is a great deal of wisdom, I believe, only it is couched so simply that people can't believe it to be real absolute wisdom . . .

12 To Allen

L.F., I, 33–5　　　　　　　　Castle Irwell. May 23, 1835

By this time, FitzGerald and Tennyson knew each other well enough to spend a holiday together in the Lakes with their common friend James Spedding, whose father, a rich Cumberland farmer, lived at Mirehouse. Spedding had been at school and at Cambridge with FitzGerald, and they remained lifelong friends. FitzGerald greatly admired Spedding, though he often made jokes about Spedding's lofty forehead and his absorption in the works of Francis Bacon, which Spedding devoted his life to editing, though he earned his living as a civil servant in the Colonial Office. Nearly fifty years later, just after Spedding's death, FitzGerald recalled details of this visit to the Lakes (see Letter 221).

. . . I staid at Mirehouse till the beginning of May, and then, going homeward, spent a week at Ambleside, which, perhaps you don't know, is on the shores of Winander-mere. It was very pleasant there: though it was to be wished that the weather had been a little better. I have scarce done anything since I saw you but abuse the weather: but these four last days have made amends for all: and are, I hope, the beginning of summer at last. Alfred Tennyson stayed with me at Ambleside: Spedding was forced to go home, till the last two days of my stay there. I will say no more of Tennyson than that the more I have seen of him, the more cause I have to think him great. His little humours and grumpinesses were so droll, that I was always laughing: and was often put in mind (strange to say) of my little unknown friend, Undine – I must however say, further, that I felt what Charles Lamb describes, a sense of depression at times from the overshadowing of a so much more lofty intellect than my own: this (though it may seem vain to say so) I never experienced before, though I have often been with much greater intellects: but I could not be mistaken in the universality of his mind; and perhaps I have received some benefit in the now more distinct consciousness of my dwarfishness. I think that you should keep all this to yourself, my dear Allen: I mean, that it is only to you that I would write so freely about myself. You know most of my secrets, and I am not afraid of entrusting even my vanities to so true a man . . .

I have not been reading very much – (as if you ever expected that I did!) – but I mean, not very much for me – some Dante, by the aid of a Dictionary: and some Milton – and some Wordsworth – and some Selections from Jeremy Taylor, Barrow, etc., compiled by Basil Montagu – of course you know the book: it is published by Pickering. I do not think it is very well done: but it has served to delight, and, I think, to instruct me much. Do you know South? He must be very great, I think. It seems to me that our old Divines will hereafter be considered our Classics – (in Prose, I mean) – I am not aware that any other nations have such books. A single selection from Jeremy Taylor is fine: but it requires a skilful hand to put many detached bits from him together: for a common editor only picks out the flowery, metaphorical, morsels: and so rather cloys: and gives quite a wrong estimate of the Author, to those who had no previous acquaintance with him: for, rich as Taylor's illustrations, and grotesque as his images, are, no one keeps a grander proportion: he never huddles illustration upon the matter so as to overlay it, nor crowds images too thick together: which these Selections might make one unacquainted with him suppose. This is always the fault of Selections: but Taylor is particularly liable to injury on this score. What a man he is! He has such a knowledge of the nature of man, and such powers of expressing its properties, that I sometimes feel as if he had some exact counterpart of my own individual character under his eye, when he lays open the depths of the heart, or traces some sin to its root. The eye of his portrait expresses this keen intuition: and I think I should less like to have stood with a lie on my tongue before him, than before any other I know of . . .

13 To Alfred Tennyson
Glyde, 110–11   London. July 2, 1835

During the Westmorland holiday, FitzGerald had learned more about Tennyson's personal circumstances, and he now wrote, with anxious delicacy, to offer financial help.

. . . I have heard you sometimes say that you are bound by the want of such and such a sum, and I vow to the Lord that I could not have a greater pleasure than transferring it to you on such occasions; I should not dare to say such a thing to a small man, but you are not a small man assuredly; and even if you do not make use of my offer, you will not be offended, but put it to the right account. It is very difficult to persuade people in this world that one can part with a bank-note without a pang. It is one of the most simple things I have ever done to talk thus to you, I believe; but here is an end, and be charitable to me.

14 To Allen

L.F., I, 35–7   Wherstead. July 4, 1835

John was FitzGerald's eldest brother. His wife was still alive two years later.

... My brother John's wife, always delicate, has had an attack this year, which she can never get over: and while we are all living in this house cheerfully, she lives in separate rooms, can scarcely speak to us, or see us: and bears upon her cheek the marks of death. She has shown great Christian dignity all through her sickness: was the only cheerful person when they supposed she could not live: and is now very composed and happy. You say sometimes how like things are to dreams: or, as I think, to the shifting scenes of a play. So does this place seem to me. All our family, except my mother, are collected here: all my brothers and sisters, with their wives, husbands, and children: sitting at different occupations, or wandering about the grounds and gardens, discoursing each their separate concerns, but all united into one whole. The weather is delightful: and when I see them passing to and fro, and hear their voices, it is like the scenes of a play. I came here only yesterday ...

What you say of Tennyson and Wordsworth is not, I think, wholly just. I don't think that a man can turn himself so directly to the service of morality, unless naturally inclined: I think Wordsworth's is a natural bias that way. Besides, one must have labourers of different kinds in the vineyard of morality, which I certainly look up to as the chief object of our cultivation: Wordsworth is first in the craft: but Tennyson does no little by raising and filling the brain with noble images and thoughts, which, if they do not direct us to our duty, purify and cleanse us from mean

and vicious objects, and so prepare and fit us for the
reception of the higher philosophy. A man might forsake
a drunken party to read Byron's Corsair: and Byron's
Corsair for Shelley's Alastor: and the Alastor for the
Dream of Fair Women or the Palace of Art: and then I
won't say that he would forsake these two last for anything
of Wordsworth's, but his mind would be sufficiently refined and spiritualised to admit Wordsworth, and profit by
him: and he might keep all the former imaginations as so
many pictures, or pieces of music, in his mind. But I think
that you will see Tennyson acquire all that at present you
miss: when he has *felt* life, he will not die fruitless of instruc-
tion to man as he is. But I dislike this kind of criticism,
especially in a letter. I don't know anyone who has thought
out anything so little as I have. I don't see to any end, and
should keep silent till I have got a little more, and that little
better arranged . . .

15 To Thackeray

L.F., I, 38–9 and Terhune 136   Wherstead. July, 1835

*This summer FitzGerald's father decided to leave Wherstead and move
to the family estate at Boulge, near Woodbridge. Wherstead Lodge was
an imposing eighteenth-century house with a fine hall and staircase and a
park of splendid trees. Boulge Hall (now demolished) was a roomy but
less impressive house, said to have been Queen Anne in origin, but with
nineteenth-century additions. The un-named girl whom FitzGerald
mentions to Thackeray as a possible wife may have been either Caroline,
daughter of George Crabbe, the Vicar of Bredfield and son of the poet
Crabbe, or Elizabeth Charlesworth, who later married FitzGerald's
friend E. B. Cowell.*

My Father is determined to inhabit an empty house of his
about fourteen miles off: and we are very sorry to leave

this really beautiful place. The other house has no great merit. So there is nothing now but packing up sofas, and pictures, and so on. I rather think I shall be hanging about this part of the world all the winter: for my two sisters are about to inhabit this new house alone, and I cannot but wish to add my company to them now and then . . .

And now, my dear Boy, do you be very sensible, and tell me one thing – think of it in your bed, and over your cigar, and for a whole week, and then send me word directly – shall I marry? – I vow to the Lord that I am upon the brink of saying 'Miss – do you think you could marry me?' to a plain, sensible, girl, without a farthing! There now you have it. The pro's and con's are innumerable, and not to be consulted . . . A'nt I in a bad way? Do you not see that I am far gone? I should be as poor as a rat, and live in a windy tenement in these parts, giving tea to acquaintances. I shall lose all my bachelor trips to London and Cambridge, I should no more, oh never more! – have the merry chance of rattling over to see thee, old Will, in Paris, or at Constantinople, at my will. I should be tied down. These are to be thought of: but then I get a settled home, a good companion, and the other usual pro's that desperate people talk of. Now write me word quickly: lest the deed be done! To be sure, there is one thing: I think it is extremely probable that the girl wouldn't have me: for her parents are very strict in religion, and look upon me as something of a Pagan. When I think of it, I know what your decision will be – No! How you would hate to stay with me and my spouse, dining off a mutton chop, and a draught of sour, thin, beer, in a clay-cold country. You would despair. You would forsake me. If I know anything of myself, no imp would ever turn me against you: besides, I think no person that I should like would be apt to dislike you: for I must have a woman of some humour lurking about her somewhere: humour half hidden under modesty. But enough of these things . . .

My dear boy, God bless thee a thousand times over! When are we to see thee? How long are you going to be at Paris? What have you been doing? The drawing you sent was very pretty. So you don't like Raphael! Well, I am his inveterate admirer: and say, with as little affectation as I can, that his worst scrap fills my head more than all Rubens and Paul Veronese together – 'the mind, the mind, Master Shallow!' You think this cant, I dare say: but I say it truly, indeed. Raphael's are the only pictures that cannot be described: no one can get words to describe their perfection. Next to him, I retreat to the Gothic imagination, and love the mysteries of old chairs, Sir Rogers, etc. in which thou, my dear boy, art and shall be a Raphael. To depict the true old English gentleman, is as great a work as to depict a Saint John, and I think in my heart I would rather have the former than the latter . . .

16 To Allen
Terhune, 137   Boulge. February 4, 1836

Seven months later FitzGerald was still hesitating about proposing marriage to his un-named love. The mention in this letter of her piety and her understanding of children makes it more likely that she was Caroline Crabbe, a parson's daughter who looked after her younger brothers and sisters. This was FitzGerald's last mention of the idea of this marriage; either he never brought himself to the point of proposing, or he proposed and was refused.

I have just returned from a dance round my room to the tune of Sir Roger de Coverley, which I daresay you never heard . . . Here we are all wading through mire, owing to the heavy rains: but I dance and sing merrily. Now you must know that there has been staying here for a fortnight the young damsel I have often told you about: & I like her more than ever. She has shown sense and clear sightedness in some matters that have made me wonder: judging by the rest of the world. Yet have I not committed myself – no, my Johnny, I am still a true Bachelor. What do you think of me? You would like this woman very much, I am sure. She is very pious, but very rational ('poor FitzGerald!' say you internally . . .) she is healthy, and stout, and a good walker, and a gardener, and fond of the country, and thinks everything beautiful, and can jump over stiles with the nimblest modesty that ever was seen. Item, eats very little meat – humph! – drinks no wine – understands good house-keeping – understands children (ill-omened consolation!) – ay, there's the rub. Should I dance round my room to the tune of Sir Roger de Coverley if I were married and had seven children? Answer me that.

17 To Donne
F.F., 5–6   London. October 23, 1836

FitzGerald was an ardent and discriminating theatre-goer whenever he visited London. The comic actor Charles Kemble, brother of Mrs Siddons and John Philip Kemble, was sixty-one in 1836, so it is not surprising that FitzGerald found him not light enough for young roles like Cassio and Faulconbridge. The whole Kemble family were friends of the FitzGeralds, Charles's son John Mitchell Kemble was a school friend of FitzGerald's, and his daughter Fanny later became one of Fitz-Gerald's most regular correspondents. At this time Macready, at forty-three, was at his peak as a tragic actor.

. . . I have been to the play nearly every night since I have been here: and they have really mustered all the strength of England at Covent Garden, even at the present low prices – I have seen King John, and Othello, there – Charles Kemble has lost all his lightness in Falconbridge & Cassio: and is become very burdensome on the stage, I think. Vandenhoff really plays Iago very well: not so well as Young, to my taste: I don't think he has made up his mind so clearly as to Iago's real character – But he plays with great ease, and point – Macready's Othello is fine, in parts, very fine: but not so good as some of his other parts – Miss Helen Faucit is a very considerable bore: and Mrs. W. West persists in softening whore into *whoore*: an old item of stage delicacy . . .

18 To Donne
W.B.D.F. 30   Boulge. March 29, 1837

. . . The man you ask me about was there: Alfred Tennyson . . . When I spoke to you of inviting him, you comprehend, I am sure, the tone in which I did so; half jokingly, not seriously desiring you to fulfil a duty.

Letters look very grave, while all the time there is a smile on the writer's lips: nor will lines of writing repre-sent the modulations of the voice that is speaking half in jest, and half in earnest. Perhaps one might write more intelligibly in waving lines on those recessions.

'Why do you not ask Alfred Tennyson to your house?'

This would at least characterise the wondering and un-
certain mood of mind in which we often are: in which I am
more than half my life, I believe. Seriously however, I think
you will be much enriched with his acquaintance, and he
with yours, and one wishes to bind together all good spirits
and to dispose an electric chain of intelligence throughout
the country. But I suppose I spoke of this chiefly from an
instinctive desire we all have to share good things with
those we love . . .

19 To Allen
L.F., I, 48–9   Boulge. April 21, 1837

*After the FitzGerald family moved to Boulge Hall, FitzGerald decided
to set up house on his own in a small thatched cottage at the gates of the
park, into which he moved in 1837. He lived in two rooms, a parlour and
a bedroom, papered in green, crammed with books, pictures and a piano,
and generally dusty and tobacco-smelling. The walls were thin and the
cottage was damp, so in his first years there he sometimes moved back into
Boulge Hall for the winter.*

. . . Ah! I wish you were here to walk with me now that the
warm weather is come at last. Things have been delayed
but to be more welcome, and to burst forth twice as thick
and beautiful. This is boasting however, and counting of
the chickens before they are hatched: the East winds may
again plunge us back into winter: but the sunshine of this

morning fills one's pores with jollity, as if one had taken laughing gas. Then my house is getting on: the books are up in the bookshelves and do my heart good: then Stothard's Canterbury Pilgrims are over the fireplace: Shakespeare in a recess: how I wish you were here for a day or two! My sister is very well and cheerful and we have kept house very pleasantly together. My brother John's wife is, I fear, declining very fast: it is very probable that I shall have to go and see her before long: though this is a visit I should gladly be spared. They say that her mind is in a very beautiful state of peacefulness. She *may* rally in the summer: but the odds are much against her. We shall lose a perfect Lady, in the complete sense of the word, when she dies.

I have been doing very little since I have been here: having accomplished only a few Idylls of Theocritus, which harmonize with this opening of the fine weather. Is all this poor occupation for a man who has a soul to account for? My dear Allen, you, with your accustomed humility, asked me if I did not think you changed when I was last in London: never did I see man less so: indeed you stand on too sure a footing to change, I am persuaded. But you will not thank me for telling you these things: but I wish you to believe that I rejoice as much as ever in the thought of you, and feel confident that you will ever be to me the same best of friends that you have ever been. I owe more to you than to all others put together. I am sure, for myself, that the main difference in our opinions (considered so destructive to friendship by so many pious men) is a difference in the Understanding, not in the Heart: and though you may not agree entirely in this, I am confident that it will never separate you from me.

20 To Bernard Barton

L.F., I, 50–51 London. April, 1838

Bernard Barton, a Quaker banker's clerk living at Woodbridge, made some name as a poet in his day, and was a correspondent of Lamb and Byron. Although he was twenty-five years older that FitzGerald, they became close friends, with disastrous consequences for FitzGerald. The John mentioned at the beginning of the letter is FitzGerald's eldest brother. Carlyle's French Revolution *had been published the previous summer.*

John, who is going down into Suffolk, will I hope take this letter and despatch it to you properly. I write more on account of this opportunity than of anything I have to say: for I am very heavy indeed with a kind of Influenza, which has blocked up most of my senses, and put a wet blanket over my brains. This state of head has not been improved by trying to get through a new book much in fashion – Carlyle's French Revolution – written in a German style. People say the book is very deep: but it appears to me that the meaning *seems* deep from lying under mystical language. There is no repose, nor equable movement in it: all cut up into short sentences half reflective, half narrative; so that one labours through it as vessels do through what is called a short sea – small, contrary going waves caused by shallows, and straits, and meeting tides, etc. I like to sail before the wind over the surface on an even-rolling eloquence, like that of Bacon or the Opium-Eater. There is also pleasant fresh water sailing with such writers as Addison; is there any *pond*-sailing in literature? that is, drowsy, slow, and of small compass? Perhaps we may say, some Sermons. But this is only conjecture. Certainly Jeremy Taylor rolls along as majestically as any of them. We have had Alfred Tennyson here; very droll, and very wayward: and much sitting up of nights till two and three in the morning with pipes in our mouths: at which good hour we would get Alfred to give us some of his magic music, which he does between growling and smoking; and so to bed. All this has not cured my Influenza as you may imagine: but these hours shall be remembered long after the Influenza is forgotten . . .

21 To Barton

L.F., I, 52, 54   London. June 8, 1838

One of the links between FitzGerald and Barton was their interest in, and collection of, pictures. Much of FitzGerald's visits to London was spent in visiting art dealers.

. . . I have been ruralising in Bedfordshire. Delicious has it been there: such weather, such meadows, to enjoy: and the Ouse still wandering along at his ease through pretty villages and vales of his own beautifying. I am much in love with Bedfordshire: it beats our part of the world: and I am sure you would like it. But here I am come back to London for another three weeks I suppose . . .

I wish you were in London to see all these pictures: I am sure their greatness would not diminish your pleasure in you own small collection. Why should it? There is as genuine a feeling of Nature in one of Nursey's sketches as in the Rubenses and Claudes here: and if that is evident, and serves to cherish and rekindle one's own sympathy with the world about one, the great end is accomplished. I do not know very much of Salvator: is he not rather a melodramatic painter? No doubt, very fine in his way. But Claude and the two Poussins are the great ideal painters of Landscape. Nature looks more stedfast in them than in other painters: all is wrought up into a quietude and harmony that seems eternal. This is also one of the mysterious charms in the Holy Families of Raffaelle and of the early painters before him: the faces of the Madonnas are beyond the discomposure of passion, and their very draperies betoken an Elysian atmosphere where wind never blew. The best painter of the unideal Christ is, I think, Rembrandt: as one may see in his picture in the National Gallery, and that most wonderful one of our Saviour and the Disciples at Emmaus in the Louvre: there they sit at supper as they might have sat. Rubens and the Venetian painters did neither one thing nor the other: their Holy figures are neither ideal nor real: and it is incongruous to see one of Rubens' brawny boors dressed up in the ideal red and blue drapery with which the early Italians clothed their figures of Christ . . .

22 To Allen

L.F., I, 55–6   Lowestoft. August 28, 1838

FitzGerald's yearly visits to Bedfordshire were to stay with William Kenworthy Browne at Cauldwell House in Bedford. They had first met in Tenby in 1833, and for the next twenty-six years their friendship gave warmth and animation to FitzGerald's life. Browne, eight years younger than FitzGerald, was a cheerful athletic young squire, not intellectual but intelligent enough to sympathize with some of FitzGerald's interests. He appears as the admired Phidippus in FitzGerald's Socratic dialogue Euphranor.

. . . When I left town I went into Bedfordshire and loitered about there and in Northamptonshire till ten days ago: when I came to join my sisters at this watering place on the Suffolk coast. I have been spending a very pleasant time; but the worst of it is that the happier I am with Browne the sorrier I am to leave him. To put off this most evil day I have brought him out of Bedfordshire here: and here we are together in a pleasant lodging looking out upon the sea, teaching a great black dog to fetch and carry, playing with our neighbour's children, doing the first five propositions of Euclid (which *I* am teaching him!), shooting gulls on the shore, going out in boats, etc. All this must have an end: and as usual my pleasure in his stay is proportionably darkened by the anticipation of his going, and go he must in a very few days. Well, Carlyle told us that we are not to expect to be so happy. I have thought once or twice how equally happy I was with you by the sea-side at Tenby. You and Browne (though in rather different ways) have certainly made me more happy than any men living. Sometimes I behave very ill to him, and am much ashamed of myself: but enough of this.

I have been to see two shew places lately: Boughton in Northamptonshire, a seat of the Duke of Buccleugh's, of the Versailles or Clare Hall style of building, in a very great park planted with the longest avenues I ever saw. But I thought the whole affair gloomy and deserted. There are some fine pictures: and two cartoons said to be by Raffaelle: of which one is the vision of Ezechiel – I could not judge of their genuineness. The other place I have seen is Woburn Abbey – the Duke of Bedford's – a fine place but not much to my taste either. There are very fine pictures there of all kinds – one room hung with brilliant Canalettis – and altogether the pictures are better arranged and hung than in any place I have seen. But these kind of places have not much character in them: an old Squire's gable-ended house is much more English and aristocratic to my mind. I wish you had been with me and Browne at an old seat of Lord Dysart's, Helmingham in Suffolk, the other day. There is a portrait there of the present Lady Dysart in the prime of her beauty, by Sir Joshua. She is now 95.

23 To F. Tennyson
L.F., I, 58–9   Geldestone. April 10, 1839

Frederick Tennyson, eldest brother of the poet and himself a writer, met FitzGerald in London in the 1830s, and became one of his regular correspondents. Frederick Tennyson spent much of his life in Italy, often at this time in company with an Irish art student called Saville Morton. The 'pickle' in which the French king Louis Philippe found himself was that French support of the Egyptian ruler Mehmet Ali against Turkey was aligning England, Austria, Prussia and Russia in support of Turkey. This eventually forced France to back down, which made Louis Philippe very unpopular with his subjects. Talleyrand, who had been French Ambassador in London and Louis Philippe's mentor on foreign affairs, died in 1838.

. . .I live on in a very seedy way, reading occasionally in books which everyone else has gone through at school: and what I do read is just in the same way as ladies work: to pass the time away. For little remains in my head. I daresay you think it very absurd that an idle man like me should poke about here in the country, when I might be in London seeing my friends: but such is the humour of the beast. But it is not always to be the case: I shall see your good physiognomy one of these days, and smoke one of your cigars, and listen to Morton saying fine and wild things, 'startling the dull ear of night' with paradoxes that perhaps are truisms in the world where spirits exist independent of matter. You two men have made great commotion in my mind, and left your marks upon it, I can tell you: more than most of the books I read. What is Alfred about, and where is he? Present my homage to him. Don't you rather rejoice in the pickle the King of the French finds himself in? I don't know why, but I have a sneaking dislike of the old knave. How he must pine to summon up Talleyrand's Ghost, and what a Ghost it must be, wherever it is!

24 To Allen
L.F., I, 59–60   Geldestone. April 28, 1839

. . . Here I live with tolerable content: perhaps with as much as most people arrive at, and what if one were properly grateful one would perhaps call perfect happiness. Here is a glorious sunshiny day: all the morning I read about Nero in Tacitus lying at full length on a bench in the garden: a nightingale singing, and some red anemones eyeing the sun manfully not far off. A funny mixture all this: Nero, and the delicacy of Spring: all very human however. Then at half past one lunch on Cambridge cream cheese: then a ride over hill and dale: then spudding up some weeds from the grass: and then coming in, I sit down to write to you, my sister winding red worsted from the back of a chair, and the most delightful little girl in the world chattering incessantly. So runs the world away. You think I live in Epicurean ease: but this happens to be a jolly day: one isn't always well, or tolerably good, the weather is not always clear, nor nightingales singing, nor Tacitus full of pleasant atrocity. But such as life is, I believe I have got hold of a good end of it . . .

25 To Barton
L.F., I, 61–2   Bedford. July 24, 1839

FitzGerald is again staying with Browne, whose nickname 'Piscator' (from Izaak Walton's name for himself in The Compleat Angler*) was earned by his fondness for fishing. FitzGerald generally remained a spectator on their fishing expeditions. The pleasantry about the Ouse is* *from Thomas Fuller's* Worthies of England.

Here I am again in the land of old Bunyan – better still in the land of the more perennial Ouse, making many a fantastic winding and going much out of his direct way to fertilize and adorn. Fuller supposes that he lingers thus in the pleasant fields of Bedfordshire, being in no hurry to enter the more barren fens of Lincolnshire. So he says. This house is just on the edge of the town: a garden on one side skirted by the public road which again is skirted by a row of such Poplars as only the Ouse knows how to rear – and pleasantly they rustle now – and the room in which I write is quite cool and opens into a greenhouse which opens into said garden: and it's all deuced pleasant. For in half an hour I shall seek my Piscator, and we shall go to a Village two miles off and fish, and have tea in a pot-house, and so walk home. For all which idle ease I think I must be damned. I begin to have dreadful suspicions that this fruitless way of life is not looked upon with satisfaction by the open eyes above. One really ought to dip for a little misery: perhaps however all this ease is only intended to turn sour by and bye, and so to poison one by the very nature of self-indulgence. Perhaps again as idleness is so very great a trial of virtue, the idle man who keeps himself tolerably chaste, etc., may deserve the highest reward; the more idle, the more deserving. Really I don't jest: but I don't propound these things as certain.

26 To W. F. Pollock

M.L., 4–6   Boulge. August 14, 1839

Frederick Pollock was at Cambridge just after FitzGerald, and they first met some years later in London, and corresponded for the rest of their lives. Pollock was a barrister, who eventually became Queen's Remembrancer, and was knighted. He translated Dante and edited

Macready's diaries.

... I have been in my dear old Bedfordshire ever since I saw you: lounging in the country, lying on the banks of the Ouse, smoking, eating copious teas (prefaced with beer) in the country pot-houses, and have come mourning here: finding an empty house when I expected a full one, and no river Ouse, and no jolly boy to whistle the time away with. Such are the little disasters and miseries under which I labour: quite enough, however, to make one wish to kill oneself at times. This all comes of having no occupation or sticking-point: so one's thoughts go floating about in a gossamer way. At least, this is what I hear on all sides . . . I think I shall probably be in Ireland all September . . . I love Ireland very much, I don't know why: the country and the people and all are very homogeneous: mournful and humorous somehow: just like their national music. Some of Tommy Moore's Irish Ballads (the airs, I mean) are the spirits of the Waterford women made music of. You should see them, Pollock, on a Sunday, as they come from Chapel in their long blue cloaks. Don't you think that blue eyes with black hair, and especially with long black eyelashes, have a mystery about them? This day week a dozen poor fellows who had walked all the way from the county Mayo into Bedfordshire came up to the door of the Inn where we were fishing, and called for small beer. We made their hearts merry with good Ale: and they went off flourishing their sticks, hoping all things, enduring all things, and singing some loose things. You must contrive to see something of the people when you go to Ireland: I think that is the great part of the fun. You should certainly go some miles in or on an Irish Stage Coach, and also on a jaunting Car. I never saw Wimpole near Cambridge till the other day when I passed it in my way from Bedfordshire. Did you ever go and see it? People always told me it was not

31

worth seeing: which is another reason for believing nothing that people tell on.: it is a very noble old Queen Anne's building of red brick, in the way of Hampton Court (not half so fine, but something in that way), looking down two miles of green sward as broad as itself, skirted on each side with fine elms. I did not go inside, but I believe the pictures are worth seeing. Houses of that style have far more mark and character than Woburn and the modern bastard Grecian . . . Cambridge looked very ghastly, and the hard-reading, pale, dwindled students walking along the Observatory road looked as if they were only fit to have their necks wrung. I scorn my nerveless carcase more and more every day – but there's no good in talking.

27 To Barton

L.F., I, 63–4   Halverstown. October 20, 1839

FitzGerald spent part of the autumn of 1839 in Ireland with Browne, staying with his uncle at Halverstown. The reminiscences in this letter are of his birthplace, the White House, Bredfield. The book about the Zulus to which he refers was by Captain A. F. Gardiner.

. . . Thank you for the picture of my dear old Bredfield which you have secured for me: it is most welcome . . . Some of the tall ash trees about it used to be visible at sea: but I think their topmost branches are decayed now. This circumstance I put in, because it will tell in your verse illustration of the view. From the road before the lawn, people used plainly to see the topmasts of the men-of-war lying in Hollesley bay during the war. I like the idea of this: the old English house holding up its enquiring chimneys and weathercocks (there is great physiognomy in weather-cocks) toward the far-off sea, and the ships upon it. How well I remember when we used all to be in the Nursery, and from the window see the hounds come across the lawn, my Father and Mr Jenney in their hunting caps, with their long whips . . .

I have gone through Homer's Iliad – sorry to have finished it. The accounts of the Zoolu people, with Dingarn their king, etc., give one a very good idea of the Homeric heroes, who were great brutes: but superior to the Gods who governed them: which also has been the case with most nations. It is a lucky thing that God made Man, and that Man has not to make God: we should fare badly, judging by the specimens already produced – Frankenstein Monster Gods, formed out of the worst and rottenest scraps of humanity – gigantic – and to turn destructively upon their Creators –

'But be ye of good cheer! I have overcome the world –'

So speaks a gentle voice . . .

28 To Barton
N.L., 19–20   London. February 17, 1840

. . . When I got to my lodgings, I found A. Tennyson installed in them: he has been here ever since in a very uneasy state: being really ill, in a nervous way: what with an hereditary tenderness of nerve, and having spoiled what strength he had by incessant smoking etc. – I have also made him very out of sorts by desiring a truce from complaints and complainings – Poor fellow: he is quite magnanimous, and noble natured, with no meanness or vanity or affectation of any kind whatever – but very perverse, according to the nature of his illness – So much for Poets, who, one must allow, are many of them a somewhat tetchy race – There's that great metaphysical, Doric, moral, religious, psychological, poet of the Age, W. Wordsworth, who doesn't like to be contradicted at all: nor to be neglected in any way.

Well, my dear Sir, you are made of a happier compound, and take the world easily – Your nerves will not irritate you with a sense of neglected genius, if I do not quite fill up this sheet to the end – Prepare yourself: take a little bottled Porter if you have it: I am going to end: no offence intended: now are you ready? – quite ready? – Well, then, I am ever yours

29 To Allen
 L.F., I, 66   Boulge. April 4, 1840

. . . The country is now showing symptoms of greenness and warmth. Yesterday I walked (not a common thing for me) eleven miles; partly over a heath, covered with furze bushes just come out into bloom, whose odour the fresh wind blew into my face. Such a day it was, only not so warm aş when you and I used to sit on those rocks overlooking the sea at Tenby, just eight years ago. I am afraid you are growing too good a Christian for me, Master Allen, if you know what I mean by that. Don't be alarmed however . . .

30 To Pollock

M.L., 7–9   Geldestone. May 3, 1840

Brougham was one of the founders of the Edinburgh Review *and wrote regularly for it, as did Macaulay, who had recently returned from India. FitzGerald's reading was desultory but at a high level. The sonorous prose of seventeenth-century historians and divines like Clarendon and Jeremy Taylor, and of their nineteenth-century imitators like De Quincey, suited his taste. The new work by Dickens was* Master Humphrey's Clock.

I received a second letter of yours from York – how many months ago? certainly when no leaves were out as they are now in a wonderful way for this season of the year. You in London do not know that the country is in great want of rain. What does it signify to you? What effect would it have on your dry wigs, which, like Achilles' sceptre, will never, never bud again. Today we have been drinking the Duke of Wellington's health, as my brother-in-law is a staunch Tory, and I am not disinclined – so far. Then, after a walk which was illuminated by a cigar – *lanterna pedibus meis* – we are come back to the library: where, after tea, we are in some danger of falling asleep. So I take this sheet of paper and this pen that lie opposite me on the table, and write to you. So far so good.

   You told me to read Clarendon – which I have begun to do: and like him much. It is really delightful to read his manly, noble English after Lord Brougham's spick-and-span Birmingham ware in the Edinburgh. Is the article on Sir W. Raleigh by Macaulay? It is not so good as most of his, I think. I never was one of those who cared much for the vindication of Raleigh's character: he was a blackguard, it seems: and the chief defence is that he lived among blackguards – Bacon, for instance. Does Spedding think him immaculate? I think the portraits of Raleigh are not favourable: there is great finesse in his eyes and in the shape of his face. Old James the First was a better man than any of his courtiers, I do believe.

It must be very nearly half-past 9 I am sure: ring the bell for the tea-things to be removed – pray turn the lamp – at 10 the married people go to bed: I sit up till 12, sometimes diverging into the kitchen, where I smoke amid the fumes of cold mutton that has formed (I suppose) the maids' supper. But the pleasant thing is to wake early, throw open the window, and lie reading in bed. Morning, noon and night we look at the barometer, and make predictions about the weather. The wheat begins to look yellow; the clover layers are beginning to blossom, before they have grown to any height; and the grass won't grow: stock, therefore, will be very cheap, because of the great want of keep. That is poetry . . .

My brother-in-law is fallen fast asleep over Buckland's Bridgewater Treatise – his breathing approaches a snore. Now could I drink hot blood. I will write no more. Clarendon shall wind up the night with me. What do people say of Dickens's new work? I saw the 1st No. – a very seedy framework, I thought: but the little conversation between the Lord Mayor and Mr Toddyhigh wonderful . . .

31 To F. Tennyson
  L.F., I, 67–9   Bedford. June 7, 1840

. . . While you are wandering among ruins, waterfalls, and temples, and contemplating them as you sit in your lodgings, I poke about with a book and a colour-box by the side of the river Ouse – quiet scenery enough – and make horrible sketches. The best thing to me in Italy would be that you are there. But I hope you will soon come home and install yourself again in Mornington Crescent. I have just come from Leamington: while there, I met Alfred by chance: we made two or three pleasant excursions together: to Stratford upon Avon and Kenilworth, etc. Don't these names sound very thin amid your warm southern nomenclature? But I'll be bound you would be pleased to exchange all your fine burnt up places for a look at a Warwickshire pasture every now and then during these hot days . . .

The sun shines very bright, and there is a kind of bustle in these clean streets, because there is to be a grand True Blue dinner in the town Hall. Not that I am going: in an hour or two I shall be out in the fields rambling alone. I read Burnet's History – ex pede Herculem. Well, say as you will, there is not, and never was, such a country as Old England – never were there such a Gentry as the English. They will be the distinguishing mark and glory of England in History, as the Arts were of Greece, and War of Rome. I am sure no travel would carry me to any land so beautiful, as the good sense, justice, and liberality of my good countrymen make this. And I cling the closer to it, because I feel that we are going down the hill, and shall perhaps live ourselves to talk of all this independence as a thing that has been. To none of which you assent perhaps. At all events, my paper is done, and it is time to have done with this solemn letter. I can see you sitting at a window that looks out on the bay of Naples, and Vesuvius with a faint smoke in the distance: a half-naked man under you cutting up watermelons, etc. Havn't I seen it all in Annuals, and in the Ballet of Massaniello long ago?

32 To Allen

L.F., I, 69–71   Boulge. July 12, 1840

The 'Lusia' of this letter is FitzGerald's eldest sister Andalusia.

I wrote a good bit of a letter to you three weeks ago: but, being non-plussed suddenly, tore it up. Lusia says she has had a letter from Mrs. Allen, telling how you had a troublesome and even dangerous passage to Tenby: but that there you arrived at last. And there I suppose you are. The *veteris vestigia flammae*, or old pleasant recollections of our being together at that place make me begin another sheet to you. I am almost convicted in my own mind of ingratitude for not having travelled long ago to Pembroke-shire, to show my most kind friends of Freestone that I remember their kindness, and that they made my stay so pleasant as to make me wish to test their hospitality again. Nothing but my besetting indolence (the strongest thing about me) could have prevented my doing this. I should like much to see Mr. and Mrs. Allen again, and Carew Castle, and walk along the old road traversed by you and me several times between Freestone and Tenby. Does old Penelly Top stand where it did, faintly discernible in these rainy skies? Do you sit ever upon that rock that juts out by Tenby harbour, where you and I sat one day seven years ago, and quoted G. Herbert? Lusia tells me also that nice Mary Allen is to be married to your brother – Charles, I think. She is really one of the pleasantest remembrances of womanhood I have. I suppose she sits still in an upper room, with an old turnip of a watch (tell her I remember this) on the table beside her as she reads wholesome books. As I write, I remember different parts of the house and the garden, and the fields about. Is it absolutely *that* Mary

Allen that is to become Mrs. Charles Allen? Pray write, and let me hear of this from yourself. Another thing also: are you to become our Rector in Sussex? This is another of Lusia's scandals. I rather hope it is true: but not quite. Lusia is pretty well: better, I think, than when she first came down from London . . . She makes herself tolerably happy down here: and wishes to exert herself: which is the highest wish a FitzGerald can form. I go on as usual, and in a way that needs no explanation to you: reading a little, drawing a little, playing a little, smoking a little, etc. I have got hold of Herodotus now: the most interesting of all Historians. But I find the disadvantage of being so ill-grounded and bad a scholar: I can get at the broad sense: but all the delicacies (in which so much of the beauty and character of an author lie) escape me sadly. The more I read, the more I feel this. But what does it all signify? Time goes on, and we get older; and whether my idleness comprehends the distinctions of the 1st and 2nd Aorist will not be noted much in the Book of Life, either on this or the other side of the leaf . . .

33 To Barton

L.F., I, 74   Bedford. August 31, 1840

I duly received your letter. I am just returned from staying three days at a delightful Inn by the river Ouse, where we always go to fish. I dare say I have told you about it before. The Inn is the cleanest, the sweetest, the civillest, the quietest, the liveliest, and the cheapest that ever was built or conducted. Its name, the Falcon of Bletsoe. On one side it has a garden, then the meadows through which winds the Ouse: on the other, the public road, with its coaches, its farmers, horsemen, and foot travellers. So, as one's humour is, one can have whichever phase of life one pleases: quietude or bustle; solitude or the busy hum of men: one can sit in the principal room with a tankard and a pipe and see both these phases at once through the windows that open upon either. But through all these delightful places they talk of leading railroads: a sad thing, I am sure: quite impolitic. But Mammon is blind . . .

34 To Samuel Laurence

L.F., I, 75–6   Boulge. November 9, 1840

Laurence was a portrait painter, whom FitzGerald met through Sped-ding, and from whom he commissioned portraits of several of his family and friends. The person indicated by a dash in the last sentence was Hartley Coleridge, son of the poet, who was notoriously bohemian in his habits.

. . . We have had much rain which has hindered the sporting part of our company: but has not made much difference to me. One or two sunshiny days have made me say within myself, 'how felicitously and at once would Laurence hit off an outline in this clear atmosphere'. For this fresh sunlight is not a mere dead medium of light, but is so much vital champagne both to sitter and to artist. London will become worse as it becomes bigger, which it does every hour.

I don't see much prospect of my going to Cumberland this winter: though I should like to go snipe-shooting with that literary shot James Spedding. Do you mean to try and go up Skiddaw? You will get out upon it from your bedroom window: so I advise you to begin before you go down to Breakfast. There is a mountain called Dod, which has felt me upon its summit. It is not one of the highest in that range. Remember me to Grisedale Pike, a very well-bred mountain. If you paint — put him not only in a good light, but to leeward of you in a strong current of air . . .

35 To F. Tennyson

L.F., I, 76–8　　　　　　　London. January 16, 1841

FitzGerald's collection of pictures eventually included, as well as the Constable, the 'great enormous' Venetian Holy Family mentioned in this letter, a copy of a Raphael, what he believed to be a Giorgione, and an Abraham and Isaac *which he believed to be a Titian, but was actually by Scarsella (now in the Fitzwilliam Museum, to which FitzGerald bequeathed it).*

I have just concluded, with all the throes of imprudent pleasure, the purchase of a large picture by Constable, of which, if I can continue in the mood, I will enclose you a sketch. It is very good: but how you and Morton would abuse it! Yet this, being a sketch, escapes some of Constable's faults, and might escape some of your censures. The trees are not splashed with that white sky-mud, which (according to Constable's theory) the Earth scatters up with her wheels in travelling so briskly round the sun; and there is a dash and felicity in the execution that gives one a thrill of good digestion in one's room, and the thought of which makes one inclined to jump over the children's heads in the streets. But if you could see my great enormous Venetian Picture you would be extonished. Does the thought ever strike you, when looking at pictures in a house, that you are to run and jump at one, and go right through it into some behind-scene world on the other side, as Harlequins do? A steady portrait especially invites one to do so: the quietude of it ironically tempts one to outrage it: one feels it would close again over the panel, like water, as if nothing had happened. That portrait of Spedding, for instance, which Laurence has given me: not swords, nor cannon, nor all the Bulls of Bashan butting at it, could, I feel sure, discompose that venerable forehead. No wonder that no hair can grow at such an altitude: no wonder his view of Bacon's virtue is so rarefied that the common consciences of men cannot endure it. Thackeray and I occasionally amuse ourselves with the idea of Spedding's forehead: we find it somehow or other in all things, just peering out of all things: you see it in a milestone, Thackeray says. He also draws the forehead rising with a sober light over Mont Blanc, and reflected in the lake of Geneva. We have great laughing over this. The forehead is at present in Pembrokeshire, I believe: or Glamorganshire: or Monmouthshire: it is hard to say which. It has gone to spend its Christmas there.

[A water-colour sketch of Constable's picture.]

This you see is a sketch of my illustrious new purchase. The two animals in the water are cows: that on the bank a dog: and that in the glade of the wood a man or woman as you may choose. I can't say my drawing gives you much idea of my picture, except as to the composition of it: and even that depends on the colour and disposition of light and shade. The effect of the light breaking under the trees is very beautiful in the original: but this can only be given in water-colours on thick paper, where one can scratch out the lights. One would fancy that Constable had been looking at that fine picture of Gainsborough's in the National: the Watering Place: which is superior, in my mind, to all the Claudes there. But this is perhaps because I am an Englishman and not an Italian.

36 To F. Tennyson

L.F., I, 82–5   Boulge. March 21, 1841

Carlyle's 'insane' book was On Heroes and Hero-Worship, *published in 1841. The talk of war with America was because of the disputed boundary between the U.S.A. and Canada. FitzGerald's friend Sped-*

. . . Day follows day with unvaried movement: there is the same level meadow with geese upon it always lying before my eyes: the same pollard oaks: with now and then the butcher or the washerwoman trundling by in their carts. As you have lived in Lincolnshire I will not further describe Suffolk. No new books (except a perfectly insane one of Carlyle, who is becoming very obnoxious now that he is become popular), nor new pictures, no music. A game at picquet of two hours duration closes each day. But for that I might say with Titus – perdidi diem. Oh Lord! all this is not told you that you may admire my philosophic quietude, etc.; pray don't think that. I should travel like you if I had the eyes to see that you have: but, as Goethe says, the eye can but see what it brings with it the power of seeing. If anything I had seen in my short travels had given me any new ideas worth having I should travel more: as it is, I see your Italian lakes and cities in the Picturesque Annuals as well as I should in the reality. You have a more energetic, stirring, acquisitive, and capacious soul . . .

Perhaps you are coming back. Bring Morton back with you. I will then go to London and we will smoke together and be as merry as sandboys. We will all sit under the calm shadow of Spedding's forehead. People talk of a war with America. Poor dear old England! she makes a gallant shew in her old age. If Englishmen are to travel, I am glad that such as you are abroad – good specimens of Englishmen: with the proper *fierté* about them. The greater part are poor wretches that go to see oranges growing, and hear Bellini for eighteenpence. I hope the English are as proud and disagreeable as ever . . .

This is Sunday March 21 – a fine sunny blowing day. We shall dine at one o'clock – an hour hence – go to Church –

then walk – have tea at six, and pass rather a dull evening, because of no picquet. You will be sauntering in St. Peter's perhaps, or standing on the Capitol while the sun sets. I should like to see Rome after all . . .

37 To W. H. Thompson
L.F., I, 85–6   Boulge. March 26, 1841

William Hepworth Thompson was a contemporary of FitzGerald's at Trinity. He remained in Cambridge, becoming a Fellow, Regius Professor of Greek, and eventually Master of Trinity.

. . . I had a long letter from Morton the other day – he is still luxuriating at Venice. Also a letter from Frederic Tennyson, who has been in Sicily, etc., and is much distracted between enjoyment of those climates and annoyance from Fleas. These two men are to be at Rome together soon: so if any one wants to go to Rome, now is a good time. I wish I was there. F. Tennyson says that he and a party of Englishmen fought a cricket match with the crew of the Bellerophon on the *Parthenopœan hills* (query about the correctness of this – I quote from memory), and *sacked* the sailors by 90 runs. Is not this pleasant? – the notion of good English blood striving in worn out Italy – I like that such men as Frederic should be abroad: so strong, haughty and passionate. They keep up the English character abroad . . . Have you read poor Carlyle's raving book about heroes? Of course you have, or I would ask you to buy my copy. I don't like to live with it in the house. It smoulders. He ought to be laughed at a little. But it is pleasant to retire to the Tale of a Tub, Tristram Shandy, and Horace Walpole, after being tossed on his canvas waves. This is blasphemy. Dibdin Pitt of the Coburg could enact one of his heroes . . .

38 To Barton

N.L., 38–9   Lowestoft. June 17, 1841

*Donne's version of the mishap described by FitzGerald in this letter is
also extant; he wrote on 3rd July to Barton 'If E.F.G. is within your
reach, pray tell him I was punctual at twelve o'clock where he wots of.
That I afterwards went to various public houses, and finally before the
mayor and into the prisons in search of him, but I returned disconsolate,
and the very skies sympathized with me, and wetted me through. To make
matters worse I had in some measure been the cause of my own disappointment, by putting him off coming the week before.' Probably the
postponing message never reached FitzGerald, and the two men therefore
kept their tryst in Norwich a week apart.*

. . . I left Geldestone yesterday to go to Norwich: when I
expected Donne to carry me back to Mattishall: no Donne
came: so, after sitting 7 hours in the commercial Room I
got up on the Coach by which I had set out, and vowed in
desperation that I would not descend from it till it stopped.
It stopped here at the sea – I was satisfied: I felt that it could
not reasonably be expected to go further – so here have I
spent the day: and like a naughty boy wont go home to
Geldestone quite yet. Such fine weather: such heaps of
mackerel brought to shore: pleasant flippant Magazines at
the Circulating Libraries – above all an Inn to live in!
After living some time at my brother in law's expense,
there is something very refreshing in launching out at
one's own . . .

39 To Barton

L.F., I, 88–90   Edgeworthstown. September 2, 1841

F. B. Edgeworth, half-brother of the novelist Maria Edgeworth, was a Cambridge contemporary of FitzGerald, who visited his family home while spending the summer of 1841 in Ireland.

. . . I came to this house a week ago to visit a male friend, who duly started to England the day before I got here. I therefore found myself domiciled in a house filled with ladies of divers ages – Edgeworth's wife, aged – say 28 – his mother aged 74 – his sister (the great Maria) aged 72 – and another cousin or something – all these people very pleasant and kind: the house pleasant: the grounds ditto: a good library . . . so here I am quite at home . . . I am now writing in the Library here: and the great Authoress is as busy as a bee making a catalogue of her books beside me, chattering away. She is as lively, active, and cheerful as if she were but twenty; really a very entertaining person. We talk about Walter Scott whom she adores, and are merry all the day long. I have read about thirty-two sets of novels since I have been here: it has rained nearly all the time . . .

I have now begun to sketch heads on the blotting paper on which my paper rests – a sure sign, as Miss Edgeworth tells me, that I have said quite enough. She is right. Goodbye. In so far as this country is Ireland I am glad to be here: but inasmuch as it is not England I wish I were there.

40 To F. Tennyson

L.F., I, 91–3   Naseby. October 1841

Naseby Wooleys in Northamptonshire was one of the family estates which FitzGerald visited from time to time. The battlefield on which

Fairfax and Cromwell defeated the Royalist forces in 1645 was on the estate.

I am surprised you think my scanty letters are worth encouraging, especially with such long and excellent answers as that I have just got from you. It has found its way down here: and oddly enough does your Italian scenery, painted, I believe, very faithfully upon my inner eye, contrast with the British barrenness of the Field of Naseby. Yet here was fought a battle of some interest to Englishmen: and I am persuading farmers to weed well the corn that grows over those who died there. No, no; in spite of your Vesuviuses and sunshine, I love my poor dear brave barren ugly country. Talk of your Italians! why, they are extinguished by the Austrians because they don't blaze enough of themselves to burn the extinguisher. Only people who deserve despotism are forced to suffer it. We have at last good weather: and the harvest is just drawing to a close in this place. It is a bright brisk morning, and the loaded waggons are rolling cheerfully past my window. But since I wrote what is above a whole day has passed: I have eaten a bread dinner: taken a lonely walk: made a sketch of Naseby (not the least like yours of Castellamare): played for an hour on an old tub of a piano: and went out in my dressing-gown to smoke a pipe with a tenant hard by. That tenant (whose name is Love, by the bye) was out with his folks in the stack yard: getting in all the corn they can, as the night looks rainy. So, disappointed of my pro-jected 'talk about runts' and turnips, I am come back – with a good deal of animal spirits at my tongue's and fingers' ends. If I were transported now into your room at Castella-mare, I would wag my tongue far beyond midnight with you. These fits of exultation are not very common with me: as (after leaving off beef) my life has become of an even grey paper character: needing no great excitement, and as pleased with Naseby as Naples . . .

41 To Barton

L.F., I, 98–9   Geldestone. January, 1842

. . . If I do not see you before I go to London, I shall assuredly be down again by the latter part of February: when toasted cheese and ale shall again unite our souls. You need not however expect that I can return to such familiar intercourse as once (in former days) passed between us. New honours in society have devolved upon me the necessity of a more dignified deportment. A letter has been sent from the Secretary of the Ipswich Mechanics' Institution asking me to Lecture – any subject but Party Politics or Controversial Divinity. On my politely declining, another, a fuller, and a more pressing, letter was sent urging me to comply with their demand: I answered to the same effect, but with accelerated dignity. I am now awaiting the third request in confidence: if you see no symptoms of its being mooted, perhaps you will kindly propose it. I have prepared an answer. Donne is mad with envy. He consoles himself with having got a Roman History to write for Lardner's Cabinet Cyclopædia. What a pity it is that only Lying Histories are readable. I am afraid Donne will stick to what is considered the Truth too much.

This is a day like May: I and the children have been scrambling up and down the sides of a pit till our legs ache.

42 To Barton

N.L., 47–8   London. January, 1842

. . . We have had trouble at home. Captain Allen, Lusia's betrothed lover, is dead with nearly all his crew on the shore of the fatal Niger. He wrote to her in good health and spirits the day before he was taken ill: and lay ill more than 30 days – He was a gallant fellow, true to the cause to the last: for when they proposed to turn back to the River's mouth and take him out of the evil air, he bid them hold on – You may imagine it was a sad thing to break this to poor Lusia, who was sanguine of his return: I shall not easily forget doing it. I knew of what had happened all day, and she was not to be told till night. It is an awful thing to be as it were in the secret of Fate, and see another smiling unconscious of the bolt that you know must fall. She was much benumbed: and finally taking off a golden bracelet which her lover had sent her from Africa, and which she had worn night and day, from the moment she had received it, crushed it into my Father's hand and fell upon his bosom, in a way that no affectation of passion could reach, however novel-like it may seem to read. She has shown great fortitude and determination to bear up since.

You may wonder how with all this going on I have the heart to run about picture dealing. I cannot however help it: though I wish I had a stronger sense of these afflictions. What I can do for my poor dear Lusia I hope to do now and as long as I live. She is a noble-hearted girl: and should be married to a good fellow . . .

43 To F. Tennyson

L.F., I, 101–4   London. February 6, 1842

During his London visits, FitzGerald lived in lodgings and only dined occasionally at his parents' house in Portland Place. Many evenings were spent at the theatre; this letter is FitzGerald's fullest description of audience, performance and production in the lavish operatic style of the period.

. . . Last night I went to see Acis and Galatea brought out, with Handel's music, and Stanfield's scenery: really the best done thing I have seen for many a year. As I sat alone (alone in spirit) in the pit, I wished for you: and now Sunday is over: I have been to church: I have dined at Portland Place: and now I come home to my lodgings: light my pipe: and will whisper something over to Italy. You talk of your Naples: and that one cannot understand Theocritus without having been on those shores. I tell you, you can't understand Macready without coming to London and seeing his revival of Acis and Galatea. You enter Drury Lane at a quarter to seven: the pit is already nearly full: but you find a seat, and a very pleasant one. Box doors open and shut: ladies take off their shawls and seat themselves: gentlemen twist their side curls: the musicians come up from under the stage one by one: 'tis just upon seven. Macready is very punctual: Mr. T. Cooke is in his place with his marshal's baton in his hand: he lifts it up: and off they set with old Handel's noble overture. As it is playing, the red velvet curtain (which Macready has substituted, not wisely, for the old green one) draws apart: and you see a rich drop scene, all festooned and arabesqued with River Gods, Nymphs, and their emblems; and in the centre a delightful, large, good copy of Poussin's great landscape (of which I used to have a print in my rooms) where the Cyclops is seen seated on a mountain, looking over the sea-shore. The overture ends, the drop scene rises, and there is the sea-shore, a long curling bay: the sea heaving under the moon, and breaking upon the beach, and rolling the surf down – the stage! This is really capitally done. But enough of description. The choruses were well sung, well acted, well dressed, and well grouped; and the whole thing creditable and pleasant. Do you know the music? It is of Handel's best: and as classical as any man who wore a full-bottomed wig could write. I think Handel never gets out of his wig: that is, out of his age: his Hallelujah chorus is a chorus not of angels, but of well-fed earthly choristers, ranged tier above tier in a Gothic cathedral, with princes for audience, and their military trumpets flourishing over the full volume of the organ. Handel's gods are like Homer's, and his sublime never reaches beyond the region of the clouds. Therefore I think that his great marches, triumphal pieces, and coronation anthems, are his finest works. There is a little bit of Auber's, at the end of the Bayadère when the God resumes his divinity and retires into the sky, which has more of pure light and mystical solemnity than anything I know of Handel's: but then this is only a scrap: and Auber could not breathe in that atmosphere long: whereas old Handel's coursers, with necks with thunder clothed and long resounding pace, never tire. Beethoven thought more deeply also: but I don't know if he could sustain himself so well. I suppose you will resent this praise of Beethoven: but you must be tired of the whole matter, written as it is in this vile hand: and so here is an end of it . . . And now I am going to put on my night-cap: for my paper is nearly ended, and the iron tongue of St. Paul's, as reported by an East wind, has told twelve. This is the last news from the city. So Good night. I suppose the violets will be going off in the Papal dominions by the time this letter reaches you: my country cousins are making much of a few aconites.

44 To Barton
L.F., I, 104–6   London. February 21, 1842

Up to this time, FitzGerald had published nothing except some occasional verses in magazines, and more than ten years were still to pass before he turned his hand to poetic translation. He never felt a strong vocation to be a writer, as he acknowledges in this letter.

... When I rate you (as you call it) about shewing my verses, letters, etc., you know in what spirit I rate you: thanking you all the time for your generous intention of praising me. It would be very hard, and not desirable, to make you understand why my Mama need not have heard the verses: but it is a very little matter: so no more of it. As to my doing anything else in that way, I know that I could write volume after volume as well as others of the mob of gentlemen who write with ease: but I think unless a man can do better, he had best not do at all; I have not the strong inward call, nor cruel-sweet pangs of parturition, that prove the birth of anything bigger than a mouse. With you the case is different, who have so long been a follower of the Muse, and who have had a kindly, sober, English, wholesome, religious spirit within you that has communicated kindred warmth to many honest souls. Such a creature as Augusta – John's wife – a true Lady, was very fond of your poems: and I think that is no mean praise: a very good assurance that you have not written in vain. I am a man of taste, of whom there are hundreds born every year: only that less easy circumstances than mine at present are compel them to one calling: that calling perhaps a mechanical one, which overlies all their other, and naturally perhaps more energetic impulses. As to an occasional copy of verses, there are few men who have leisure to read, and are possessed of any music in their souls, who are not capable of versifying on some ten or twelve occasions during their natural lives: at a proper conjunction of the stars. There is no harm in taking advantage of such occasions.

This letter-writing fit (one must suppose) can but happen once in one's life: though I hope you and I shall live to have many a little bargain for pictures. But I hold communion with Suffolk through you. In this big London all full of intellect and pleasure and business I feel pleasure in dipping down into the country, and rubbing my hand over the cool dew upon the pastures, as it were. I know very few people here: and care for fewer; I believe I should like to live in a small house just outside a pleasant English town all the days of my life, making myself useful in a humble way, reading my books, and playing a rubber of whist at night. But England cannot expect long such a reign of inward quiet as to suffer men to dwell so easily to themselves . . .

45 To F. Tennyson
L.F., I, 111–13   London. March 31, 1842

. . . Concerning the bagwigs of composers. Handel's was not a bagwig, which was simply so named from the little stuffed black silk watch-pocket that hung down behind the back of the wearer. Such were Haydn's and Mozart's – much less influential on the character: much less ostentatious in themselves: not towering so high, nor rolling down in following curls so low as to overlay the nature of the brain within. But Handel wore the Sir Godfrey Kneller wig: greatest of wigs: one of which some great General of the day used to take off his head after the fatigue of the battle, and hand over to his valet to have the bullets combed out of it. Such a wig was a fugue in itself. I don't understand your theory about trumpets, which have always been so little spiritual *in use*, that they have been the provocatives and celebrators of physical force from the beginning of the world. '*Power*,' whether spiritual or physical, is the meaning of the trumpet: and so, well used, as you say, by Handel in his approaches to the Deity. The fugue in the overture to the Messiah expresses perhaps the thorny wandering ways of the world before the voice of the one in the wilderness, and before 'Comfort ye my people, etc.' Mozart, I agree with you, is the most universal musical genius: Beethoven has been too analytical and erudite: but his inspiration is nevertheless true. I have just read his Life by Moscheles: well worth reading. He shewed no very decided preference for music when a child, though he was the son of a composer: and I think that he was, strictly speaking, more of a thinker than a musician. A great genius he was somehow. He was very fond of reading: Plutarch and Shakespeare his great favourites. He tried to think in music: almost to reason in music: whereas perhaps we should be contented with *feeling* in it. It can never speak very definitely. There is that famous 'Holy, Holy, Lord God Almighty, etc.,' in Handel: nothing can sound more simple and devotional: but it is only lately adapted to these words, being originally (I believe) a love song in Rodelinda. Well, lovers adore their mistresses more than their God. Then the famous music of 'He layeth the beams of his chambers in the waters, etc.,' was originally fitted to an Italian pastoral song – 'Nasce al bosco in rozza cuna, un felice pastorello, etc.' That part which seems so well to describe 'and walketh on the wings of the wind' falls happily in with 'e con l'aura di fortuna' with which this pastorello sailed along. The character of the music is ease and largeness: as the shepherd lived, so God Almighty walked on the wind. The music breathes ease: but words must tell us who takes it easy. Beethoven's Sonata – Op. 14 – is meant to express the discord and gradual atonement of two lovers, or a man and his wife: and he was disgusted that every one did not see what was meant: in truth, it expresses any resistance gradually overcome – Dobson shaving with a blunt razor, for instance. Music is so far the most universal language, that any one piece in a particular strain symbolizes all the analogous phenomena spiritual or material – if you can talk of spiritual phenomena. The Eroica symphony describes the battle of the passions as well as of armed men . . .

46 To Pollock
    L.F., I, 115–16   Geldestone. May 22, 1842

The 1842 edition of Tennyson's poems, which contained some of his finest work but also some of his namby-pamby juvenilia, had just been published.

. . . Alfred, whatever he may think, cannot trifle – many are the disputes we have had about his powers of badinage, compliment, waltzing, etc. His smile is rather a grim one. I am glad the book is come out, though I grieve for the insertion of these little things, on which reviewers and dull readers will fix; so that the right appreciation of the book will be retarded a dozen years . . .

The rain will not come and we are burnt up, and in despair. But the country never looked more delicious than it does. I am as happy here as possible, though I don't like to boast. I am going to see my friend Donne in ten days, he is writing the dullest of histories – one of Rome. What the devil does it signify setting us in these days right as to the Licinian Rogation, and Livy's myths? Every school-boy knew that Livy lied; but the main story was clear enough for all the purposes of experience; and, that being so, the more fabulous and entertaining the subsidiary matter is the better. Tell Thackeray not to go into Punch yet.

47 To Laurence
    L.F., I, 116–17   Geldestone. May 22, 1842

Spedding had gone to America as a member of the Ashburton Commission.

... You have of course read the account of Spedding's forehead landing in America. The English sailors hail it in the Channel, mistaking it for Beachy Head. There is a Shakespeare cliff, and a Spedding cliff. Good old fellow! I hope he'll come back safe and sound, forehead and all.

I sit writing this at my bedroom window, while the rain (long-looked for) patters on the window. We have a housefull of the most delightful children: and if the rain would last, and the grass grow, all would be well. I think the rain will last: I shall prophesy so when I go down to our early dinner. For it is Sunday: and we dine children and all at one o'clock: and go to afternoon church, and a great tea at six – then a pipe (except for the young ladies) – a stroll – a bit of supper – and to bed. Wake in the morning at five – open the window and read Ecclesiasticus. A proverb says that 'everything is fun in the country' . . .

48 To Pollock

M.L., 18–19 Geldestone. June 24, 1842

FitzGerald spent 1842 at Boulge and in his usual round of visits to London, Bedford and Geldestone. His failure to accompany Thackeray to Ireland in 1842 is curious, as he went there in 1841 and 1843. More and more he was restricting his meetings with his more intellectually demanding friends to his visits to London, preferring to travel, or stay in the country, with less competitive friends like Browne.

There is that poor fellow Thackeray gone off to Ireland: and what a lazy beast I am for not going with him. But except for a journey of two days, I get as dull as dirt . . . I mean to go to Blenheim to see a Raffaelle this year, and that is all I propose to do. No sights recompense the often undoing and doing up of a carpet-bag. What then is the stamping down, strapping, and locking up of a trunk, with all the blood in your head! If one were rich, and travelled with a valet to do all, it would be well. The only other alternative is to travel with nothing but the clothes on one's back . . .

49 To F. Tennyson

FitzGerald rarely commented on public affairs in his letters. Here he gives a prophetically sceptical glance at Britain's industrial revolution and imperial expansion, at a date when both seemed to be still gathering momentum. His opinions of other nations tended to be insular and contemptuous. Mendelssohn's new work was his Scotch Symphony.

. . . As to poor England, I never see a paper, but I think with you that she is on the go. I used to dread this: but somehow I now contemplate it as a necessary thing, and, till the shoe begins to pinch me sorely, walk on with some indifference. It seems impossible the manufacturers can go on as they are: and impossible that the demand for our goods can continue as of old in Europe: and impossible but that we must get a rub and licking in some of our colonies: and if all these things come at once, why then the devil's in it. I used to think as you do about France and the French: and we all agreed in London that France should be divided among the other powers as Poland was: but Donne has given me pause: he says that France is the great counteracting democratic principle to Russia. This may be: though I think Russia is too unwieldly and rotten-ripe ever to make a huge progress in conquest. What is to be thought of a nation where the upper classes speak the language of another country, and have varnished over their honest barbarism with the poorest French profligacy and intrigue? Russia does not seem a whole to me. In the mean time, all goes on toward better and better, as is my firm belief: and humanity grows clear by flowing, (very little profited by any single sage or hero), and man shall have wings to fly and something much better than that in the end . . .

I draw a very little, and think of music as I walk in the fields: but have no piano in this part of the world . . . I hear there is a fine new Symphony by Mendelssohn, who is by far our best writer now, and in some measure combines Beethoven and Handel. I grow every day more and more to love only the old God save the King style: the common chords, those truisms of music, like other truisms so little understood in the full. Just look at the mechanism of Robin Adair . . .

50 To Barton

L.F., I, 135–7   Naseby. September 22, 1842

Samuel Laurence took FitzGerald to call on Carlyle in Cheyne Row in mid-September 1842. Carlyle was then writing his Cromwell *and had recently visited Naseby to inspect the battlefield. FitzGerald, whose family owned the site, put him right about the actual area of the battle and, visiting Naseby himself in the following week, arranged for excavations to satisfy Carlyle's enquiries, FitzGerald and Carlyle became friends and correspondents from this time.*

. . . Here I am as before: but having received a long and interesting letter from Carlyle asking information about this Battle field, I have trotted about rather more to ascertain names of places, positions, etc. After all he will make a mad book. I have just seen some of the bones of a dragoon and his horse who were found foundered in a morass in the field – poor dragoon, much dismembered by time: his less worthy members having been left in the owner's summer-house for the last twenty years have disappeared one by one: but his skull is kept safe in the hall: not a bad skull neither: and in it some teeth yet holding, and *a bit of the iron heel of his boot*, put into the skull by way of convenience.

This is what Sir Thomas Browne calls 'making a man act his Antipodes'. I have got a fellow to dig at one of the great general graves in the field: and he tells me to-night that he has come to bones: to-morrow I will select a neat specimen or two. In the meantime let the full harvest moon wonder at them as they lie turned up after lying hid 2400 revolutions of hers. Think of that warm 14th of June when the Battle was fought, and they fell pell-mell: and then the country people came and buried them so shallow that the stench was terrible, and the putrid matter oozed over the ground for several yards: so that the cattle were observed to eat those places very close for some years after. Every one to his taste, as one might well say to any woman who kissed the cow that pastured there.

Friday, 23rd. We have dug at a place, as I said, and made such a trench as would hold a dozen fellows: whose remains positively make up the mould. The bones nearly all rotted away, except the teeth which are quite good. At the bottom lay the *form* of a perfect skeleton: most of the bones gone, but the pressure distinct in the clay: the thigh and leg bones yet extant: the skull a little pushed forward, as if there were scanty room. We also tried some other reputed graves, but found nothing: indeed it is not easy to distinguish what are graves from old marl-pits, etc. I don't care for all this bone-rummaging myself: but the identification of the graves identifies also where the greatest heat of the battle was. Do you wish for a tooth?

As I began this antiquarian account in a letter to you, so I have finished it, that you may mention it to my Papa, who perhaps will be amused at it. Two farmers insisted on going out exploring with me all day: one a very solid fellow, who talks like the justices in Shakespeare: but who certainly was inspired in finding out this grave: the other a Scotchman full of intelligence, who proposed the flesh-soil for manure for turnips. The old Vicar, whose age reaches halfway back to the day of the Battle, stood tottering over the verge of the trench. Carlyle has shewn great sagacity in guessing at the localities from the vague descriptions of contemporaries: and his short *pasticcio* of the battle is the best I have seen. But he will spoil all by making a demi-god of Cromwell, who certainly was so far from wise that he brought about the very thing he fought to prevent – the restoration of an unrestricted monarchy.

51 To F. Tennyson

L.F., I, 141–2   Halverstown. July, 1843

FitzGerald spent the summer of 1843 in Ireland, visiting his brother Peter, his uncle and the Edgeworths. The Anti-Corn Law League under Cobden's leadership was agitating for the Repeal of the Corn Laws; these were the Hungry Forties in England, but Ireland's chronically low standard of living seemed no worse than usual in 1842; the Great Hunger was four years ahead.

. . . You would rave at this climate which is wetter far than that of England. There are the Wicklow Hills (mountains we call them) in the offing – quite high enough. In spite of my prejudice for a level, I find myself every day unconsciously verging towards any eminence that gives me the freest view of their blue ranges. One's thoughts take wing to the distance. I fancy that moderately high hills (like these) are the ticket – not to be domineered over by Mont Blancs, etc. But this may only be a passing prejudice.

We hear much less of Repeal here than in London: and people seemed amused at the troops and waggons of gunpowder that are to be met now and then upon the roads . . .

52 To Barton

L.F., I, 143   Ballysax. August 17, 1843

FitzGerald was staying with his second brother Peter at Ballysax in Co. Kildare when he attended this cheerful picnic.

... We have at last delightful weather, and we enjoy it. Yesterday we went to Pool-a-Phooka, the Leap of the Goblin Horse. What is that, do you suppose? Why, a cleft in the mountains down and through which the river Liffey (not very long born from the earth) comes leaping and roaring. Cold veal pies, champagne, etc., make up the enchantment. We dabbled in the water, splashed each other, forded the river, climbed the rocks, laughed, sang, eat, drank, and were roasted, and returned home, the sun sinking red . . .

53 To F. Tennyson

L.F., I, 144–6   Boulge. December 10, 1843

Fitzgerald had moved into Boulge Hall from his cottage for the coldest part of the winter.

... You see I am not settled at the Florence of Suffolk, called Ipswich, yet: but I am perhaps as badly off; being in this most dull country house quite alone; a grey mist, that seems teeming with half formed snow, all over the landscape before my windows. It is also Sunday morning: ten of the clock by the chime now sounding from the stables.

I have fed on bread and milk (a dreadfully opaque diet) and I await the morning Church in humble hope. It will begin in half an hour. We keep early hours in the country. So you will be able exactly to measure my aptitude and fullness for letter writing by the quantity written now, before I bolt off for hat, gloves, and prayerbook. I always put on my thickest great coat to go to our Church in: as fungi grow in great numbers about the communion table. And now, to turn away from Boulge, I must tell you that I went up to London a month ago to see old Thackeray, who had come there to have his eyes doctored. I stayed with him ten days and we were as usual together. Alfred came up 'in transitu' from Boxley to Cheltenham; he looked, and said he was, ill: I have never seen him so hopeless: and I am really anxious to know how he is . . . I remember the days of the summer when you and I were together, quarrelling and laughing – these I remember with pleasure. Our trip to Gravesend has left a perfume with me. I can get up with you on that everlastingly stopping coach on which we tried to travel from Gravesend to Maidstone that Sunday morning: worn out with it, we got down at an inn, and then got up on another coach – and an old smiling fellow passed us holding out his hat – and you said, 'That old fellow must go about as Homer did' – and numberless other turns of road and humour, which sometimes pass before me as I lie in bed . . . Now before I turn over, I will go and see about Church, as I hear no bell, pack myself up as warmly as I can, and be off. So good-bye till twelve o'clock. – 'Tis five minutes past twelve by the stable clock: so I saw as I returned from Church through the garden. Parson and Clerk got through the service see saw like two men in a sawpit. In the garden I see the heads of the snowdrops and crocuses just out of the earth. Another year with its same flowers and topics to open upon us . . .

54 To F. Tennyson

L.F., I, 150–52   Boulge. February 24, 1844

Alfred Tennyson's 'water life' was the drastic water-cure treatment, which included being wrapped in wet sheets for hours at a time.

... We have had the mildest winter known; but as good weather, when it does come in England, is always unseasonable, and as an old proverb says that a green Yule makes a fat kirkyard, so it has been with us: the extraordinary fine season has killed heaps of people with influenza, debilitated others for their lives long, worried everybody with colds, etc. I have had three influenzas: but this is no wonder: for I live in a hut with walls as thin as a sixpence: windows that don't shut: a clay soil safe beneath my feet: a thatch perforated by lascivious sparrows over my head. Here I sit, read, smoke, and become very wise, and am already quite beyond earthly things. I must say to you, as Basil Montagu once said, in perfect charity, to his friends: 'You see, my dear fellows, I like you very much, but I continue to advance, and you remain where you are (you see), and so I shall be obliged to leave you behind me. It is no fault of mine.' You must begin to read Seneca, whose letters I have been reading: else, when you come back to England, you will be no companion to a man who despises wealth, death, etc. What are pictures but paintings – what are auctions but sales! All is vanity. Erige animum tuum, mî Lucili, etc. I wonder whether old Seneca was indeed such a humbug as people now say he was: he is really a fine writer. About three hundred years ago, or less, our divines and writers called him the divine Seneca; and old Bacon is full of him. One sees in him the upshot of all the Greek philosophy, how it stood in Nero's time, when

63

the Gods had worn out a good deal. I don't think old Seneca believed he should live again. Death is his great resource. Think of the *rocococity* of a gentleman studying Seneca in the middle of February 1844 in a remarkably damp cottage.

I have heard from Alfred also, who hates his water life – βίος ἄβιος he calls it – but hopes to be cured in March. Poor fellow, I trust he may. He is not in a happy plight, I doubt. I wish I lived in a pleasant country where he might like to come and stay with me – but this is one of the ugliest places in England – one of the dullest – it has not the merit of being bleak on a grand scale – pollard trees over a flat clay, with regular hedges . . .

55 To Barton

L.F., I, 158–60   London. April 11, 1844

Though FitzGerald still came up to London every year to stay in his old lodgings in Charlotte Street, he was beginning to dislike the city more and more, and while there to think regretfully of his country cottage at Boulge and its inhabitants, Mrs Faiers his housekeeper and Beauty Bob his parrot. Timothy Matthews was a Nonconformist preacher whose crowded chapel in Bedford FitzGerald sometimes attended when he was staying with Browne.

I am still indignant at this nasty place London. Thackeray, whom I came up to see, went off to Brighton the night after I arrived, and has not re-appeared: but I must wait some time longer for him. Thank Miss Barton much for the *kit*; if it is but a kit: my old woman is a great lover of cats, and hers has just *kitted*, and a wretched little blind puling tabby lizard of a thing was to be saved from the pail for me: but if Miss Barton's is a *kit*, I will gladly have it: and my old lady's shall be disposed of – not to the pail . . .

I smoked a pipe with Carlyle yesterday. We ascended from his dining room carrying pipes and tobacco up through two stories of his house, and got into a little dressing room near the roof: there we sat down: the window was open and looked out on nursery gardens, their almond trees in blossom, and beyond, bare walls of houses, and over these, roofs and chimneys, and roofs and chimneys, and here and there a steeple, and whole London crowned with darkness gathering behind like the illimitable resources of a dream. I tried to persuade him to leave the accursed den, and he wished – but – but – perhaps he *didn't* wish on the whole.

When I get back to Boulge I shall recover my quietude which is now all in a ripple . . . A cloud comes over Charlotte Street and seems as if it were sailing softly on the April wind to fall in a blessed shower upon the lilac buds and thirsty anemones somewhere in Essex; or, who knows?, perhaps at Boulge. Out will run Mrs Faiers, and with red arms and face of woe haul in the struggling windows of the cottage and make all tight. Beauty Bob will cast a bird's eye out at the shower, and bless the useful wet. Mr Loder will observe to the farmer for whom he is doing up a dozen of Queen's Heads, that it will be of great use: and the farmer will agree that his young barleys wanted it much. The German Ocean will dimple with innumerable pin points, and porpoises rolling near the surface sneeze with unusual pellets of fresh water –

> Can such things be,
> And overcome us like a summer cloud,
> Without our special wonder &

Oh this wonderful wonderful world, and we who stand in the middle of it are all in a maze, except poor Matthews of

Bedford, who fixes his eye upon a wooden Cross and has no misgiving whatsoever. When I was at his chapel on Good Friday, he called at the end of his grand sermon on some of the people to say merely this, that they believed Christ had redeemed them: and first one got up and in sobs declared she believed it: and then another, and then another – I was quite overset: – all poor people: how much richer than all who fill the London Churches. Theirs is the kingdom of Heaven! . . .

56 To Barton
N.L., 86   London. April 27, 1844

Morison's Pills were a purge, or alterative. FitzGerald's compassion for the poor of this hungry period did not lead him to any political action, but he was a generous alms-giver.

. . . Yesterday at a tavern I drank a poor man's week's wages in a bottle of Champagne – It was scarcely my fault – but what beastly wickedness! – Till all this is set right, I shall look on Revolutions to be as just alteratives as Morison's Pills . . .

57 To F. Tennyson
L.F., I, 164–5   Boulge. May 24, 1844

. . . I daresay I should have stayed longer in London had you been there: but the wits were too much for me. Not Spedding, mind: who is a dear fellow. But one finds few in London *serious* men: I mean *serious* even in fun: with a true purpose and character whatsoever it may be. London melts away all individuality into a common lump of cleverness. I am amazed at the humour and worth and noble feeling in the country, however much railroads have mixed us up with metropolitan civilization. I can still find the heart of England beating healthily down here, though no one will believe it.

You know my way of life so well that I need not describe it to you, as it has undergone no change since I saw you. I read of mornings; the same old books over and over again, having no command of new ones: walk with my great black dog of an afternoon, and at evening sit with open windows, up to which China roses climb, with my pipe, while the blackbirds and thrushes begin to rustle bedwards in the garden, and the nightingale to have the neighbourhood to herself. We have had such a spring (bating the last ten days) as would have satisfied even you with warmth. And such verdure! white clouds moving over the new fledged tops of oak trees, and acres of grass striving with buttercups. How old to tell of, how new to see! . . .

58 To Barton

L.F., I, 168–9   London. June, 1844

FitzGerald's suspicion that Browne's marriage this summer to Elizabeth Elliott would cool their friendship proved not to be justified; he continued to stay and travel with Browne, and later he was very fond of Browne's wife and sons. 'The Daddy who wrote that Sonnet against damned Riches' is Wordsworth; the sonnet is presumably the one of 1803, 'These times strike moneyed worldlings with dismay', and 'Daddy Wordsworth' was a nickname invented by FitzGerald and current in his circle (see Letter 192).

I got here but yesterday, from Bedford, where I left W. Browne to be married to a rich woman. When I heard that they would not have less than five hundred a year, I gave up all further interest in the matter: for I could not wish a reasonable couple more. W.B. may be spoilt if he grows rich: that is the only thing that could spoil him. This time ten years I first went to ride and fish with him about the river Ouse – he was then 18 – quick to love and quick to fight – full of confidence, generosity, and the glorious spirit of Youth . . . I shall go to Church and hope he mayn't be defiled with the filthy pitch. Oh! if we could be brought to open our eyes. I repent in ashes for reviling the Daddy who wrote that Sonnet against damned Riches.

I heard a man preach at Bedford in a way that shook my soul. He described the crucifixion in a way that put the scene before his people – no fine words, and metaphors: but first one nail struck into one hand, and then into another, and one through both feet – the cross lifted up with God in man's image distended upon it. And the sneers of the priests below – 'Look at that fellow there – look at him – he talked of saving others, etc.'. And then the sun veiled his face in Blood, etc. I certainly have heard oratory now – of the Lord Chatham kind, only Matthews has more faith in Christ than Pitt in his majority. I was almost as much taken aback as the poor folks all about me who sobbed: and I hate this beastly London more and more. It stinks all through of churchyards and fish shops . . .

59 To Barton
L.F., I, 175   Leamington. September 28, 1844

FitzGerald's friendship with Carlyle had stimulated his interest in the Civil War and its battles, including Edgehill, where Prince Rupert's cavalry tactics saved the day for the Royalists.

. . . I expect to be here about a week, and I mean to give a day to looking over the field of Edgehill, on the top of which, I have ascertained, there is a very delightful pot-house, commanding a very extensive view. Don't you wish to sit at ease in such a high tower, with a pint of porter at your side, and to see beneath you the ground that was galloped over by Rupert and Cromwell two hundred years ago, in one of the richest districts of England, and on one of the finest days in October, for such my day is to be?

In the meanwhile I cast regretful glances of memory back to my garden at Boulge, which I want to see dug up and replanted. I have bought anemone roots which in the Spring shall blow Tyrian dyes, and Irises of a newer and more brilliant prism than Noah saw in the clouds . . .

60 To Barton

N.L., 90–91   Geldestone. November 20, 1844

FitzGerald's dog Ginger was a Skye terrier; he also had a black retriever, Bletsoe.

I am here, as you say, in some glory – and I am going this very afternoon to Beccles with a train of 5 children to buy *bull's eyes* (dost thou remember them?) and other sweet-meats. The children here are so simple by nature, and simply brought up, that a visit to Beccles is to them some-thing what a visit to London is to others. My heart always sinks within me when I see them really interested in the piddling shops here, and think of the unutterable staleness of all such things to oneself . . .

Ginger came with me here and takes great delight in the rabbit burrows which belong to this sandy soil. We have no rabbits at Boulge: and the dog's talents go to waste. I am not permitted to have him in the room; so he lives in the stable, and will lose some manners in consequence, which Mrs Faiers and I shall have to restore at our leisure . . .

61 To Barton

L.F., I, 179   Geldestone. November 27, 1844

My return to Boulge is delayed for another week, because we expect my Father here just now. But for this, I should have been on the Union Coach this day. The children here are most delightful; the best company in all the world, to my mind. If you could see the little girl dance the Polka with her sisters! Not set up like an Infant Terpsichore, but seriously inclined, with perfect steps in perfect time.

We see a fine white frost over the grass this morning; and I suppose you have rubbed your hands and cried 'Oh Lauk, how cold it is!' twenty times before I write this. Now one's pictures become doubly delightful to one. I certainly love winter better than summer. Could one but know, as one sits within the tropic latitude of one's fireside, that there was not increased want, cold, and misery beyond it! . . .

62 To F. Tennyson

L.F., I, 180–85   Boulge. December 8, 1844

This is FitzGerald's fullest statement of his deliberate choice of a quiet monotonous country life, his 'talent for dullness'. Though no politician, he aligned himself with Tory countrymen against the smart superficial gibes of Liberal London journalists like the Punch *contributor Douglas Jerrold. The reference to Arnold is to the* Life of Dr Arnold of Rugby, *which he had just been reading.*

What is a poor devil to do? You tell me quite truly that my letters have not two ideas in them, and yet you tell me to write my two ideas as soon as I can. So indeed it is so far easy to write down one's two ideas, if they are not very abstruse ones; but then what the devil encouragement is it to a poor fellow to expose his nakedness so? All I can say is, to say again that if you lived in this place, you would not write so long a letter as you have done, full of capital description and all good things; though without any compliment I am sure you would write a better than I shall. But you see the original fault in me is that I choose to be in such a place as this at all; that argues certainly a talent for dullness which no situation nor intercourse of men could much improve. It is true; I really do like to sit in this doleful place with a good fire, a cat and dog on the rug, and an old woman in the kitchen. This is all my live stock. The house is yet damp as last year; and the great event of this winter is my putting up a trough round the eaves to carry off the wet. There was discussion whether the trough should be of iron or of zinc: iron dear and lasting; zinc the reverse. It was decided for iron; and accordingly iron is put up.

Why should I not live in London and see the world? you say. Why then *I* say as before, I don't like it. I think the dullness of country people is better than the impudence of Londoners; and the fresh cold and wet of our clay fields better than a fog that stinks *per se*; and this room of mine, clean at all events, better than a dirty room in Charlotte St. If you, Morton, and Alfred, were more in London, I should be there more; but now there is but Spedding and Allen whom I care a straw about . . . Don't suppose I think it good philosophy in myself to keep here out of the world, and sport a gentle Epicurism; I do not; I only follow something of a natural inclination, and know not if I could do better under a more complex system. It is very smooth sailing hitherto down here. No velvet waistcoat and ever-lustrous pumps to be considered; no bon mots got up; no information necessary. There is a pipe for the parsons to smoke, and quite as much bon mots, literature, and philosophy as they care for without any trouble at all. If we could but feed our poor! It is now the 8th of December; it has blown a most desperate East wind, all razors; a wind like one of those knives one sees at shops in London, with 365 blades all drawn and pointed; the wheat is all sown; the fallows cannot be ploughed. What are all the poor folks to do during the winter? And they persist in having the same enormous families they used to do; a woman came to me two days ago who had seventeen children! What farmers are to employ all these? What landlord can find room for them? The law of Generation must be repealed. The London press does nothing but rail at us poor country folks for our cruelty. I am glad they do so; for there is much to be set right. But I want to know if the Editor of the Times is more attentive to his devils, their wives and families, than our squires and squiresses and parsons are to their fellow parishioners. Punch also assumes a tone of virtuous satire, from the mouth of Mr. Douglas Jerrold! It is easy to sit in arm chairs at a club in Pall Mall and rail on the stupidity and brutality of those in High Suffolk.

Come, I have got more than two ideas into this sheet; but I don't know if you won't dislike them worse than mere nothing. But I was determined to fill my letter. Yes, you are to know that I slept at Woodbridge last night, went to church there this morning, where every one sat with a purple nose, and heard a dismal well-meant sermon; and the organ blew us out with one grand idea at all events, one of old Handel's Coronation Anthems; that I dined early, also in Woodbridge; and walked up here with a tremendous East wind blowing sleet in my face from over the German Sea, that I found your letter when I entered my room; and reading it through, determined to spin you off a sheet incontinently, and lo! here it is! Now or never! I shall now have my tea in, and read over your letter again while at it. You are quite right in saying that Gravesend excursions with you do me good. When did I doubt it? I remember them with great pleasure; few of my travels so much so. I like a short journey in good company; and I like you all the better for your Englishman's humours. One doesn't find such things in London; something more like it here in the country, where every one, with whatever natural stock of intellect endowed, at least grows up his own way, and flings his branches about him, not stretched on the espalier of London dinner-table company.

P.S. Next morning. Snow over the ground. We have our wonders of inundation in Suffolk also, I can tell you. For three weeks ago such floods came, that an old woman was carried off as she was retiring from a beer house about 9 p.m., and drowned. She was probably half seas over before she left the beer house.

And three nights ago I looked out at about ten o'clock at night, before going to bed. It seemed perfectly still; frosty, and the stars shining bright. I heard a continuous moaning sound, which I knew to be, not that of an infant exposed, or female ravished, but of the sea, more than ten miles off! What little wind there was carried to us the murmurs of the waves circulating round these coasts so far over a flat country. But people here think that this sound so heard is not from the waves that break, but a kind of prophetic voice from the body of the sea itself announcing great gales. Sure enough we have got them, however heralded. Now I say that all this shows that we in this Suffolk are not so completely given over to prose and turnips as some would have us. I always said that being near the sea, and being able to catch a glimpse of it from the tops of hills, and of houses, redeemed Suffolk from dullness; and at all events that our turnip fields, dull in themselves, were at least set all round with an undeniably poetic element. And so I see Arnold says; he enumerates five inland counties as the only parts of England for which nothing could be said in praise. Not that I agree with him there neither; I cannot allow the valley of the Ouse about which some of my pleasantest recollections hang to be without its great charm. W. Browne, whom you despised, is married, and I shall see but little of him for the future. I have laid by my rod and line by the willows of the Ouse for ever. 'He is married and cannot come.' This change is the true meaning of those verses,

> Friend after friend departs;
> Who has not lost a friend?

and so on. If I were conscious of being stedfast and good humoured enough, I would marry to-morrow. But a humourist is best by himself.

63 To Barton

N.L., 94–5   London. January 11, 1845

. . . I spent one evening with Carlyle, but was very dull somehow, and delighted to get out into the street. An organ was playing a polka even so late in the street: and Carlyle was rather amazed to see me polka down the pavement – He shut his street door – to which he always accompanies you – with a kind of groan. He was looking well – but he says he gets no sleep at nights. This comes of having a great idea, which germinates once in the mind, grows like a tape worm, and consumes the vitals. What a nasty idea –

Last night I went to hear Handel's Messiah – nobly done.

But here again I was glad to get into the street before it was half over. So I doubt I cant hold out the heroic long. 'Let me plant cabbages!' was the well considered prayer of Panurge; and it is rather mine. But honour to the Carlyles, who, giving up their own prospect of cabbages, toil and sweat in the spirit that we may plant ours in peace . . .

64 To Barton

N.L., 97–8   London. January 17, 1845

Tennyson had been persuaded in 1840 by a Dr Allen to invest all his small fortune in a scheme for carving wood by machinery, which failed in 1843. Tennyson was shattered by the catastrophe, but his brother-in-law, by insuring in Tennyson's favour the life of Allen, who died in January 1845, enabled Tennyson to recover most of his loss.

I was all prepared for going into Suffolk today: but I got a note from A. Tennyson yesterday, saying he was coming to London, and wished to see me. So I waited: and last night he came: looking much better: but a valetudinarian almost: – not in the effeminate way; but yet in as bad a man's way. Alas for it, that great thoughts are to be lapped in such weakness. Dr. Allen, who had half swindled his money, is dead: and A.T. having a Life insurance, and Policy, on him, will now, I hope, retrieve the greater part of his fortune again. Apollo certainly did this: shooting one of his swift arrows at the heart of the Doctor; whose perfectly heartless conduct certainly upset A.T.'s nerves in the first instance.

I have sent your letter and enclosure to Mrs Jones: – for you do not specify *what* the situation is – But I hope she will enquire directly, and satisfy herself. It is very good of you to remember her. Ah! I shall be glad to be back in the land where such little offices are thought of! Could it be offered to me to write another Iliad, or to live down to my three score years and ten (if it is for me to fulfil that number) in the daily remembrance of such small charities, I should not hesitate which to choose. Of all sayings, none is to me so touching as that of the good Emperor Titus – 'I have lost a day!'. I always wonder Dante did not expatiate more on one who certainly was so Christian at heart . . .

65 To Donne
L.F., I, 187   Boulge. January 25, 1845

Tennyson had been working on In Memoriam, *his tribute to Arthur Hallam, since 1833, and several of his friends had already seen sections of it, but it was not to be published for another five years.*

. . . A.T. has near a volume of poems – elegiac – in memory of Arthur Hallam. Don't you think the world wants other notes than elegiac now? Lycidas is the utmost length an elegiac should reach. But Spedding praises: and I suppose the elegiacs will see daylight, public daylight, one day. Carlyle goes growling on with his Cromwell: whom he finds more and more faultless every day. So that *his* paragon also will one day see the light also, an elegiac of a different kind from Tennyson's; as far apart indeed as Cromwell and Hallam . . .

66 To Donne
F.F., 10   Boulge. February 28, 1845

FitzGerald's onslaught on the melodious tears of Elizabeth Barrett was no doubt provoked by her 1844 Poems *which contained several sonnets about her drowned brother, but she is oddly classed with the contemporary novelist Geraldine Jewsbury and with the seventeenth-century poet William Browne, writer of epitaphs on Lady Pembroke and others, whom FitzGerald presumably included as the prototype of the modern elegist.*

... If one could have good Lyrics, I think the World wants them as much as ever. Tennyson's are good: but not of the *kind* wanted. We have surely had enough of men reporting their sorrows: especially when one is aware all the time that the poet wilfully protracts what he complains of, magnifies it in the Imagination, puts it into all the shapes of Fancy: and yet we are to condole with him, and be taught to ruminate our losses & sorrows in the same way. I felt that if Tennyson had got on a horse & ridden 20 miles, instead of moaning over his pipe, he would have been cured of his sorrows in half the time. As it is, it is about 3 years before the Poetic Soul walks itself out of darkness & Despair into Common Sense – Plato wd. not have allowed such querulousness to be published in his Republic, to be sure: and when we think of the Miss Barretts, Brownes, Jewsburys etc who will set to work to feel friends' losses in melodious tears, in imitation of A.T.'s – one must allow Plato was no such prig as some say he was ...

67 To Barton

L.F., I, 189–90   Geldestone. April 3, 1845

FitzGerald's statement that he had abjured authorship can only refer to the occasional verse which he wrote, but did not publish, in the 1830s and 1840s. It was to be another four years before he undertook a work of professional authorship.

. . . I have been loitering out in the garden here this golden day of Spring. The wood-pigeons coo in the covert; the frogs croak in the pond; the bees hum about some thyme, and some of my smaller nieces have been gathering prim-roses, 'all to make posies suitable to this present month'. I cannot but think with a sort of horror of being in London now: but I doubt I must be ere long . . . I have abjured all Authorship, contented at present with the divine Poem which Great Nature is now composing about us. These primroses seem more wonderful and delicious Annuals than Ackerman ever put forth. I suppose no man ever grew so old as not to feel younger in Spring . . .

68 To F. Tennyson
L.F., I, 193–5   Boulge. June 12, 1845

Thackeray wrote criticisms of contemporary artists in the Royal Academy exhibitions for Fraser's Magazine. It would not have been an easy task for any infuriated artist to horse-whip the tall and powerful Thackeray, hence FitzGerald's laughter. His critique of French superficiality was provoked by a French opera recently given in London.

. . . If you want to know something of the Exhibition however, read Fraser's Magazine for this month; there Thackeray has a paper on the matter, full of fun. I met Stone in the street the other day; he took me by the button, and told me in perfect sincerity, and with increasing warmth, how, though he loved old Thackeray, yet these yearly out-speakings of his sorely tried him; not on account of himself (Stone), but on account of some of his friends, Charles Landseer, Maclise, etc. Stone worked himself up to such a pitch under the pressure of forced calmness that he at last said Thackeray would get himself horse-whipped one day by one of these infuriated Apelleses. At this I, who partly agreed with Stone that ridicule, though true, needs not always to be spoken, began to laugh: and told him two could play at that game. These painters cling together, and bolster each other up, to such a degree, that they really have persuaded themselves that any one who ventures to laugh at one of their drawings, exhibited publickly for the express purpose of criticism, insults the whole corps. In the mean while old Thackeray laughs at all this; and goes on in his own way; writing hard for half a dozen Reviews and Newspapers all the morning; dining, drinking, and talking of a night; managing to preserve a fresh colour and perpetual flow of spirits under a wear-and-tear of thinking and feeding that would have knocked up any other man I know two years ago, at least . . .

. . . So it is with nearly all French things; there is a clever showy surface; but no Holy of Holies far withdrawn; conceived in the depth of a mind, and only to be received into the depths of ours after much attention. Poussin must spend his life in Italy before he could paint as he did; and what other Great Man, out of the exact Sciences, have they to show? This you will call impudence. Now Beethoven, you see by your own experience, has a depth not to be reached all at once. I admit with you that he is too bizarre, and, I think, morbid; but he is original, majestic, and profound. Such music *thinks*; so it is with Gluck; and with Mendelssohn. As to Mozart, he was, as a musical Genius, more wonderful than all. I was astonished at the Don Giovanni lately. It is certainly the Greatest Opera in the world. I went to no concert, and am now sorry I did not . . .

69 To Barton

N.L., 100–101   Halverstown, Ireland. August 15, 1845

FitzGerald's summer visit to Ireland in 1845 coincided with a moment of great optimism about the abundant potato crop of that year. The blight which was to destroy the crop, and produce the 1846 famine, did not reach Ireland till September 1845.

Tomorrow I leave Paddyland and draw homeward, staying some while at Bedford. I may also go to Naseby for a day or two. But my easily-wearied heart yearns to be at home again – I was to have gone to meet Allen in Wales; but I have refreshed myself with the opal tints of the Wicklow hills here, and I want no more. A line of distant hills is all we want in Suffolk. A landscape should have that image of futurity in it . . .

I suppose Carlyle's book must be on the point of appearing. At all events he must have almost done *his* part. He told me that he had done so much for the illustration of Cromwell's letters etc. that he doubted if he should ever write any further Life of him – So get this; it is sure to have much more good than bad in it. I told C. that the more I read of Cromwell the more I was forced to agree with the verdict of the world about him. Carlyle only grunted and sent forth a prodigious blast of tobacco smoke. He smokes indignantly –

You say nothing of the state of harvest etc, in Suffolk. The crops about here are very good, and only want sunshine now to crown a full cup of harvest. Ireland is wonderfully improved (this part of it, at least) in the last two years even . . .

70 To Barton

N.L., 105   Geldestone. February 14, 1846

. . . And now I must go out: for a covey of children with bonnets on are waiting for Uncle Edward to take them to a great gravel-pit in the middle of a fir-wood, where they may romp and slide down at pleasure – This is Saturday, and they may dirty stockings and frocks as much as they please . . .

71 To F. Tennyson

L.F., I, 201   Boulge. March, 1846

. . . I believe that I, as men usually do, grow more callous and indifferent daily: but I am sure I would as soon travel to see your face, and my dear old Alfred's, as any one's. But beside my inactivity, I have a sort of horror of plunging into London: which, except for a shilling concert, and a peep at the pictures, is desperate to me. This is my fault, not London's: I know it is a lassitude and weakness of soul that no more loves the ceaseless collision of Beaux Esprits, than my obese ill-jointed carcase loves bundling about in coaches and steamers. And, as you say, the dirt, both of earth and atmosphere, in London, is a real bore. But enough of that. It is sufficient that it is more pleasant to me to sit in a clean room, with a clear air outside, and hedges just coming into leaf, rather than in the Tavistock or an upper floor of Charlotte Street. And how much better one's books read in country stillness, than amid the noise of wheels, crowds, etc., or after hearing them eternally discussed by no less active tongues ! . . .

72 To Barton

N.L., 121–3   London. April, 1846

Thomas Churchyard was a Woodbridge solicitor, a painter and collector of pictures, and one of the Woodbridge 'wits' (the others being Barton and George Crabbe) with whom FitzGerald often foregathered to dine and smoke. Portland Place, where FitzGerald met the novelist Harrison Ainsworth, was his parents' house. Edward Cowell, the linguist and orientalist, later became one of FitzGerald's closest friends. His 'Lady', Elizabeth Charlesworth, whom he married in 1847, was fourteen years older than he was, and has been conjectured to be FitzGerald's own early love (see Letter 15).

I have been very bilious and very resentful of this London atmosphere. And all epistolary power has left me. I have been able to manage no book but Mrs Trollope's novels: of which one, 'The Robertses on their Travels' is very entertaining and, I think, instructive. I wish our good folks who go abroad yearly to stare, make fools of themselves, and learn much less good than evil, would read and take to heart the true picture of so many of them drawn in that novel –

I sent Churchyard a note some days ago, apprizing him of my locality, and hoping I should see him ere long. I keep all my picture expeditions till he comes up. Indeed, I have lost all appetite for such sights: and I think would go further to see a bit of clear blue sky over a furze-blossomed heath than any Titian in the world.

On Thursday I dined with a large party at Portland Place, among the company your friend *Ainsworth* figures: and your friend *Wilson* comes to sing to us in the evening. Ainsworth is, in my opinion, a *Snob*; but I don't reveal my opinion at P.P. Tennyson and I sometimes get a walk and a talk together. He is no Snob. He has lately been standing as Godfather to one of Dickens's children – Count d'Orsay being the other Godfather – insomuch that the poor child will be named 'Alfred d'Orsay Tennyson Dickens'! proving clearly enough, I think, that Dickens is a *Snob* – For what is Snobbishness and Cockneyism but all such pretension and parade? It is one thing to worship Heroes; and another to lick up their spittle –

I expect Edward Cowell to-day. He comes to London to see his Lady, and to buy Persian books. I shall be glad to see him; he will bring up a waft of Suffolk air with him – O! the bit of salmon I eat yesterday! I feel it within me like churchyard fat – I scratch out a capital C because I mean like a burial place and not any person. Farewell for the present.

73 **To Barton**

N.L., 123–4   London. May 4, 1846

. . . Tomorrow Tennyson and I are going to get a pint or two of fresh air at Richmond: and we are to wind up our day at Carlyle's by way of a refreshing evening's entertainment. I met C. last night at Tennyson's; and they two discussed the merits of this world, and the next, till I wished myself out of *this*, at any rate. Carlyle gets more wild, savage, and unreasonable every day; and, I do believe, will turn mad. 'What is the use of ever so many rows of stupid, fetid, animals in cauliflower wigs – and clean lawn sleeves – calling themselves Bishops – Bishops, I say, of the Devil – not of God – obscene creatures, parading between men's eyes, and the eternal light of Heaven', etc. etc. This, with much abstruser nonconformity for 2 whole hours! – and even as it was yesterday, so shall it be to-morrow, and the day after that – in saecula saeculorum! . . .

74 To Pollock

M.L., 19–21   Boulge. Autumn, 1846

Pollock had just been appointed a Master of the Court of Exchequer.
Tennyson went to Belgium, Germany and Switzerland with his publisher
Moxon in August. Sir Edward Lytton Bulwer, the novelist, was the
flatterer of Caroline Norton who, after her separation from her husband,
supported herself by writing and editing.

I was glad to hear from you; and I congratulate you on
having secured stedfast office and revenue that will put
you at ease, and end all trouble and disappointment.
Henceforth you may sit on your bench and look down
complacently on the *mare magnum* of wigs all striving which
shall rise topmost. And as you say, you can now set about
finding out what to do with much spare time; a thing hard
to do at all times (how tiresome was a whole holiday at
school!), but most hard to men who have for the greater
part of their lives been accustomed to a regular day-full of
work. And all must leave it at some time. I have been all
my life apprentice to this heavy business of idleness; and
am not yet master of my craft; the Gods are too just to
suffer that I should . . .

Tennyson . . . is come back from Switzerland rather
disappointed, I am glad to say. How could such herds of
gaping idiots come back enchanted if there were much
worth going to see? I think that tours in Switzerland and
Italy are less often published now than formerly: but there
is all Turkey, Greece, and the East to be prostituted also:
and I fear we shan't hear the end of it in our lifetimes.
Suffolk turnips seem to me so classical compared to all that
sort of thing.

I believe I shall be in London shortly before, or after,
Christmas: and shall assuredly look for you. Do you ever

see Thackeray? I read some pretty verses of his in Mrs Norton's Drawing Room Scrap Book; and *such* a copy of verses to her Ladyship by Sir Edward! It is impossible to read verses worse in sense or sound. And how Mrs Norton could admit such vulgar flattery! I am afraid the Suffolk turnips are better than her too: and they are not particularly good this year.

75 To E. B. Cowell
L.F., I, 208   Bedford. September 15, 1846

Here I am at last, after making a stay at Lowestoft, where I sailed in boats, bathed, and in all ways enjoyed the sea air. I wished for you upon a heathy promontory there, good museum for conversation on old poets, etc. What have you been reading, and what tastes of rare Authors have you to send me? I have read (as usual with me) but very little, what with looking at the sea with its crossing and recrossing ships, and dawdling with my nieces of an evening. Besides a book is to me what Locke says that watching the hour hand of a clock is to all; other thoughts (and those of the idlest and seemingly most irrelevant) will intrude between my vision and the written words: and then I have to read over again; often again and again till all is crossed and muddled. If Life were to be very much longer than is the usual lot of men, one would try very hard to reform this lax habit, and clear away such a system of gossamer associations: even as it is, I try to turn all wandering fancy out of doors, and listen attentively to Whately's Logic, and old Spinoza still! I find some of Spinoza's Letters very good, and so far useful as that they try to clear up some of his abstrusities at the earnest request of friends as dull as myself. I think I perceive as well as ever how the quality of his mind forbids much salutary instinct which widens the system of things to more ordinary men, and yet helps to keep them from wandering in it. I am now reading his Tractatus Theologico-Politicus, which is very delightful to me because of its clearness and acuteness . . .

76 To Cowell
L.F., I, 211   Boulge. Winter, 1846

This is the first mention of FitzGerald's Euphranor, a Dialogue on Youth, which was not completed and published till 1851. The reference at the end of the letter is to Walter Savage Landor's The Hellenics, published 1846–7.

. . . I have been doing some of the dialogue, which seems the easiest thing in the world to do but is not. It is not easy to keep good dialectic, and yet keep up the disjected sway of natural conversation. I talk, you see, as if I were to do some good thing: but I don't mean that. But any such trials of one's own show one the art of such dialogues as Plato's, where the process is so logical and conversational at once: and the result so plain, and seemingly so easy. They remain the miracles of that Art to this day: and will do for many a day: for I don't believe they will ever be surpassed; certainly not by Landor.

77 To Barton
N.L., 135–6   Geldestone. April 1, 1847

FitzGerald's brother-in-law John Kerrich had invested his capital in the mining speculations of FitzGerald's father, which were now nearing a disaster which was to involve the fortunes of the whole family.

. . . You may imagine I have seen this house under happier circumstances than at present; – Kerrich is gone with his brother to London for a while: Eleanor has acted, and acts, with great sagacity and firmness. She has to learn to put off the yoke of submission to which she has so happily sub-jected herself for 20 years, and to be the *Master*; for a time at least: – a thing not agreeable to the good feminine nature; – but necessary here, – and in so many cases beside. Her present to me on my birthday was a pair of plain cloth gloves! more touching to me, as coming out of the small funds of a large family, than if they were filled with gold . . .

78 To Barton

L.F., I, 222–3   Gloucester. August 29, 1847

FitzGerald's sister Andalusia, whose first fiancé died in Africa (see Letter 42), married in 1844 the Rev. Francis de Soyres. The parson with whom FitzGerald stayed in Dorset was Francis Duncan, a Cam-bridge friend. FitzGerald, whose religious leanings, such as they were, were Low Church, had no sympathy for the Tractarian Movement whose adherents were at this time mostly called after Edward Pusey, the best known of their leaders within the Anglican Church.

. . . After I wrote to you at Exeter, I went for three days to the Devonshire coast; and then to Lusia's home in Somer-setshire. I never saw her look better or happier. De Soyres pretty well; their little girl grown a pretty and strong child; their baby said to be very thriving. They live in a fine, fruitful, and picturesque country: green pastures, good arable, clothed with trees, bounded with hills that almost reach mountain dignity, and in sight of the Bristol Channel which is there all but Sea. I fancy the climate is moist, and I should think the trees are too many for health: but I was there too little time to quarrel with it on that score. After being there, I went to see a parson friend in Dorsetshire; a quaint, humorous man. Him I found in a most out-of-the-way parish in a fine open country; not so much wooded; chalk hills. This man used to wander about the fields at Cambridge with me when we both wore caps and gowns, and then we proposed and discussed many ambitious schemes and subjects. He is now a quiet, saturnine, parson with five children, taking a pipe to soothe him when they bother him with their noise or their misbehaviour: and I! – as the Bishop of London said, 'By the grace of God I am what I am.' In Dorsetshire I found the churches much occupied by Puseyite Parsons; new chancels built with altars, and painted windows that officiously displayed the Virgin Mary, etc. The people in those parts call that party 'Pugicides', and receive their doctrine and doings peacefully. I am vext at these silly men who are dishing themselves and their church as fast as they can.

79 To Carlyle

L.F., I, 226–8   Bedford. September 20, 1847

FitzGerald's preference for the Evangelicalism typified by Exeter Hall (a building in the Strand, London, where many religious and philanthropical meetings were held) over the 'wretched Oxford business' of the Tractarian Movement did not drive him as far as Carlyle's total condemnation of any Established Church; he remained a supporter of Anglicanism.

I was very glad of your letter: especially as regards that part in it about the Derbyshire villages. In many other parts of England (not to mention my own Suffolk) you would find the same substantial goodness among the people, resulting (as you say) from the funded virtues of many good humble men gone by. I hope you will continue to teach us all, as you have done, to make some use and profit of all this: at least, not to let what good remains die away under penury and neglect. I also hope you will have some mercy now, and in future, on the 'Hebrew rags' which are grown offensive to you; considering that it was these rags that really did bind together those virtues which have transmitted down to us all the good you noticed in Derbyshire. If the old creed was so commendably effective in the Generals and Counsellors of two hundred years ago, I think we may be well content to let it work still among the ploughmen and weavers of to-day; and even to suffer some absurdities in the Form, if the Spirit does well upon the whole. Even poor Exeter Hall ought, I think, to be borne with; it is at least better than the wretched Oxford business. When I was in Dorsetshire some weeks ago, and saw chancels done up in sky-blue and gold, with niches, candles, an *Altar*, rails to keep off the profane laity, and the parson (like your Reverend Mr Hitch) *intoning* with his back to the people, I thought the Exeter Hall War-cry of 'The Bible – the whole Bible – and nothing but the Bible' a good cry: I wanted Oliver and his dragoons to march in and put an end to it all. Yet our Established Parsons (when quiet and in their senses) make good country gentlemen, and magistrates; and I am glad to secure one man of means and education in each parish of England: the people can always resort to Wesley, Bunyan, and Baxter, if they want stronger food than the old Liturgy, and the orthodox Discourse . . .

80 To Barton

N.L., 157–8   Geldestone. April 8, 1848

The 'Cedar Parlour' was the scene of some of the principal events in Samuel Richardson's novel Sir Charles Grandison. *FitzGerald was*

Thomas Carlyle. Photograph by Julia Margaret Cameron.
(*National Portrait Gallery*)

right about the Chartists; their attempt on 10 April 1848 to carry their
petition for electoral reform to Parliament was turned back by the police.
An abortive rebellion in Ireland ended in the arrest of its leaders in
March 1848.

. . . I have spent a very pleasant week here with my
delightful nieces – so simple-minded, affectionate, and
open to all innocent pleasure. Here I am like the Father of a
delightful family, without the responsibilities attached.
These girls are now all grown up, or growing up; *ladies* in
the only true sense of the word: finding their luxury in
going among the poor: and doing what good they can . . .

We had indeed wondrous weather for the first three days
of my stay: but in this house one is independent of weather.
Kerrich is pretty well. Eleanor so-so. This morning I read
some of my old friend Sir Charles Grandison in bed – the
old 'Cedar Parlour'. It is a curious history of old manners:
but we are greatly improved since. You see people are all
agog as to what the Chartists are to do on Monday: – I
think, nothing. Ireland gets worse and worse.

81 To F. Tennyson
L.F., I, 236–8   Boulge. May 4, 1848

FitzGerald's father was now nearing bankruptcy, and FitzGerald's own
income was partly endangered, though on his mother's death he was due to
inherit a further modest fortune, and he was philosophical about the
necessary retrenchment in his expenditure meanwhile. 1848 was a year of
literary landmarks, including Thackeray's Vanity Fair *and Dickens's*
Dombey and Son. *The stirring political events in Europe, where*
revolutions were breaking out everywhere – in this month of May the
Lombards had driven out their Austrian overlords, and Mazzini's ideal
of a unified Italian republic looked like coming true – still seemed to

. . . You know England has had a famous winter of it for commercial troubles: my family has not escaped the agitation: I even now doubt if I must not give up my daily two-pennyworth of cream and take to milk: and give up my Spectator and Athenæum. I don't trouble myself much about all this: for, unless the kingdom goes to pieces by national bankruptcy, I shall probably have enough to live on: and, luckily, every year I want less. What do you think of my not going up to London this year; to see exhibitions, to hear operas, and so on? Indeed I do not think I shall go: and I have no great desire to go. I hear of nothing new in any way worth going up for. I have never yet heard the famous Jenny Lind, whom all the world raves about. Spedding is especially mad about her, I understand: and, after that, is it not best for weaker vessels to keep out of her way? Night after night is that bald head seen in one particular position in the Opera house, in a stall; the miserable man has forgot Bacon and philosophy, and goes after strange women. There is no doubt this lady is a wonderful singer; but I will not go into hot crowds till another Pasta comes; I have heard no one since her worth being crushed for. And to perform in one's head one of Handel's choruses is better than most of the Exeter Hall performances. I went to hear Mendelssohn's Elijah last spring: and found it wasn't at all worth the trouble. Though very good music it is not original: Haydn much better. I think the day of Oratorios is gone, like the day for painting Holy Families, etc. But we cannot get tired of what has been done in Oratorios more than we can get tired of Raffaelle. Mendelssohn is really original and beautiful in *romantic* music: witness his Midsummer

Night's Dream, and Fingal's Cave.

I had a note from Alfred three months ago. He was then in London: but is now in Ireland, I think, adding to his new poem, the Princess. Have you seen it? I am considered a great heretic for abusing it; it seems to me a wretched waste of power at a time of life when a man ought to be doing his best; and I almost feel hopeless about Alfred now. I mean, about his doing what he was born to do . . . On the other hand, Thackeray is progressing greatly in his line: he publishes a Novel in numbers – Vanity Fair – which began dull, I thought: but gets better every number, and has some very fine things indeed in it. He is become a great man I am told: goes to Holland House, and Devonshire House: and for some reason or other, will not write a word to me. But I am sure this is not because he is asked to Holland House. Dickens has fallen off in his last novel, just completed; but there are wonderful things in it too. Do you ever get a glimpse of any of these things?

As to public affairs, they are so wonderful that one does not know where to begin. If England maintains her own this year, she must have the elements of long lasting in her. I think People begin to wish we had no more to do with Ireland: but the Whigs will never listen to a doctrine which was never heard of in Holland House. I am glad Italy is free: and surely there is nothing for her now but a Republic. It is well to stand by old kings who have done well by us: but it is too late in the day to *begin* Royalty . . .

82 To Donne

F.F., 22   July, 1848?

. . . I have been to London – a visit of business – my poor Father's affairs all in the worst confusion, so that now he is obliged to give up his rents etc into Creditors' hands – I am so far mixed up in this, that I am also a Creditor to the amount of £10,000 – as are all my brethren and sisters; out of the interest of which we live for the present. It remains to be seen how much we and others shall get of our money; in the meantime I keep on the windy side of care, & don't care half so much for all these matters as I should for my finger aching – To each his troubles . . .

83 To Barton

N.L., 162–3 London. September 9, 1848

The Rev. J. B. Wilkinson was the husband of FitzGerald's third sister Jane, and the source of Tennyson's and FitzGerald's disputed claim to responsibility for the worst blank verse line in English poetry (see Letter 229).

. . . I suppose you will have heard of our Creditors' meeting on Thursday: a room in the City filled with miserable, avaricious, hungry, angry, degraded, cunning, faces – amid them Wilkinson, like the good man in a den of thieves – attorney Ward's sharp voice grinding disreputable reports and surmises – a drunken green-grocer clamouring for two years' pay etc. Wilkinson told me afterward that he was on the point of getting up to open the meeting with prayer, a thought to fill the eyes with tears.

Of the result, all I can say is that, so far so well. All depends on a meeting on the 4th October; which I shall help on as much as I can – I do so because I am convinced it is best for the Creditors, who are the *only* party I consider. I am now going to Bedford to see about the raising of some money – But I shall soon be back in Suffolk; where I want to be to push on affairs. I believe Boulge furniture will be sold.

I have seen no one in London but Lawyers and Creditors

and the one poor Debtor.

84 To Cowell
M.L., 22   London. November, 1848

Tennyson did in fact inherit the Poet Laureateship from Wordsworth two years later. The last sentence of this letter might have been suggested by the last part of Tennyson's Locksley Hall *('I will take some savage woman, she shall rear my dusky race'), published in 1842.*

... Tennyson is emerged half-cured, or half-destroyed, from a water establishment: has gone to a new Doctor who gives him iron pills; and altogether this really great man thinks more about his bowels and nerves than about the Laureate wreath he was born to inherit. Not but he meditates new poems; and now the Princess is done, he turns to King Arthur – a worthy subject indeed – and has consulted some histories of him, and spent some time visiting his traditionary haunts in Cornwall. But I believe the trumpet can wake Tennyson no longer to do great deeds; I may mistake and prove myself an owl; which I hope may be the case. But how are we to expect heroic poems from a valetudinary? I have told him he should fly from England and go among savages ...

85 To Cowell
L.F., I, 240–41   ? 1848

... As to Sophocles, I will not give up my old Titan. Is there not an infusion of Xenophon in Sophocles, as compared to Aeschylus, – a dilution? Sophocles is doubtless the better artist, the more complete; but are we to expect anything but glimpses and ruins of the divinest? Sophocles

Bernard Barton. Lithograph by J. H. Lynch after Samuel Lawrence. (*National Portrait Gallery*)

96

is a pure Greek temple; but Aeschylus is a rugged mountain, lashed by seas, and riven by thunderbolts: and which
is the more wonderful, and appalling? Or if one will have
Aeschylus too a work of man, I say he is like a Gothic
Cathedral, which the Germans say did arise from the genius
of man aspiring up to the immeasurable, and reaching after
the infinite in complexity and gloom, according as
Christianity elevated and widened men's minds. A dozen
lines of Aeschylus have a more Almighty power on me
than all Sophocles' plays; though I would perhaps rather
save Sophocles, as the consummation of Greek art, than
Aeschylus' twelve lines, if it came to a choice which must
be lost. Besides these Aeschyluses *trouble* us with their
grandeur and gloom; but Sophocles is always soothing,
complete, and satisfactory.

86 To Allen

L.F., I, 244   London. Spring, 1849

*During the winter of 1848 and the spring of 1849 FitzGerald shuttled
between Suffolk, where his old friend Bernard Barton was ailing (he died
on 19 February 1849) and London, to see lawyers and creditors about his
father's affairs. His visits to London were cheered by the company of
Tennyson, Carlyle, Spedding and Thackeray, whose novel* Pendennis
had begun appearing in parts in November 1848.

. . . I have seen Thackeray three or four times. He is just
the same. All the world admires Vanity Fair; and the
Author is courted by Dukes and Duchesses, and wits of
both sexes. I like Pendennis much; and Alfred said he
thought 'it was quite delicious: it seemed to him so
mature', he said. You can imagine Alfred saying this over
one's fire, spreading his great hand out.

87 To F. Tennyson

L.F., I, 245–7   Boulge. June 19, 1849

Monckton Milnes's Life, Letters and Literary Remains of John
Keats, *published in 1848, was the first revelation to the public of Keats's
wonderful letters, as well as of some of his most famous sonnets and odes,
unpublished in his lifetime. The mention of Bernard Barton's death and
his daughter's financial plight is ominous of FitzGerald's later disastrous
chivalry. FitzGerald's 'Memoir of Bernard Barton', his first publication
in prose, appeared in 1849 as the introduction to a volume of Barton's
poems and letters.*

. . . Of my own affairs I have nothing agreeable to tell . . .
When I met you in London, I was raising money for myself
on my reversionary property: and so I am still: and of
course the lawyers continue to do so in the most expensive
way; a slow torture of the purse. But do not suppose I
want money: I get it, at a good price: nor do I fret myself
about the price: there will be quite enough (if public
securities hold) for my life under any dispensation the
lawyers can inflict. As I grow older I want less. I have not
bought a book or a picture this year: have not been to a
concert, opera, or play: and, what is more, I don't care to
go. Not but if I meet you in London again I shall break out
into shilling concerts, etc., and shall be glad of the
opportunity . . .

By the by, beg, borrow, steal, or buy Keats' Letters and
Poems; most wonderful bits of Poems, written off hand at
a sitting, most of them: I only wonder that they do not
make a noise in the world . . .

I am now helping to edit some letters and poems of –
Bernard Barton! Yes: the poor fellow died suddenly of
heart disease; leaving his daughter, a noble woman, almost
unprovided for: and we are getting up this volume by
subscription . . .

Now there are some more things I could tell you, but you see where my pen has honestly got to in the paper. I remember you did not desire to hear about my garden, which is now gorgeous with large red poppies, and lilac irises – satisfactory colouring: and the trees murmur a continuous soft *chorus to the solo which my soul discourses within*. If that be not Poetry, I should like to know what is? and with it I may as well conclude . . .

88 To F. Tennyson

L.F., I, 250–51   Bedford. December 7, 1849

. . . In a week I go to London, where I hope to see Alfred. Oddly enough, I had a note from him this very day on which I receive yours: he has, he tells me, taken chambers in Lincoln's Inn Fields. Moxon told me he was about to publish another edition of his Princess, with interludes added between the parts: and also that he was about to print, but (I think) not to publish, those Elegiacs on Hallam. I saw poor old Thackeray in London: getting very slowly better of a bilious fever that had almost killed him. Some one told me that he was gone or going to the Water Doctor at Malvern. People in general thought Pendennis got dull as it got on; and I confess I thought so too: he would do well to take the opportunity of his illness to discontinue it altogether. He told me last June he himself was tired of it: must not his readers naturally tire too? Do you see Dickens' David Copperfield? It is very good, I think: more carefully written than his later works. But the melodramatic parts, as usual, bad. Carlyle says he is a showman whom one gives a shilling to once a month to see his raree-show, and then sends him about his business.

I have been obliged to turn Author on the very smallest scale. My old friend Bernard Barton chose to die in the early part of this year . . . We have made a Book out of his Letters and Poems, and published it by subscription . . . and I have been obliged to contribute a little dapper Memoir, as well as to select bits of Letters, bits of Poems, etc. All that was wanted is accomplished: many people subscribed. Some of B.B.'s letters are pleasant, I think, and when you come to England I will give you this little book of incredibly small value. I have heard no music but two concerts at Jullien's a fortnight ago; very dull, I thought: no beautiful new Waltzes and Polkas which I love. It is a strange thing to go to the Casinos and see the coarse whores and apprentices in bespattered morning dresses, pea-jackets, and bonnets, twirl round clumsily and indecently to the divine airs played in the Gallery; 'the music yearning like a God in pain' indeed . . .

89 To Allen
L.F., I, 256   Boulge. March 9, 1850

. . . I believe I love poetry almost as much as ever: but then I have been suffered to doze all these years in the enjoyment of old childish habits and sympathies, without being called on to more active and serious duties of life. I have not put away childish things, though a man. But, at the same time, this visionary inactivity is better than the mischievous activity of so many I see about me; not better than the useful and virtuous activity of a few others: John Allen among the number.

90 To F. Tennyson
L.F., I, 257–8   London. April 17, 1850

FitzGerald's father was now a sick and ruined man, separated from his wife; the clearing up after his bankruptcy chiefly fell on FitzGerald's shoulders, and this was a time of many anxieties for him.

You tell me to write soon: and this letter is begun, at least, on the day yours reaches me. This is partly owing to my having to wait an hour here in the Coffee room of the Portland Hotel: whither your letter has been forwarded to me from Boulge. I am come up for one week: once more to haggle with Lawyers; once more to try and settle my own affairs as well as those of others for a time . . .

I don't think of drowning myself yet: and what I wrote to you was a sort of safety escape for my poor flame . . . It is only idle and well-to-do people who kill themselves; it is ennui that is hopeless: great pain of mind and body 'still, still, on hope relies'; the very old, the very wretched, the most incurably diseased never put themselves to rest. It really gives me pain to hear you or any one else call me a philosopher, or any good thing of the sort. I am none, never was; and, if I pretended to be so, was a hypocrite. Some things, as wealth, rank, respectability, I don't care a straw about; but no one can resent the toothache more, nor fifty other little ills beside that flesh is heir to. But let us leave all this.

I am come to London; but I do not go to Operas or Plays: and have scarce time (and, it must be said, scarce inclination) to hunt up many friends. Dear old Alfred is out of town; Spedding is my sheet-anchor, the truly wise and fine fellow: I am going to his rooms this very evening: and there I believe Thackeray, Venables, etc., are to be. I hope not a large assembly: for I get shyer and shyer even of those I knew. Thackeray is in such a great world that I am afraid of him; he gets tired of me: and we are content to regard each other at a distance. You, Alfred, Spedding, and Allen, are the only men I ever care to see again . . .

91 To F. Tennyson

M.L., 23–6   Boulge. August 15, 1850

Alfred Tennyson married Emily Sellwood, and published In Memoriam, *in 1850. FitzGerald's visit to 'where the Lady of my old Love resides' would have been to Bredfield if the old love was Caroline Crabbe, or to Bramford, where the Cowells were now living, if his old love was Elizabeth Charlesworth, now Mrs Cowell. His reference to his study of Spanish 'with the help of a friend' supports the latter identification, since the friend who inspired him to study, and later translate, Calderon was Cowell. Carlyle's* Latterday Pamphlets *were published in 1850. Wordsworth died on 23 April of this year. 'Cider Phillips' was John Philips, author of a blank verse poem,* Cyder, *published in 1708. John Gay was the author of* The Beggar's Opera.

Let me hear something of you. The last I heard was three months and more ago, when you announced I was a Godfather. I replied instantly. Since all this, Alfred has got married. Spedding has seen him and his wife at Keswick: and speaks very highly of her. May all turn out well! Alfred has also published his Elegiacs on A. Hallam: these sell greatly: and will, I fear, raise a host of Elegiac scribblers.

Since I wrote to you, I have been down here, leading a life of my usual vacuity. My garden shows Autumn asters about to flower: chrysanthemums beginning to assert their places in the beds. The corn cutting all round. I have paid no visits except where the Lady of my old Love resides . . . I have begun to nibble at Spanish: at their old Ballads: which are fine things – like *our*, or rather the North Country, old Ballads. I have also bounced through a play of Calderon with the help of a friend – a very fine play of its kind. This Spanish literature is alone of its kind in

Europe, I fancy: with some *Arabian* blood in it. It was at one time over-rated perhaps: I think lately it has undergone the natural reaction of undervaluing. But I am not a fit judge perhaps: and after all shall never make much study of it.

I was in London for only ten days this Spring: and those ten days not in the thick of the season. So I am more than usually deficient in any news. The most pleasurable remembrance I had of my stay in town was the last day I spent there; having a long ramble in the streets with Spedding, looking at Books and Pictures: then a walk with him and Carlyle across the Park to Chelsea, where we dropped that Latter Day Prophet at his house; then getting upon a steamer, smoked down to Westminster: dined in a chophouse by the Bridge: and then went to Astley's: old Spedding being quite as wise about the Horsemanship as about Bacon and Shakespeare. We parted at midnight in Covent Garden: and this whole pleasant day has left a taste on my palate like one of Plato's lighter, easier, and more picturesque dialogues.

When I speak of the Latter Day Prophet, I conclude you have read, or heard of, Carlyle's Pamphlets so designed. People are tired of them and of him: he only foams, snaps, and howls, and no progress, people say: this is almost true: and yet there is vital good in all he has written . . .

You see Daddy Wordsworth is dead, and there is a huge subscription going on for his monument in Westminster Abbey. I believe he deserves one; but I am against stuffing Westminster Abbey with any one's statue till a hundred years or so have proved whether Posterity is as warm about a Man's Merits as we are. What a vast monument is erected to Cider Phillips – to Gay? – the last of whom I love, but yet would not interfere with the perfect Gothic of the Abbey to stick up his ugly bust in it . . . Thackeray goes on with Pendennis: which people think very clever, of course, but rather dull. It is nothing but about selfish London people.

92 To F. Tennyson

To FitzGerald's dismay, Mrs Cowell persuaded her husband to give up his job in the family business and go to Oxford to get a degree. FitzGerald feared that Oxford might divert Cowell from his Oriental studies, and also felt a more selfish regret for the idyllic life at the Bramford cottage which he had often shared. The 'neighbouring Parson' was George Crabbe.

. . . The delightful lady . . . is going to leave this neighbourhood and carry her young Husband to Oxford, there to get him some Oriental Professorship one day. He is a delightful fellow, and, *I* say, will, if he live, be the best Scholar in England. Not that I think Oxford will be so helpful to his studies as his counting house at Ipswich was. However, being married he cannot at all events become Fellow, and, as so many do, dissolve all the promise of Scholarship in Sloth, Gluttony, and sham Dignity. I shall miss them both more than I can say, and must take to Lucretius! to comfort me. I have entirely given up the *Genteel* Society here about; and scarce ever go anywhere but to the neighbouring Parson, with whom I discuss Paley's Theology, and the Gorham Question. I am going to him tonight, by the help of a Lantern, in order to light out the Old Year with a Cigar. For he is a great Smoker, and a very fine fellow in all ways.

I have not seen any one you know since I last wrote; nor heard from anyone: except dear old Spedding, who really came down and spent two days with us, me and that Scholar and his Wife in their Village, in their delightful little house, in their pleasant fields by the River side. Old Spedding was delicious there; always leaving a mark, I say, in all places one has been at with him, a sort of Platonic perfume. For has he not all the beauty of the Platonic Socrates, with some personal Beauty to boot? He explained to us one day about the laws of reflection in water: and I said then one never could look at the willow whose branches furnished the text without thinking of him. How beastly this reads! As if he gave us a lecture! But you know the man, how quietly it all came out; only because I petulantly denied his plain assertion. For I really often cross him only to draw him out; and vain as I may be, he is one of those that I am well content to make shine at my own expense . . .

As to Alfred, I have heard of his marriage, etc., from Spedding, who also saw and was much pleased with her indeed. But you know Alfred himself never writes, nor indeed cares a halfpenny about one, though he is very well satisfied to see one when one falls in his way. You will think I have a spite against him for some neglect, when I say this, and say besides that I cannot care for his In Memoriam. Not so, if I know myself: I always thought the same of him, and was just as well satisfied with it as now. His poem I never did greatly affect: nor can I learn to do so: it is full of finest things, but it is monotonous, and has that air of being evolved by a Poetical Machine of the highest order. So it seems to be with him now, at least to me, the Impetus, the Lyrical oestrus, is gone . . . It is the cursed inactivity (very pleasant to me who am no Hero) of this 19th century which has spoiled Alfred, I mean spoiled him for the great work he ought now to be entering upon; the lovely and noble things he has done must remain. It is dangerous work this prophesying about great Men . . .

I hear little music but what I make myself, or help to

make with my Parson's son and daughter. We, with not a voice among us, go through Handel's Coronation Anthems! Laughable it may seem; yet it is not quite so; the things are so well-defined, simple, and grand, that the faintest outline of them tells; my admiration of the old Giant grows and grows: his is the Music for a Great, Active, People. Sometimes too, I go over to a place elegantly called *Bungay*, where a Printer lives who drills the young folks of a manufactory there to sing in Chorus once a week . . . They sing some of the English Madrigals, some of Purcell, and some of Handel, in a way to satisfy me, who don't want perfection, and who believe that the *grandest* things do not depend on delicate finish. If you were here now, we would go over and hear the Harmonious Blacksmith sung in Chorus, with words, of course. It almost made me cry when I heard the divine Air rolled into vocal harmony from the four corners of a large Hall. One can scarce comprehend the Beauty of the English Madrigals till one hears them done (though coarsely) in this way and on a large scale: the play of the parts as they alternate from the different quarters of the room . . .

I am now going to sit down and play one of Handel's Overtures as well as I can – Semele, perhaps, a very grand one – then, lighting my lantern, trudge through the mud to Parson Crabbe's. Before I take my pen again to finish this letter the New Year will have dawned – on some of us. 'Thou fool! this night thy soul may be required of thee!' Very well: while it is in this Body I will wish my dear old F.T. a happy New Year. And now to drum out the Old with Handel. Good Night.

New Year's Day, 1851. A happy New Year to you! I sat up with my Parson till the Old Year was past, drinking punch and smoking cigars, for which I endure some headache this morning. Not that we took much; but a very little punch disagrees with me. Only I would not disappoint my old friend's convivial expectations. He is one of those happy men who has the boy's heart throbbing and trembling under the snows of sixty-five.

93 To Mrs Cowell
M.L., 27–8   London. February, 1851

It will be a great pleasure to me to do all I can for your poems . . . It is now just upon a year since I was looking at some of them at Bramford, after my return from Bedford: the spring flowers then coming out in your garden when I used to walk home laden with Keziah's cakes, stopped by a fall of snow at the Hockley's, too late for Mr Hughes' farewell sermon!

You talk of having all Suffolk about you. I think you should spare me a bit of Bramford. What shall it be? Enclosed with your Poems you shall send either one of Cowell's *slippers* – which I used to wear for him – or a little piece of green ribbon cut into a leaf pattern, which I remember you used to wear this time last year. Yes, send me that, a memorial of the past, and that (elderly knight as I am) I may be encouraged to venture on my critical labours with something like the scarf of fair Lady as a guerdon. This suggestion, begun but half earnestly, really is the one I will abide by in good earnest. Send me this; that while I look on it,

> I may seem
> As in the nights of old, to lie
> Beside the mill wheel in the stream,
> While *Spedding's Willow* whispers by.

It is a very odd thing, but quite true, I assure you, that before your letter came I was sitting at breakfast alone, and reading some of Moore's Songs, and thinking to myself how it was fame enough to have written but one song – air, or words – which should in after days solace the sailor at the wheel, or the soldier in foreign places! – be taken up into the life of England! No doubt 'The Last Rose of Summer' will accomplish this . . .

94 To Cowell
Terhune, 256   Boulge. June 13, 1851

The unexpectedly favourable opinion of Elizabeth Barrett Browning's poetry in this letter is interesting to compare with FitzGerald's crushingly anti-feminist verdict after her death (see Letter 121) which, when published after FitzGerald's own death, gave Browning such mortal offence.

. . . I see extracts in the *Athenaeum* from a new poem of Mrs Barrett Browning – 'Casa Guidi Windows' – a Dantesque survey of Italy – and really I am compelled to think *her* now a greater poet than Tennyson! That it should come to this! I don't mean that what she writes is equal to what he *wrote*, and was born to write; but better than what he has lately done or (as I fear) ever will do again. Mrs Browning writes on a noble, stirring, and nineteenth century subject; dashing away at rhyme and rhythm; often failing, often succeeding; at all events preserving the charm of impulse and *go*; not 'added and altered many times till all is ripe and rotten'. Yet I do not believe that her Poems are good enough to live . . .

95 To F. Tennyson

L.F., I, 269–70   Boulge. August 25, 1851

FitzGerald's fitful but genuine sense of social responsibility quite often led him to contribute to the musical education and enjoyments of his country neighbours; he sometimes enabled local organists to take a holiday by taking over their duties for a week or so, and he gave music classes.

. . . I do indeed take a survey of old Handel's Choruses now and then; and am just now looking with great delight into Purcell's King Arthur, real noble *English* music, much of it; and assuredly the prototype of much of Handel. It is said Handel would not admire Purcell; but I am sure he adapted himself to English ears and sympathies by means of taking up Purcell's vein. I wish you were here to consider this with me; but you would grunt dissent, and smile bitterly at my theories. I am trying to teach the bumpkins of the united parishes of Boulge and Debach to sing a second to such melodies as the women sing by way of Hymns in our Church: and I have invented (as I think) a most simple and easy way of teaching them the little they need to learn. How would you like to see me, with a bit of chalk in my hand, before a black board, scoring up semibreves on a staff for half a dozen Rustics to vocalize? Laugh at me in Imagination . . .

96 To F. Tennyson

L.F., I, 271–3   London. December, 1851

The Μαραθωνομάχους ἄνδρας *: the men who fought at the Battle of Marathon and saved Greece from the Persians.*

I have long been thinking I would answer a long and kind letter I had from you some weeks ago, in which you condoled with me about my finances, and offered me your house as a Refuge for the Destitute. I can never wonder at generosity in you: but I am sorry I should have seemed to complain so much as to provoke so much pity from you. I am not worse off than I have been these last three years; and so much better off than thousands who deserve more that I should deserve to be kicked if I whined over my decayed fortunes . . .

I have long felt about England as you do, and even made up my mind to it, so as to sit comparatively, if ignobly, easy on that score. Sometimes I envy those who are so old that the curtain will probably fall on them before it does on their Country. If one could save the Race, what a Cause it would be! not for one's own glory as a member of it, nor even for its glory as a Nation: but because it is the only spot in Europe where Freedom keeps her place. Had I Alfred's voice, I would not have mumbled for years over In Memoriam and the Princess, but sung such strains as would have revived the Μαραθωνομάχους ἄνδρας to guard the territory they had won. What can 'In Memoriam' do but make us all sentimental? . . .

97 To F. Tennyson

L.F., I, 275–8   Bedford. June 8, 1852

FitzGerald's financial affairs had now been sorted out, and he spent 1852 in visits to Allen in his parish at Press, near Shrewsbury, to Browne (now living at Goldington Hall, near Bedford) and to his mother, who had settled in a house near Richmond. FitzGerald's father died in March of this year. Thackeray's novel was Henry Esmond.

. . . Your letter found me at my Mother's house, at Ham, close to Richmond; a really lovely place, and neighbourhood, though I say it who am all prejudiced against London and 'all the purtenances thereof'. But the copious woods, green meadows, the Thames and its swans gliding between, and so many villas and cheerful houses and terraced gardens with all their associations of Wits and Courtiers on either side, all this is very delightful. I am not heroic enough for Castles, Battlefields, etc. Strawberry Hill for me! I looked all over it: you know all the pictures, jewels, curiosities were sold some ten years ago; only bare walls remain: the walls indeed here and there stuck with Gothic woodwork, and the ceilings with Gothic gilding, sometimes painted Gothic to imitate woodwork; much of it therefore in less good taste: all a Toy, but yet the Toy of a very clever man. The rain is coming through the Roofs, and gradually disengaging the confectionary Battlements and Cornices. Do you like Walpole? did you ever read him? Then close by is Hampton Court: with its stately gardens, and fine portraits inside: all very much to my liking. I am quite sure gardens should be formal, and unlike general Nature. I much prefer the old French and Dutch gardens to what are called the English . . .

Thackeray I saw for ten minutes: he was just in the agony of finishing a Novel: which has arisen out of the Reading necessary for his Lectures, and relates to those Times – of Queen Anne, I mean. He will get £1000 for his Novel. He was wanting to finish it, and rush off to the Continent, I think to shake off the fumes of it . . . Carlyle I did not go to see, for I really have nothing to tell him, and I have got tired of hearing him growl: though I do not cease to admire him as much as ever. I also went once to the pit of the Covent Garden Italian Opera, to hear Meyerbeer's Huguenots, of which I had only heard bits on the Pianoforte. But the first Act was so noisy, and ugly, that I came away, unable to wait for the better part, that, I am told, follows. Meyerbeer is a man of Genius: and works up *dramatic* Music: but he has scarce any melody, and is rather grotesque and noisy than really powerful. I think this is the fault of modern music; people cannot believe that Mozart is *powerful* because he is so Beautiful: in the same way as it requires a very practised eye (more than I possess) to recognize the consummate power predominating in the tranquil Beauty of Greek Sculpture. I think Beethoven is rather spasmodically, than sustainedly, grand . . .

I do not think I told you my Father was dead; like poor old Sedley in Thackeray's Vanity Fair, all his Coal schemes at an end. He died in March, after an illness of three weeks, saying 'that engine works well' (meaning one of his Colliery steam engines) as he lay in the stupor of Death. I was in Shropshire at the time, with my old friend Allen; but I went home to Suffolk just to help to lay him in the Grave . . .

Don't write Politics – I agree with you beforehand.

98 To Thackeray

Terhune, 183–4   Boulge. November 15, 1852

In October of this year Thackeray went on a lecture tour in the U.S.A. Before leaving he wrote an affectionate letter to FitzGerald, his 'best and oldest friend', asking him to be his literary executor and guardian of his daughters. FitzGerald, deeply touched, replied promising legacies to the Thackeray girls, and after Thackeray had left for America, sent the following letter. 'Bouillebaisse' is Thackeray's 'Ballad of the Bouillebaisse'. The sense of failure in life which FitzGerald expresses is characteristic of his undervaluation of his own achievement, for he was now launched into literature; his dialogue Euphranor *had been published in*

1851, his anthology Polonius, a Collection of Wise Saws and Modern Instances *appeared in 1852, he had already begun the translations from Spanish which were to be published in the following year, and in this winter of 1852 he began the Persian studies which were to lead him to fame. Those early works were, however, little noticed and his readers were few.*

I had your note – I dare scarce read it as it lies in my desk. It affects me partly as those old foolscap letters did, of which I told you I burned so many this spring: and why: – I was really ashamed of their kindness! If ever we get to another world, you will perhaps know why all this is so. I must not talk any more of what I have so often tried to explain to you. Meanwhile, I truly believe there is no man alive loves you (in his own way of love) more than I do. Now you are gone out of England, I can feel something of what I should feel if you were dead: I sit in this seedy place and read over Bouillebaisse till I cry again. This really is so: and is poor work: were you back again, I should see no more of you than before. But this is not from want of love on my part: it is because we live in such different worlds: and it is almost painful to me to tease anybody with my seedy dullness, which is just bearable by myself. Life every day seems a more total failure and mess to me: but it is yet bearable: and I am become a sad Epicurean – just desirous to keep on the windy side of bother and pain . . .

99 To George Crabbe the Younger

L.F., I, 282–3   Boulge. July 22, 1853

Six Dramas of Calderon, Freely Translated by Edward Fitz-Gerald *was published in July 1853, and got a rather cool reception.*

. . . I am very glad you like the plays and am encouraged

to hope that other persons who are not biassed by pedantic prejudices or spites might like them too. But I fully expect that (as I told you, I think) the London press, etc., will either sink them, or condemn them as on too free a principle: and all the more if they have not read the originals. For these are safe courses to adopt. All this while I am assuming the plays are well done in their way, which of course I do. On the other hand, they may really not be as well done as I think; on their own principle: and that would really be a fair ground of condemnation.

100 To F. Tennyson

L.F., I, 288–9   Bath. May 7, 1854

In the autumn of 1853 FitzGerald gave up his cottage at Boulge, and for the next few years he had no settled home but shifted around staying in lodgings and with the Crabbes at Bredfield, the Cowells at Oxford, at Geldestone, at Bedford, in London, and with his sister Andalusia, now living at Bath. 'Old Vathek's Tower' is the tower that William Beckford, author of Vathek, *built when he lived at Bath after his loss of Fonthill Abbey, whose jerry-built tower later collapsed, hence FitzGerald's comment 'while it stood'. Walter Savage Landor lived in Bath from 1838 to 1858, but died in Italy. Samuel Rogers died in 1855, aged 92.*

. . . If ever you live in England you must live here at Bath. It really is a splendid City in a lovely, even a noble, Country. Did you ever see it? One beautiful feature in the place is the quantity of Garden and Orchard it is all through embroidered with. Then the Streets, when you go into them, are as handsome and gay as London, gayer and handsomer because cleaner and in a clearer Atmosphere; and if you want the Country you get into it (and a very fine Country) on all sides and directly. Then there is such Choice of Houses, Cheap as well as Dear, of all sizes, with good

W. M. Thackeray. Oil sketch by Samuel Laurence.
(*National Portrait Gallery*)

Markets, Railways, etc. I am not sure I shall not come here for part of the Winter. It is a place you would like, I am sure: though I do not say but you are better in Florence. Then on the top of the hill is old Vathek's Tower, which he used to sit and read in daily, and from which he could see his own Fonthill, while it stood. Old Landor quoted to me 'Nullus in orbe locus, etc.,' apropos of Bath: he, you may know, has lived here for years, and I should think would die here, though not yet. He seems so strong that he may rival old Rogers; of whom indeed one Newspaper gave what is called an 'Alarming Report of Mr. Rogers' Health' the other day, but another contradicted it directly and indignantly, and declared the Venerable Poet never was better. Landor has some hundred and fifty Pictures; each of which he thinks the finest specimen of the finest Master, and has a long story about, how he got it, when, etc. I dare say some are very good: but also some very bad. He appeared to me to judge of them as he does of Books and Men; with a most uncompromising perversity which the Phrenologists must explain to us after his Death . . .

101 To Stephen Spring Rice
Terhune, 194   Bury St Edmunds. October 21, 1856

From 1854 to the late summer of 1856 FitzGerald led a fairly tranquil life, studying Persian, visiting the Tennysons at Farringford, being visited by Carlyle at the farmhouse at Farlingay in Suffolk where he lodged at intervals during these years, sailing along the South Coast, touring France, Belgium and Germany with Browne and the younger Crabbe. His mother died in January 1855 and he came into his share of her estate. But the summer of 1856 brought three events which profoundly affected his life. Cowell found in the Bodleian and copied for FitzGerald a manuscript of the Rubaiyat *of Omar Khayyam; Cowell accepted a post in Calcutta, and the Cowells left for India in August, to Fitz-*

Gerald's sorrow; and he decided, now that his financial position was secure, that he must honour the undertaking which he apparently gave to Bernard Barton on his death-bed, to look after his daughter. How FitzGerald's mistaken chivalry had turned this undertaking from a financial commitment into a promise of marriage has been explained in the Introduction. The next few letters relate to the brief and disastrous marriage, from which all his friends tried to dissuade him, and to his regret for the Cowells.

I am going to be married to Miss Barton, a very doubtful experiment – long thought of – not fixt beyond all Cause and Impediment till lately – and now 'Vogue la Galère!' I shut my eyes to the Consequences, and read trash in Hafiz . . . Oh, I am very tired of writing this News to Relatives etc.

102 **To Cowell**

L.F., I, 310–11, and Terhune, 196

London.
January 22, 1857

FitzGerald married Lucy Barton on 4 November 1856; they spent six unhappy weeks at Brighton, then they parted for a month, but rejoined in London where they lived in lodgings for February and March 1857. FitzGerald, aware even before his marriage that it was bound to fail, made no secret of his misery to Cowell. His Persian studies were his only consolation; this letter to Cowell ended with pages of learned detail about Persian literature. Already in 1856 FitzGerald had published his first translation from the Persian, Jami's Salaman and Absal.

My marriage . . . had good Sense and Experience prevailed instead of Blind Regard on one side . . . never *would* have been completed! You know my opinion of a 'Man of Taste' – never so dangerous as when tied down to daily Life Companionhood – and with one very differently complexioned and Educated, and who might have been

117

far happier and usefuller untied to me. She wants a large Field to work on, and to bestow her Labour on a Field that will answer to Tillage . . . I believe before long I shall offer a Field for some sort of Labour, if not the best; for I am not well, and shall, I really believe, very soon be laid by (if not dead) and *then* I shall put all my Taste into the Fire, I suppose; and my Wife will be rejoiced at last to be a Slave with a Master who can at last thank her for her Pains . . , I have now been five weeks alone at my old Lodgings in London where you came this time last year! My wife in Norfolk. She came up yesterday; and we have taken Lodgings for two months in the Regent's Park. And I positively stay behind here in the old Place on purpose to write to you in the same condition you knew me in and I you! I believe there are new Channels fretted in my Cheeks with many unmanly Tears since then, 'remembering the Days that are no more', in which you two are so mixt up. Well, well; I have no news to tell you. Public matters you know I don't meddle with; and I have scarce seen any Friends even while in London here. Carlyle but once; Thackeray not once; Spedding and Donne pretty often . . . I hear Tennyson goes on with King Arthur; but I have not seen or heard from him for a long long while.

Oddly enough, as I finished the last sentence, Thackeray was announced; he came in looking gray, grand, and good-humoured; and I held up this Letter and told him whom it was written to and he sends his Love! He goes Lecturing all over England; has fifty pounds for each Lecture: and says he is ashamed of the Fortune he is making. But he deserves it.

And now for my poor Studies. I have read really very little except Persian since you went: and yet, from want of Eyes, not very much of that. I have gone carefully over two-thirds of Hafiz again with Dictionary and Von

Hammer: and gone on with Jami and Nizami. But my great Performance all lies in the last five weeks since I have been alone here; when I wrote to Napoleon Newton to ask him to lend me his MS of Attar's Mantic uttair; and, with the help of Garcin de Tassy have nearly made out about two-thirds of it. For it has greatly interested me, though I confess it is always an old Story. The Germans make a Fuss about the Sufi Doctrine; but, as far as I understand it, it is not very abstruse Pantheism, and always the same. One becomes as wearied of the *man-i* and *du-i* in their Philosophy as of the *bulbul*, etc. in their Songs . . .

Write to me; direct – whither? For till I see better how we get on I dare fix on no place to live or die in. Direct to me at Crabbe's, Bredfield, till you hear further.

103 To Cowell
L.F., I, 318–20   London. March 12, 1857

. . . Shall we ever meet again? I think not; or not in such plight, both of us, as will make Meeting what it used to be. Only today I have been opening dear old Salaman: the original Copy we bought and began this time three years ago at Oxford; with all my scratches of Query and Explanation in it, and the Notes from you among the Leaves. How often I think with Sorrow of my many Harshnesses and Impatiences! which are yet more of manner than Intention. My wife is sick of hearing me sing in a doleful voice the old Glee of 'When shall we Three Meet again?' Especially the Stanza, 'Though in foreign Lands we sight, Parcht beneath a hostile Sky, etc.' . . . It seems to me it would be easy to get into the first great Ship and never see Land again till I saw the Mouth of the Ganges! and there live what remains of my shabby Life . . .

It is an amusement to me to take what Liberties I like

with these Persians, who (as I think) are not Poets enough to frighten one from such excursions, and who really do want a little Art to shape them. I don't speak of Jelaleddin whom I know so little of (enough to show me that he is no great Artist, however), nor of Hafiz, whose *best* is untranslatable because he is the best Musician of Words. Old Johnson said the Poets were the best Preservers of a Language: for people must go to the Original to relish them. I am sure that what Tennyson said to you is true: that Hafiz is the most Eastern – or, he should have said, most *Persian* – of the Persians. He is the best representative of their character, whether his Saki and Wine be real or mystical. Their Religion and Philosophy is soon seen through, and always seems to me *cuckooed* over like a borrowed thing, which people, once having got, don't know how to parade enough. To be sure, their Roses and Nightingales are repeated enough; but Hafiz and old Omar Khayyam ring like True Metal. The Philosophy of the Latter is, alas!, one that never fails in the World. 'Today is ours, etc.' . . .

104 To Cowell

L.F., I, 321–2   London. March 29, 1857

. . . I had a letter from your Mother telling me she had heard from you – all well – but the Heats increasing. I suppose the Crocuses we see even in these poor little Gardens hereabout would wither in a Glance of your Sun. Now the black Trees in the Regent's Park opposite are beginning to show green Buds; and Men come with great Baskets of Flowers; Primroses, Hepaticas, Crocuses, great Daisies, etc., calling as they go, 'Growing, Growing, Growing! All the Glory going!' So my wife says she heard them call: some old Street cry, no doubt, of which we have so few remaining. It will almost make you smell them all the way from Calcutta. 'All the Glory going!' . . .

I took up old Hafiz again, and began with him where I left off in November at Brighton. And this morning came to an ode we did together this time two years ago when you were at Spiers' in Oxford . . . How it brought all back to me! Oriel opposite, and the Militia in Broad Street, and the old Canary-coloured Sofa and the Cocoa or Tea on the Table! . . .

Tuesday April 21. Yours and your wife's dear good Letters put into my hand as I sit in the sunshine in a little Balcony outside the Windows looking upon the quite green hedge side of the Regent's Park. For Green it is thus early, and such weather as I never remember before at this Season. Well, your Letters, I say, were put into my hand as I was there looking into Aeschylus under an Umbrella, and waiting for Breakfast. My wife cried a good deal over your wife's Letter, I think, I think so. Ah me! I would not as yet read it, for I was already sad; but I shall answer hers to me which I did read indeed with many thoughts: perhaps I can write this post; at least I will clear off this letter to you, my dear Cowell.

105 To Cowell

L.F., I, 331–3   Yarmouth. June 5, 1857

In May FitzGerald went to stay with Browne at Goldington; in June he joined his wife at Yarmouth.

. . . Instead of the Regent's Park, and Regent Street, here before my windows are the Vessels going in and out of this River: and Sailors walking about with fur caps and their brown hands in their Breeches Pockets . . . When in

Bedfordshire I put away almost all books except Omar Khayyam!, which I could not help looking over in a Paddock covered with Buttercups and brushed by a delicious Breeze, while a dainty racing Filly of W. Browne's came startling up to wonder and snuff about me . . . Omar breathes a sort of Consolation to me! Poor Fellow; I think of him, and Oliver Basselin, and Anacreon; lighter Shadows among the Shades, perhaps, over which Lucretius presides so grimly . . .

106 To Mrs Allen

L.F., I, 337–9   Geldestone. August 15, 1857

In August, FitzGerald and his wife parted for good; he settled a generous income on her, and returned to his bachelor life, with the only kind of family relationship that suited him – the company of his sister Eleanor and her children; and to the consolation of friendship with Browne and Cowell, though there was anxiety in the thought of the latter in an India torn by the Mutiny.

One should be very much gratified at being remembered so long with *any* kindness: and how much more gratified with so kind Remembrances as yours! I may safely say that I too remember you and my Freestone days of five and twenty years ago with a particular regard; I have been telling my Nieces at the Breakfast Table this morning, after I read your letter, how I remembered you sitting in the '*Schoolroom*' – too much sheltered with Trees – with a large Watch open before you – your Sister too, with her light hair and China-rose Complexion – too delicate! – your Father, your Mother, your Brother – of whom (your Brother) I caught a glimpse in London two years ago. And all the *Place* at Freestone – I can walk about it as I lie awake here, and see the very yellow flowers in the fields, and hear that distant sound of explosion in some distant Quarry. The coast at Bosherston one could never forget once seen, even if it had no domestic kindness to frame its Memory in. I might have profited more of those good Days than I did; but it is not my Talent to take the Tide at its flow; and so all goes to worse than waste!

But it is ungracious to talk of oneself – except so far as shall answer some points you touch on. It would in many respects be very delightful to me to walk again with you over those old Places; in other respects sad: – but the pleasure would have the upper hand if one had not again to leave it all and plunge back again. I dare not go to Wales now.

I owe to Tenby the chance acquaintance of another Person who now from that hour remains one of my very best Friends. A Lad – then just 16 – whom I met on board the Packet from Bristol: and next morning at the Boarding House – apt then to appear with a little *chalk* on the edge of his Cheek from a touch of the Billiard Table Cue – and now a man of 40 – Farmer, Magistrate, Militia Officer – Father of a Family – of more use in a week than I in my Life long. You too have six sons, your Letter tells me. They may do worse than do as well as he I have spoken of, though he too has sown some wild oats, and paid for doing so.

My family consists of some eight Nieces here, whom I have seen, all of them, from their Birth upwards – perfectly good, simple, and well-bred, women and girls; varying in disposition but all agreed among themselves and to do what they can in a small Sphere. They go about in the Village here with some consolation both for Body and Mind for the Poor, and have no desire for the Opera, nor for the Fine Folks and fine Dresses there. There is however some melancholy in the Blood of some of them – but none that mars any happiness but their own: and that but so slightly as one should expect when there was no Fault, and no Remorse, to embitter it!

You will perhaps be as well entertained with this poor familiar news as any I could tell you. As to public matters, I scarcely meddle with them, and don't know what to think of India except that it is very terrible. I always think a Nation with great Estates is like a Man with them: – more trouble than Profit: I would only have a *Competence* for my Country as for myself. Two of my very dearest Friends went but last year to Calcutta: – he as Professor at the Presidency College there: and now he has to shoulder a musket, I believe, as well as deliver a Lecture. You and yours are safe at home, I am glad to think.

Please to remember me to all whom I have shaken hands with, and make my kind Regards to those of your Party I have not yet seen. I am sure all *would be* as kind to me as others who bear the name of Allen *have been*.

Once more – thank you thank you for *your* kindness; and believe me yours as ever very truly,

107 **To G. Crabbe the Younger**
M.L., 47   Goldington. September 19, 1857

FitzGerald's convivial old friend George Crabbe, Vicar of Bredfield, with whom FitzGerald had partly made his home during the last four wandering years, died in September 1857. The Crabbe family had been kind to Lucy Barton when her father died, and FitzGerald felt she might now be sustained by giving the Crabbe sisters that bossy mothering which he himself had found insupportable.

I got your Letter today. In case I should not go to the Funeral, it will only be from my nervous fear of making any Figure in it; and I can't feel sure but I might make too much of one, for it is certain I feel your Father's loss more than any I have felt – except Major Moore's perhaps, whom, if I had known longer, I had not lived nearly so much with. If I go, it will be rather for the sake of the Living. I want your Sisters so much to go to my Wife at Gorlestone, when they can, and for as long as they can: and I have had a Letter from her today, hoping so they *will* but let her in that way return them some of the Sympathy they showed her when *her* Trial was. I am convinced that their going to her would be the very thing for herself, poor Soul; taking her out of herself, and giving her the very thing she is pining for; namely, some one to devote herself to. I write to your Sister to say this. And mind you tell me any use I can be to you, for I can't say what a pleasure it will be to me, and what a heap of unrepaid obligations I feel always on my Shoulders for the kindness and all the happy peaceful Times I have experienced at Bredfield for the last ten years . . .

108 To Cowell

L.F., I, 340–41   Rushmere. October 3, 1857

When this letter was written, news had not yet reached England that Lucknow, where a thousand English men, women and children were besieged by the Mutineers, had been reached, after three agonizing months, by Havelock's relieving forces on 25 September.

I hope things will not be so black with you and us by the time this Letter reaches you, but you may be amused and glad to have it from me. Not that I have come into Suffolk on any cheerful Errand: I have come to bury dear old Mr. Crabbe! I suppose you have had some Letters of mine telling you of his Illness; Epileptic Fits which came successively and weakened him gradually, and at last put him to his Bed entirely, where he lay some while unable to move himself or to think! They said he might lie so a long time, since he eat and drank with fair Appetite: but suddenly the End came on and after a twelve hours Stupor he died. On Tuesday September 22 he was buried; and I came from Bedfordshire (where I had only arrived two days before) to assist at it. I and Mr. Drew were the only persons invited not of the Family; but there were very many Farmers and Neighbours come to pay respect to the remains of the brave old Man, who was buried, by his own desire, among the poor in the Churchyard in a Grave that he wishes to be no otherwise distinguisht than by a common Head and Footstone . . .

You may imagine it was melancholy enough to me to revisit the house when He who had made it so warm for me so often lay cold in his Coffin unable to entertain me any more! His little old dark Study (which I called the '*Cobblery*') smelt strong of its old Smoke: and the last Cheroot he had tried lay three quarters smoked in its little China Ash-pan. This I have taken as a Relic, as also a little silver Nutmeg Grater which used to give the finishing Touch to many a Glass of good hot Stuff, and also had belonged to the Poet Crabbe . . .

Last night I had some of your Letters read to me: among them one but yesterday arrived, not very sunshiny in its prospects: but your Brother thinks the Times Newspaper of yesterday somewhat bids us look up. Only, all are trembling for Lucknow, crowded with Helplessness and Innocence! I am ashamed to think how little I understand of all these things: but have wiser men, and men in Place, understood much more? or, understanding, have they *done* what they should? . . .

Love to the dear Lady, and may you be now and for time to come safe and well is the Prayer of yours . . .

109 **To Cowell**

L.F., I, 343–4   London. December 8, 1857

*So far, FitzGerald had mentioned to Cowell only some translations into
Latin which he had made of parts of the* Rubaiyat *of the twelfth-century
Persian poet Omar Khayyam, but now he revealed that he had done an
English version, and was thinking of publishing it; though he thought
Omar's scepticism, which the French scholar Garcin de Tassy had played
down in a published paper about the Persian poet, but which FitzGerald
had fully exposed in his translation, might be unacceptable. His suspicion
that* Fraser's Magazine *would not accept his translation was justified;
the editor kept it for a year but did not publish it.*

... And now about old Omar. You talked of sending a
Paper about him to Fraser and I told you, if you did, I
would stop it till I had made my Comments. I suppose you
have not had time to do what you proposed, or are you
overcome with the Flood of bad Latin I poured upon you?
Well: don't be surprised (*vext*, you won't be) if I solicit
Fraser for room for a few Quatrains in English Verse,
however – with only such an Introduction as you and
Sprenger give me – very short – so as to leave you to say
all that is Scholarly if you will, I hope this is not very
Cavalier of me. But in truth I take old Omar rather more
as my property than yours: he and I are more akin, are we
not? You see all Beauty, but you don't feel *with* him in some
respects as I do. I think you would almost feel obliged to
leave out the part of Hamlet in representing him to your
Audience: for fear of Mischief. Now I do not wish to show
Hamlet at his maddest: but mad he must be shown, or he
is no Hamlet at all. G.de Tassy eluded all that was danger-

ous, and all that was characteristic. I think these *free* opinions are less dangerous in an old Mahometan, or an old Roman (like Lucretius) than when they are returned to by those who have lived on happier Food. I don't know what you will say to all this. However I dare say it won't matter whether I do the Paper or not, for I don't believe they'll put it in . . .

110 To Mrs Tennyson

H. Tennyson, 101   London. March 19, 1858

My married life has come to an end: I am back again in the old quarters, living as for the last thirty years – only so much older, sadder, uglier, and worse! – If people want to go further for the cause of this blunder, than the fact of two people of very determined habits and temper first trying to change them at close on fifty – they may lay nine-tenths of the blame on me. I don't want to talk more of the matter, but one must say something.

111 To Cowell

L.F., I, 348   Farlingay. November 2, 1858

Parker was the publisher of FitzGerald's translation Salaman and Absal; *it was he who had suggested that* Fraser's *might take the Omar translation.*

. . . As to Omar, I hear and see nothing of it in Fraser yet: and so I suppose they don't want it. I told Parker he might find it rather dangerous among his Divines: he took it however, and keeps it. I really think I shall take it back; add some Stanzas which I kept out for fear of being too strong; print fifty copies and give away; one to you, who won't like it neither. Yet it is most ingeniously tesselated into a sort of Epicurean Eclogue in a Persian Garden.

112 To Donne
L.F., II, 3   Bedford. March 26, 1859

In January 1859, Browne was fatally injured in a riding accident; he lingered for two months. FitzGerald went to visit him when it was clear he was dying. He died on 30 March, five days after FitzGerald saw him.

Your folks told you on what Errand I left your house so abruptly. I was not allowed to see W. B. the day I came: nor yesterday till 3 p.m.; when, poor fellow, he tried to write a line to me, like a child's! and I went, and saw, no longer the gay Lad, nor the healthy Man, I had known: but a wreck of all that: a Face like Charles I. (after decapitation almost) above the Clothes: and the poor shattered Body underneath lying as it had lain eight weeks; such a case as the Doctor says he had never known. Instead of the light utterance of other days too, came the slow painful syllables in a far lower Key: and when the old familiar words, 'Old Fellow – Fitz' – etc., came forth, so spoken, I broke down too in spite of foregone Resolution.

They thought he'd die last Night: but this Morning he is a little better: but no hope. He has spoken of me in the Night, and (if he wishes) I shall go again, provided his Wife and Doctor approve. But it agitates him: and Tears he could not wipe away came to his Eyes. The poor Wife bears up wonderfully.

FitzGerald's translation of the Rubaiyat *was published at the beginning of April 1859, but passed almost entirely unnoticed for the next two years. 'The Bird Epic' mentioned in this letter is Attar's* Mantik-ut-tair. *FitzGerald completed a translation of it,* The Bird Parliament, *one of his finest works, but never published in his lifetime.*

. . . I have had a great Loss. W. Browne was fallen upon and half crushed by his horse near three months ago: and though the Doctors kept giving hopes while he lay patiently for two months in a condition no one else could have borne for a Fortnight, at last they could do no more, nor Nature neither: and he sunk. I went to see him before he died – the comely spirited Boy I had known first seven and twenty years ago lying all shattered and Death in his Face and Voice . . .

Well, this is so: and there is no more to be said about it. It is one of the things that reconcile me to my own stupid Decline of Life – to the crazy state of the world – Well – no more about it.

I sent you poor old Omar who has *his* kind of Consolation for all these Things. I doubt you will regret you ever introduced him to me. And yet you would have me print the original, with many worse things than I have translated. The Bird Epic might be finished at once: but 'cui bono?' No one cares for such things: and there are doubtless so many better things to care about. I hardly know why I print any of these things, which nobody buys; and I scarce now see the few I give them to. But when one has done one's best, and is sure that that best is better than so many will take pains to do, though far from the best that *might be done*, one likes to make an end of the matter by Print. I suppose very few People have ever taken such Pains in Translation as I have: though certainly not to be literal. But at all Cost, a Thing must *live*: with a transfusion of one's own worse Life if one can't retain the Original's better. Better a live Sparrow than a stuffed Eagle. I shall be very well pleased to see the new MS. of Omar. I shall *one day* (if I live) print the 'Birds', and a strange experiment on old Calderon's two great Plays; and then shut up Shop in the Poetic Line . . .

114 To Mrs Allen

L.F., II, 10   Lowestoft. October 26, 1859

. . . But Tenby – I don't remember a pleasanter Place. I can now hear the Band on the Steamer as it left the little Pier for Bristol, the Steamer that brought me and the poor Boy now in his Grave to that Boardinghouse. It was such weather as now howls about this Lodging when one of those poor starved Players was drowned on the Sands, and was carried past our Windows after Dinner: I often remember the dull Trot of Men up the windy Street, and our running to the Window, and the dead Head, hair, and Shoulders hurried past. That was Tragedy, poor Fellow, whatever Parts he had played before.

I think you remember me with Kindness because accidentally associated with your old Freestone in those pleasant Days, that also were among the last of your Sister's Life. Her too I can see, with her China-rose complexion: in the Lilac Gown she wore.

I keep on here from Week to week, partly because no other Place offers: but I almost doubt if I shall be here beyond next week. Not in this Lodging anyhow: which is wretchedly 'rafty' and cold; lets the Rain in when it Rains:

and the Dust of the Shore when it drives: as both have been doing by turns all Yesterday and To day. I was cursing all this as I was shivering here by myself last Night: and in the Morning I hear of three Wrecks off the Sands, and indeed meet five shipwreckt Men with a Troop of Sailors as I walk out before Breakfast. Oh Dear! . . .

115 To Pollock

L.F., II, 12–14   Lowestoft. February 23, 1860

FitzGerald spent the winter of 1859–60 in lodgings at Lowestoft, reading old favourites, new novels like Thackeray's Lovel the Widower *and Trollope's* Barchester Towers, *and magazine articles like Pollock's on 'British Novelists' in* Fraser's *Magazine. He also wandered about watching the life of the local fishermen, in whose company and pursuits a new chapter of his life was about to begin. 'Sir C. Napier' was Admiral Sir Charles Napier, known as 'Black Charley'. 'Thackeray's first Number' was the first issue of the* Cornhill, *of which Thackeray was editor.*

'Me voilà ici' still! having weathered it out so long. No bad Place, I assure you, though you who are accustomed to Pall Mall, Clubs, etc., wouldn't like it. Mudie finds one out easily: and the London Library too: and altogether I can't complain of not getting such drowsy books as I want. Hakluyt lasted a long while: then came Captain Cook, whom I hadn't read since I was a Boy, and whom I was very glad to see again . . .

Sir C. Napier came here to try and get the Beachmen to enlist in the Naval Reserve. Not one would go: they won't give up their Independence: and so really half starve here during Winter. Then Spring comes and they go and catch the Herrings which, if left alone, would multiply by Millions by Autumn: and so kill their Golden Goose.

They are a strange set of Fellows. I think a Law ought to be made against their Spring Fishing: more important, for their own sakes, than Game Laws.

I laid out half a crown on your Fraser: and liked much of it very much: especially the Beginning about the Advantage the Novelist has over the Playwriter. A little too much always about Miss Austen, whom yet I think quite capital in a Circle I have found quite unendurable to walk in. Thackeray's first Number was famous, I thought: his own little Roundabout Paper so pleasant: but the Second Number, I say, lets the Cockney in already: about Hogarth; Lewes is vulgar: and I don't think one can care much for Thackeray's Novel. He is always talking so of himself, too. I have been very glad to find I can take to a Novel again, in Trollope's Barchester Towers, etc.: not perfect, like Miss Austen: but then so much wider Scope: and perfect enough to make me feel I know the People though caricatured or carelessly drawn . . .

I suppose when the Fields and Hedges begin to grow green I shall move a little further inland to be among them.

116 To Mrs Cowell

M.L., 52–4   Farlingay. August 21, 1860

. . . I have never set foot in London since last March year, except running through to Dorsetshire last Autumn: nor have I set eyes on Donne, Spedding, or any of the Wise Men since. It is wrong not to go: but I have lost all Curiosity about what London has to see and hear: its Books come to me here from Mudie: and W. Browne is too much connected with my old Taverns and Streets not to fling a sad shadow over all. As I have not had the courage to go into Bedfordshire, Mrs B. wished her Boys to come to see me in Suffolk, So I took them to Aldbro', where they were happy Boating and Shooting with a young Sailor, who, strangely enough, reminded me something of their Father as I first knew him near thirty years ago! This was a strange thing: and my Thoughts run after that poor Fisher Lad who has now gone off in a smack to the North. I always like Seafaring People: and go now every day almost on the Water: either this old Deben here, or on the Sea. Somehow all the Country round is become a Cemetery to me: so many I loved there dead: but none I have loved have been drown'd. Perhaps this poor Sailor who played with W.B.'s Boys as a Boy, and yet took a sort of tender Care of them, will go down into the Deep and blacken that too to my Eyes . . .

I have not looked into Persian of late: but I mean if I live to take it up again, and do a little day by day: so as not quite to lose what I have learnt. I do not expect to take any great Interest in it: though I might like the Mesnavi if it were presented to me in a large clear Type. But I can't give my Eyes up to MSS. for any upshot that Persian is like to render me. What astonishes me is, Shakespeare: when I look into him it is not a Book, but People talking all round me. Instead of wearying of him, I only wonder and admire afresh. Milton seems a deadweight compared . . .

117 To G. Crabbe the Younger
L.F., II, 17–18   Woodbridge. December 28, 1860

In December 1860 FitzGerald settled into the lodgings in the centre of the Suffolk town of Woodbridge which were his home for the next fourteen years. His visits to London were now mostly only rapid excursions for an exhibition or a theatre. The Holman Hunt picture criticized in this letter was his Finding of the Saviour in the Temple, *on which he had worked for six years, which the dealer Gambart had bought for 5500 guineas (the highest sum ever till then paid for the work of a living painter) and which was exhibited by itself at a Bond Street gallery for most of 1860.*

. . . I forgot to tell you I really ran to London three weeks ago: by the morning Express, and was too glad to rush back by the Evening Ditto. I went up for a Business I of course did not accomplish: did not call on, or see, a Friend: couldn't get into the National Gallery: and didn't care a straw for Holman Hunt's Picture. No doubt, there is Thought and Care in it: but what an outcome of several Years and sold for several Thousands! What Man with the Elements of a Great Painter could come out with such a costive Thing after so long waiting! Think of the Acres of Canvas Titian or Reynolds would have covered with grand Outlines in deep Colours in the Time it has taken to niggle this Miniature! The Christ seems to me only a wayward Boy: the Jews, Jews no doubt: the Temple I dare say very correct in its Detail: but think of even Rembrandt's Woman in Adultery at the National Gallery; a much smaller Picture, but how much vaster in Space and Feeling! Hunt's Picture stifled me with its Littleness. I think Ruskin must see what his System has led to . . .

118 To Donne
W.B.D.F., 251   Woodbridge. February 28, 1861

. . . I have not been well and we're all growing old: and 'tis time to think of curling oneself up like a Dog about to lie down. Had I worked as you have done, I should have given way years and years ago: but like a selfish Beast, I have kept out of obligations and self-sacrifices. I only say *this* in self-defence: that, if I don't exert myself for other's Good, I don't do so for their harm; and if I keep selfishly to myself, at least don't intrude on others. Enough of all that. It is a very poor Business . . .

119 To G. Crabbe the Younger

L.F., II, 18–19   Woodbridge. May 20, 1861

FitzGerald was now growing ever fonder of sailing, and had had a small boat, the Waveney, *built for sailing on the river Deben and along the Suffolk coast. The version of 'manoeuvring and skirmishing' which he quotes in this letter is an example of his increasing interest in Suffolk dialect and malapropisms, which he often quoted in his later letters.*

... I take pleasure in my new little Boat: and last week went with her to Aldbro'; and she *'behaved'* very well both going and returning; though, to be sure, there was not much to try her Temper. I am so glad of this fine Whit-Monday, when so many Holiday-makers will enjoy *their*selves, and so many others make a little money by their Enjoyment. Our 'Rifles' are going to march to Grundis-burgh, *manuring* and *skrimmaging* as they go, and also (as the Captain hopes) recruiting. He is a right good little Fellow, I do believe. It is a shame the Gentry hereabout are so indifferent in the Matter: they subscribe next to nothing: and give absolutely nothing in the way of Entertainment or Attention to the Corps. But we are split up into the pettiest possible Squirarchy, who want to make the utmost of their little territory: cut down all the Trees, level all the old Violet Banks, and stop all the Footways they can. The old pleasant way from Hasketon to Bredfield is now a Desert. I was walking it yesterday and had the pleasure of breaking down and through some Bushes and Hurdles put up to block a fallen Stile. I thought what your Father would have said of it all. And really it is the sad ugliness of our once pleasant Fields that half drives me to the Water where the Power of the Squirarchy stops!

120 To Cowell

L.F., II, 20–21   Woodbridge. May 22, 1861

. . . My chief Amusement in Life is Boating, on River and Sea. The Country about here is the Cemetery of so many of my oldest Friends: and the petty race of Squires who have succeeded only use the Earth for an *Investment*: cut down every old Tree: level every Violet Bank: and make the old Country of my Youth hideous to me in my Decline. There are fewer Birds to be heard, as fewer Trees for them to resort to. So I get to the Water: where Friends are not buried nor Pathways stopt up: but all is, as the Poets say, as Creation's Dawn beheld. I am happiest going in my little Boat round the Coast to Aldbro', with some Bottled Porter and some Bread and Cheese, and some good rough Soul who works the Boat and chews his Tobacco in peace. An Aldbro' Sailor talking of my Boat said – She go like a Wiolin, she do! What a pretty Conceit, is it not? As the Bow slides over the Strings in a liquid Tune. Another man was talking yesterday of a great storm: 'and, in a moment, all as calm as a Clock' . . .

121 To Thompson

L.F. (first edition), I, 280–81   Woodbridge.
July 15, 1861

Elizabeth Barrett Browning died in Florence on 29 June 1861. Fitz-Gerald's light-hearted male-chauvinist comment to Thompson on the event, forgivable in a private letter, was most unfortunately printed in the first edition of FitzGerald's letters in 1889, after his death but while Browning was still alive. Browning, furiously resenting the apparent callousness of FitzGerald's remark about his dead wife, published in the

Athenaeum *a vitriolic sonnet, saying that, happening to look at the edition of the letters, he had read*

> *'That you, FitzGerald, whom by ear and eye*
> *She never knew, "thanked God my wife was dead".*
> *Ay, dead! and were yourself alive, good Fitz,*
> *How to return you thanks would pass my wits.*
> *Kicking you seems the common lot of curs –*
> *While more appropriate greeting lends you grace:*
> *Surely to spit there glorifies your face –*
> *Spitting from lips once sanctified by Hers.'*

... Mrs Browning's Death is rather a relief to me, I must say: no more Aurora Leighs, thank God! A woman of real Genius, I know: but what is the upshot of it all? She and her Sex had better mind the Kitchen and their Children; and perhaps the Poor: except in such things as little Novels, they only devote themselves to what Men do much better, leaving that which Men do worse or not at all ...

122 To Pollock

M.L., 56   Woodbridge. November 20, 1861

... You have had your Summer Excursions, I suppose: and pray let me hear how you both do after them, and how well prepared to face the Winter. I rather dread it: having, I think, suffered with the Cold last year: and moreover sorry to exchange Boating on the River, in such Glorious Summer as we have had, for poring one's Eyes out over Mudie's Books at a Sea-coal Fire. Oh, if you were to hear 'Where and oh where is my Soldier Laddie gone' played every three hours in a languid way by the Chimes of Woodbridge Church, wouldn't you wish to hang yourself? On Sundays we have the 'Sicilian Mariner's Hymn' – very slow indeed. I see, however, by a Handbill in the Grocer's Shop that a Man is going to lecture on the Gorilla in a few weeks. So there is something to look forward to . . .

I am extremely pleased with Sainte Beuve's Causeries du Lundi, which I get from the London Library: and try to make the most and longest of its 12 vols.! Do you know the Book? I suppose it is now almost out of Date in London: but it is as new as 'Soldier Laddie' here.

123 To Cowell
L.F., II, 26–7   Woodbridge. December 7, 1861

Throughout 1859–61 feeling against France had been running high in England; it was suspected that Nepoleon III's intervention in Italy was the prelude to another era of French aggrandisement; fear of French invasion inspired the formation of Volunteer forces like the Rifles mentioned in Letter 119. As for FitzGerald's mention of possible war with America, the Trent *incident a few days after this letter was written very nearly did draw England into intervening on the Southern side in the American Civil War. FitzGerald's anti-imperialist views were much ahead of his time, and he was in favour of conciliation over the* Trent *affair, even though he considered America 'a Continent of Pirates'.*

. . . I suppose you would think it a dangerous thing to edit Omar; else, who so proper? Nay, are you not the only Man to do it? And he certainly is worth good re-editing. I thought him from the first the most remarkable of the Persian Poets: and you keep finding out in him Evidences of logical Fancy which I had not dreamed of. I dare say these logical Riddles are not his best: but they are yet evidence of a Strength of mind which our Persian Friends rarely exhibit, I think. I always said about Cowley, Donne, etc., whom Johnson calls the metaphysical Poets, that their very Quibbles of Fancy showed a power of Logic which could follow Fancy through such remote Analogies. This is the case with Calderon's Conceits also. I doubt I have given but a very one-sided version of Omar: but what I do only comes up as a Bubble to the Surface, and breaks:

whereas you, with exact Scholarship, might make a lasting impression of such an Author . . .

I declare I should like to go to India as well as anywhere: and I believe it might be the best thing for me to do. But, always slow at getting under way as I have been all my Life, what is to be done with one after fifty! I am sure there is no longer any great pleasure living in this Country, so tost with perpetual Alarms as it is. One Day we are all in Arms about France. To-day we are doubting if To-morrow we may not be at War to the Knife with America! I say still, as I used, we have too much Property, Honour, etc., on our Hands: our outward Limbs go on lengthening while our central Heart beats weaklier: I say, as I used, we should give up something before it is forced from us. The World, I think, may justly resent our being and interfering all over the Globe. Once more I say, would we were a little, peaceful, unambitious, trading, Nation, like – the Dutch! . . .

124 To Thompson

L.F., II, 29   Woodbridge. December 9, 1861

. . . As to my own Peccadilloes in Verse, which never pretend to be original, this is the story of *Rubaiyat*. I had translated them partly for Cowell: young Parker asked me some years ago for something for Fraser, and I gave him the less wicked of these to use if he chose. He kept them for two years without using: and as I saw he didn't want them I printed some copies with Quaritch; and, keeping some for myself, gave him the rest. Cowell, to whom I sent a Copy, was naturally alarmed at it; he being a very religious Man: nor have I given any other Copy but to George Borrow, to whom I had once lent the Persian, and to old

Donne when he was down here the other Day, to whom I was showing a Passage in another Book which brought my old Omar up . . .

125 To Pollock
M.L., 59–60   Woodbridge. January 16, 1862

FitzGerald was now digging himself in with his own long-stored posses-sions in his Woodbridge lodging. He had a magpie-like acquisitiveness for quaint brightly-coloured bric-à-brac. The line of verse he quotes is from Stanza 182, Canto IV, of Byron's Childe Harold.

. . . You should see my little Room, filling with the most wonderful Gewgaws; Pictures, China, etc. I want two or three little Casts of Greek Statues (the decenter), and then I shall have samples of China, Greece, Italy, etc., all mixed. This nonsense amuses me: at least helps to make my Room gay during the long Days and Nights of Winter. When Summer comes I shall get out on the River. I assure you our little Squires have so laid bare the Land of all the merit we had, its Trees and Hedgerows, that I turn away with Disgust from my old Haunts of fifty years ago. There is no need for them further to shut up (as they do) our old Footpaths, for one no longer wants to walk them. Oh for some Great Duke to come and buy them all out; we could bear *his* Tyranny: as Swift says, one can submit to a Lion, but to be gnawed alive by Rats! So I have recourse to the River and Sea which the Squires have not yet defaced nor forbidden, have as yet

Written no Wrinkles on that azure brow.

So it isn't all Peace in one's Soul down here; we have our Grudges, as well as Thackeray his against Saturday Reviews, etc. I think Thackeray must be much spoiled, judging by all that.

126 To G. Crabbe the Younger

M.L., 60–62   Woodbridge. January 31, 1862

Although FitzGerald here describes his search for a permanent home of his own, it was not for another two years that he bought, and began to build onto, a cottage on the outskirts of Woodbridge, and not for another twelve that he finally moved into it. He liked his landlord Berry, who was a gunsmith, and in spite of the deficiencies of the service found his lodging 'cheerful, warm and convenient (only the Privy quite public)'.

. . . I am (as for the last ten years) looking out for a House . . . But all the better houses are occupied by Dowagers like Myself: the Miss Tolls: Mrs Pulham: the Miss Silvers: and Billy Whuncupp: and none of them will die, or otherwise migrate, for Love or Money: so here I go floundering on and teasing everybody without any Progress at all. I wish you were here, or could give me any Advice from where you are: for I am so certain to blunder in all I do that I quite lose heart to decide. I do really want, however, to get into a house of my own with my own servants (where and with whom, of course, I shan't do half as well as here), and this for several reasons. Do not forget me in case you hear of any likely Housekeeper or Servant, though I can't yet engage the former because I have no house for her to keep. But a good Maidservant I would almost undertake here, paying her instead of Mrs Berry's doing so: who hires at Is. a week such a Slut as even I cannot put up with. We are now, I hope getting rid of the third since I have been here, and I yesterday went to see about another at Hasketon. Also, if when you are at Norwich, you should see any pretty and quaint Furniture, I should be glad to hear of it, and would even go to Norwich if you knew of a Place where such things were in plenty. When I took my

Niece to London in November, I went to the Baker Street Bazaar: but spent what Time and Money I had in the new Chinese Department, where I bought a heap of Things which, however, have chiefly gone in Presents. I however like Oriental Things: their quaint shapes, fine Colours, and musky sandal-wood Scents; and though I do not so much look at these things individually, yet their Presence in the Room creates a cheerfulness which is good as one grows old, blind, deaf, and dull . . . I should like some of the old light Cane Chairs such as one used to see in old Inns, Watering Places, etc . . .

127 To Donne

F.F., 66–7   Woodbridge. December 2, 1862

Mrs Faiers had been FitzGerald's housekeeper at Boulge Cottage. The period 1855–65 saw the fullest expansion of the crinoline fashion of which Mrs Faiers so much disapproved.

. . . Mrs Faiers has been here, dining with me, Today; she asked much after *you* together with the other Gentlemen whom she used to see at my Cottage. I found that one of her Glories is that, *once*, she & I entertained six Divines one Evening at that same Cottage (she is not certain if not *seven*). She is grown very infirm, & sat down on a large glazed Print of St Cecilia; but only Saint Cecilia was the worse. Mrs Faiers (after a little cold Beef & Brandy & Water) began to prophesy in grand English: she was telling me how the *Gals* dress'd out nowadays – how they went about '*pomped up*' (she said) with Roundabouts that made 'em like Beer-barrels . . .

128 To Mrs Browne
Wright, II, 42–3

March, 1863

Mrs Browne had consulted FitzGerald as to whether she should go to live in Brussels or elsewhere on the Continent, so that her daughters could learn French and German. Here, as in his unlucky epitaph on Elizabeth Barrett Browning, FitzGerald expresses uncompromisingly 'Kinde, Kirche, Kuche' views about the Destiny of Women.

. . . Why do you want your daughters to learn these languages better than they are taught in England? And as to going abroad to learn, only a week ago George Crabbe (who is one of the most sensible men I know, and who is himself very fond of travel) was saying what a mistake it is to take young people, and most especially young women, abroad. They generally get their heads filled with foreign fashions and tastes, and scarcely ever settle down to English country life after. They are always wanting to go again to the charming Brussels, etc. If you would have your daughters be content with Goldington, beware of Brussels . . . so try and make good, sensible, house-keeping, home-keeping English women of your girls!

129 To Mrs Browne
Wright, II, 44

April, 1863

FitzGerald told Tennyson in 1876 that in 1863 he had had a 'vision' in which from his garden he had clearly seen his sister Eleanor and her children sitting at his dining-room table having tea; 'he then saw his sister quietly withdraw from the room so as not to disturb the children'. He later heard that at that very moment she had died in Norfolk.

. . . My dear sister Kerrich died last Tuesday . . . For herself it is well: she never, I believe, would have had tolerable health any more. But for her family! . . . so goes the world. The good die, they sacrifice themselves for others; she never thought of herself, only her children. Ay, and would fret about any cold *I* might have, when she was lying overcome with illness herself, and with the whole weight of that large and anxious family depending on her. I will not go to the wretched funeral, where there are plenty of mourners, but I shall go to Geldestone when they wish me . . .

130 To G. Crabbe the Younger

L.F., II, 42–4 Woodbridge. August 4, 1863

In the spring of 1863 FitzGerald had a yacht built for him, which he called the Scandal. *He mostly used it for sailing along the Suffolk coast. The disappointing trip to Holland described in this letter, and one to Calais next year, were his furthest expeditions in her.*

I have at last done my Holland: you won't be surprised to hear that I did it in two days, and was too glad to rush home on the first pretence, after (as usual) seeing nothing I cared the least about. The Country itself I had seen long before in Dutch Pictures, and between Beccles and Norwich: the Towns I had seen in Picturesque Annuals, Drop Scenes, etc.

But the Pictures – the Pictures – themselves?

Well, you know how I am sure to mismanage: but you will hardly believe, even of me, that I never saw what was most worth seeing, the Hague Gallery! But so it was: had I been by myself, I should have gone off directly (after landing at Rotterdam) to that: but Mr. Manby was with me: and he thought best to see about Rotterdam first: which was last Thursday, at whose earliest Dawn we arrived. So we tore about in an open Cab: saw nothing:

the Gallery not worth a visit: and at night I was half dead with weariness. Then again on Friday I, by myself, should have started for the Hague: but as Amsterdam was also to be done, we thought best to go there (as furthest) first. So we went: tore about the town in a Cab as before: and I raced through the Museum seeing (I must say) little better than what I have seen over and over again in England. I couldn't admire the Night-watch much: Van der Helst's very good Picture seemed to me to have been cleaned: I thought the Rembrandt Burgomasters worth all the rest put together. But I certainly looked very flimsily at all.

Well, all this done, away we went to the Hague: arriving there just as the Museum closed for that day; next Day (Saturday) it was not to be open at all (I having proposed to wait in case it should), and on Sunday only from 12 to 2. Hearing all this, in Rage and Despair I tore back to Rotterdam: and on Saturday Morning got the Boat out of the muddy Canal in which she lay and tore back down the Maas, etc., so as to reach dear old Bawdsey shortly after Sunday's Sunrise. Oh, my Delight when I heard them call out 'Orford Lights!' as the Boat was plunging over the Swell.

All this is very stupid, really wrong: but you are not surprised at it in me. One reason however of my Disgust was, that we (in our Boat) were shut up (as I said) in the Canal, where I couldn't breathe. I begged Mr. Manby to let me take him to an Inn: he would stick to his Ship, he said: and I didn't like to leave him. Then it was Murray who misled me about the Hague Gallery: he knew nothing about its being shut on Saturdays. Then again we neither of us knew a word of Dutch: and I was surprised how little was known of English in return.

But I shall say no more. I think it is the last foreign Travel I shall ever undertake; unless I should go with you to see the Dresden Madonna: to which there is one less impediment now Holland is not to be gone through . . . I am the Colour of a Lobster with Sea-faring: and my Eyes smart: so Good-Bye. Let me hear of you. Ever yours E. F.G.

Oh dear! – Rembrandt's Dissection – where and how did I miss that?

131 To Cowell

L.F., II, 44–8   Woodbridge. August 5, 1863

FitzGerald had consulted Cowell about his translation of the Bird Parliament, *but his interest in Persian literature was beginning to wane. The books which he took with him to read at sea in his yacht were now generally Greek and Italian classics, and he was increasingly critical of the work of contemporary writers.*

. . . Oh dear, when I do look into Homer, Dante, and Virgil, Aeschylus, Shakespeare, etc., those Orientals look – silly! Don't resent my saying so. *Don't* they? I am now a good deal about in a new Boat I have built, and thought (as Johnson took Cocker's Arithmetic with him on travel, because he shouldn't exhaust it) so I would take Dante and Homer with me, instead of Mudie's books, which I read through directly. I took Dante by way of slow digestion: not having looked at him for some years: but I am glad to find I relish him as much as ever: he atones with the sea; as you know does the Odyssey – these are the men . . .

Of Tennyson I hear but little: and I have ceased to look forward to any future Work of his. Thackeray seems dumb as a gorged Blackbird too: all growing old!

I have lost my sister, Kerrich, the only one of my family I much cared for, or who much cared for me . . .

I was told that Tennyson was writing a sort of Lincolnshire Idyll . . . he should never have left his old County, and gone up to be suffocated by London Adulation. He has lost that which caused the long roll of the Lincolnshire Wave to reverberate in the measure of Locksley Hall. Don't believe that I rejoice like a Dastard in what I believe to be the Decay of a Great Man: my sorrow has been so much about it that (for one reason) I have the less cared to meet him of late years, having nothing to say in sincere praise. Nor do I mean that his Decay is all owing to London, etc. He is growing old: and I don't believe much in the Fine Arts thriving on an old Tree: I can't think Milton's Paradise Lost so good as his Allegro, etc.; one feels the strain of the Pump all through: only Shakespeare – the exception to all rule – struck out Macbeth at past fifty . . .

132 To Herman Biddell
M.L., 69   Woodbridge. 1863

Biddell, a farmer living near Ipswich, used to visit FitzGerald on Woodbridge market-days to talk about pictures.

. . . Now, as to Frith, etc., I didn't half read the Review: but sent it to you to see what you would make of it. I quite agree with you about Hogarth, who (I always thought) made his pictures unnatural by overcrowding what was natural in Part, as also by caricature. For this reason, I always thought his Apprentices his best Series. But there are passages of Tragedy and Comedy in his Works that go very deep into Human Nature, and into one's Soul. He was also an Artist in Composition, Colour, etc., though in all respects, I think, a little over-rated of late years.

I don't say that Frith is not more natural (in the sense you use the word, I suppose) than Hogarth; but then does he take so difficult a Face of Nature to deal with, and, even on his own lower ground, does he go to the bottom of it? Is there in his Derby Day the one typical Face and Figure of the Jockey, the Gambler, etc., such as Hogarth would have painted for ever in our Imaginations? Is Frith at all better (if so good) as Leech in Punch? . . .

If we take the mere representation of common Nature as the sum total of Art, we must put the modern Everyday life Novel above Shakespeare: for certainly Macbeth and Coriolanus, etc., did not spout Blank Verse, etc. But they dealt in great, deep and terrible Passions, and Shakespeare has made them live again out of the dead Ashes of History by the force of his Imagination, and by the 'Thoughts that breathe, and Words that burn' that he has put into their Mouths. Nor can I think that Frith's veracious Portraitures of people eating Luncheons at Epsom are to be put in the Scale with Raffaelle's impossible Idealisation of the Human made Divine.

133 To G. Crabbe the Younger

L.F., II, 51   Woodbridge. January 12, 1864

Thackeray died on Christmas Eve, 1863. Since his affectionate exchange of letters with FitzGerald in 1852 (see Letter 98), the two men had rather drifted apart. Unambitious and undesirous of personal celebrity as FitzGerald was, he must have contrasted the public's indifference to his own work with the fame enjoyed by Thackeray and Tennyson, once his youthful equals. He tended to think that their later work had deteriorated, and that Thackeray was spoiled by celebrity and Tennyson weakened by hypochondria and over-sensitivity to criticism. But FitzGerald's basic affection for both men remained true.

. . . Have we exchanged a word about Thackeray since his Death? I am quite surprised to see how I sit moping about him: to be sure, I keep reading his books. Oh, the Newcomes are fine! And now I have got hold of Pendennis, and seem to like that much more than when I first read it. I keep hearing him say so much of it: and really think I shall hear his Step up the Stairs to this Lodging as in old Charlotte Street thirty years ago. Really, a great Figure has sunk under Earth.

134 To Cowell
L.F., II, 52–3   Woodbridge. January 31, 1864

I have only Today got your Letter: have been walking out by myself in the Seckford Almshouse Garden till 9 p.m. in a sharp Frost – with Orion stalking over the South before me – (do you know him in India? I forget) have come in – drunk a glass of Porter; and am minded to answer you before I get to Bed. Perhaps the Porter will leave me stranded, however, before I get to the End of my Letter.

Before this reaches you – probably before I write it – you will have heard of Thackeray's sudden Death. It was told me as I was walking alone in those same Seckford Gardens on Christmas-day Night; by a Corn-merchant – one George Manby – (do you remember him?) who came on purpose to tell me – and to wish me in other respects a Happy Christmas. I have thought of little else than of W.M.T. ever since – what with reading over his Books, and the few Letters I had kept of his; and thinking over our five and thirty years' Acquaintance as I sit alone by my Fire these long Nights. I had seen very little of him for these last ten years; *nothing* for the last five; he did not care to write; and people told me he was become a little spoiled: by London praise, and some consequent Egotism. But he was a very fine Fellow. His Books are wonderful: Pendennis; Vanity Fair; and the Newcomes; to which compared Fielding's seems to me coarse work . . .

135 To Laurence

L.F., II, 55   Woodbridge. April 23, 1864

Laurence had sent FitzGerald a copy of his portrait of Thackeray.

I only got back last Night, from Wiltshire, where I had been to see Miss Crabbe, daughter of the old Vicar whom you remember. I found your two Letters: and then your Box. When I had unscrewed the last Screw, it was as if a Coffin's Lid were raised; there was the Dead Man. I took him up to my Bedroom; and when morning came, he was there – reading; alive, and yet dead. I am perfectly satisfied with it on the whole; indeed, could only have suggested a very, very slight alteration, if any .

136 To Cowell

L.F., II, 57–9   Woodbridge. August 31, 1864

The Cowells returned to England this year. FitzGerald was almost reluctant to see them again, fearing as always that his friends would be disappointed when they actually saw him again after an interval of correspondence; but Cowell's steady affection overcame FitzGerald's evasions, and the friendship was gradually built up again, FitzGerald often consulting Cowell about his reading and the translations from Calderón on which he was now again working.

. . . I hope you don't think I have forgotten you. Your visit gave me a sad sort of Pleasure, dashed with the Memory of other Days; I now see so few People, and those all of the common sort, with whom I never talk of our old subjects; so I get in some measure unfitted for such converse, and am almost saddened with the remembrance of an old contrast when it comes. And there is something besides; a Shadow of Death: but I won't talk of such things: only believe I don't forget you, nor wish to be forgotten by you. Indeed, your kindness touched me . . .

Another Book I have had is Wesley's Journal, which I used to read, but gave away my Copy – to you? or Robert Groome was it? If you don't know it, do know it; it is curious to think of this Diary of his running almost coevally with Walpole's Letter-Diary; the two men born and dying too within a few years of one another, and with such different Lives to record. And it is remarkable to read pure, unaffected, and undying, English, while Addison and Johnson are tainted with a Style, which all the world imitated! . . .

137 To Mrs Browne
Wright, II, 55–6   Woodbridge. February 15, 1865

This enquiry of FitzGerald's to Mrs Browne about his wife enabled Mrs Browne to break her discreet silence about his marriage, and to ask questions which elicited (see Letter 139) one of FitzGerald's plainest statements about the marriage.

. . . Do you ever hear from her? She was down here twice last year for a considerable time, though I never came across her. She seems perfectly well, and to make herself quite comfortable at Brighton and visiting about. No doubt I was all to blame in not trying to make the best of the marriage, but can any one say but that we are *both* of us better as we are? Marriages between very unequal ages are bad, but it was reserved for me to make a stupider: of two elderly people very determined in their own distinct ways of life. I often think of your husband in this matter: how he foresaw all, and very properly did not spare me in the matter . . .

138 To Allen

L.F., II, 64   Woodbridge. April 10, 1865

In the previous year FitzGerald had bought a small house on the edge of Woodbridge, and started enlarging it for his own eventual occupation. He had years of trouble and expense over the building operations, aggravated by his own indecision.

. . . I am indulging in the expensive amusement of Building, though not on a very large scale. It *is* very pleasant, certainly, to see one's little Gables and Chimnies mount into Air and occupy a Place in the Landscape . . .

The piece of Literature I really could benefit Posterity with, I do believe, is an edition of that wonderful and aggravating Clarissa Harlowe; and this I would effect with a pair of Scissors only. It would not be a bit too long as it is, if it were all equally good; but pedantry comes in, and might, I think, be cleared away, leaving the remainder one of *the great, original, Works of the World*! in this line. Lovelace is the wonderful character, for Wit: and there is some grand Tragedy too. And nobody reads it!

139 To Mrs Browne

Wright, II, 56   July 11, 1865

Mrs Browne had replied to FitzGerald's letter of 15 February saying she had seen his wife at Brighton, and diffidently mentioning her regret at the breakdown of the marriage. FitzGerald's reply confirms that he did try to escape before the marriage, but Lucy Barton, insensitively confident of her power to make him conform to commonplace respectability, would not see the danger and let him go. After the marriage, FitzGerald would not let himself be dominated, but he was too high-minded – and also too indolent – to dominate, though knowing that he could have done, and that it might have made a success of the marriage.

... Not less do I thank you sincerely for what you say, than for the kindly reticence you have always shown in the matter of Mrs E.F.G. You know well enough, from your own as well as your husband's knowledge of the case, that *I* am very much most to blame, both on the score of stupidity in taking so wrong a step, and want of courageous principle in not making the best of it when taken. *She* has little to blame herself for except in fancying she knew both me and herself better than I had over and over again told her was the truth *before* marriage. Well, I won't say more. I think you will admit that she is far better off than she *was*, and as I feel sure, ever *would have been* living with me. She was brought up *to rule*; and though I believe she would have submitted to be a slave, it would have been at too great a price to her, and I doubt no advantage to me. She now can take her own way, live where she likes, have what society she likes, etc., while, every year and every day I am creeping out of the world in my own way.

140 To Allen
     L.F., II, 72–3   Woodbridge. December 3, 1865

De Soyres was the parson husband of FitzGerald's sister Andalusia. Newman's Apologia pro Vita Sua *had appeared in 1864; Mary Berry's* Journals and Correspondence *in 1865; 'Trench's Mother' was Melesina, mother of Richard Chenevix Trench, Archbishop of Dublin, who published his mother's journals and correspondence in 1862.*

I enclose you two prints which may amuse you to look at and keep.

    I have a wonderful Museum of such scraps of Portrait; about once a year a Man sends me a Portfolio of such things. But my chief Article is Murderers; and I am now having a Newgate Calendar from London. I don't ever wish to see and hear these things tried; but, when they are in print, I like to sit in Court then, and see the Judges, Counsel, Prisoners, Crowd; hear the Lawyers' Objections, the Murmur in the Court, etc.

> The Charge is prepared; the Lawyers are met,
> The Judges are rang'd, a terrible show.

De Soyres came here the other Day, and we were talking of you; he said you had invited Newman to your house. A brave thing, if you did. I think his Apology very noble; and himself quite honest, so far as he can see himself. The Passage in No. 7 of the Apology where he describes the State of the World as wholly irreflective of its Creator unless you turn – to Popery – is very grand ..

I was very disappointed in Miss Berry's Correspondence; one sees a Woman of Sense, Taste, Good Breeding, and I suppose, Good Looks; but what more, to make three great Volumes of! Compare her with Trench's Mother. And with all her perpetual travels to improve health and spirits (which lasted perfectly well to near ninety) one would have been more interested if there were one single intimation of caring about any Body but herself, helping one poor Person, etc.

I don't know if she or Mrs Delany is dullest.

141 To Frederick Spalding
Groome, 59   Lowestoft. March 28, 1866

Spalding was a merchant's clerk in Woodbridge, but his real interests were literature and painting. He acted as confidant and adviser to FitzGerald about the latter's increasing involvement with the Lowestoft fishermen's world. In the spring of 1864 FitzGerald had met an inshore fisherman, Joseph Fletcher, nicknamed 'Posh', to whom he became devoted. The beneficial change referred to in this letter was from his solitude at Woodbridge to the company of Posh and his fellows at Lowestoft.

. . . The change has been of some use, I think, in brightening me. My long solitary habit of Life now begins to tell upon me, and I am got past the very cure which only could counteract it: Company or Society: of which I have lost the Taste too long to endure again. So, as I have made my Bed, I must lie in it – and die in it . . .

142 To Thompson

L.F., II, 81–2   Lowestoft. July 21, 1866

Thompson, who had been Regius Professor of Greek at Cambridge since 1853, had just been appointed Master of Trinity, and was about to marry. FitzGerald's own experience explains the subdued irony of his congratulations to Thompson on getting married for the first time when in his fifties, and is underlined by his dry comments later in the letter on his brother-in-law's rapacity about marriage settlements, and his brother's insouciance about the loss of his wife.

I feel sure that the Lady I once saw at the Deanery is all you say; and you believe of me, as I believe of myself, that I don't deal in Compliment, unless under very strong Compulsion. I suppose, as Master of Trinity you could not do otherwise than marry, and so keep due State and Hospitality there: and I do think you could not have found one fitter to share, and do, the honours. And if (as I also suppose) there is Love, or Liking, or strong Sympathy, or what not? why, all looks well. Be it so!

I had not heard of Spedding's entering into genteel House-keeping till your Letter told me of it. I suppose he will be a willing Victim to his Kinsfolk.

A clerical Brother in law of mine has lost his own whole Fortune in four of these Companies which have gone to smash. Nor his own only. For, having, when he married my Sister, insisted on having half her Income tied to him by Settlement, *that* half lies under Peril from the 'Calls' made upon him as Shareholder.

At Genus Humanum damnat Caligo Futuri.

So I, trusting in my Builder's Honesty, have a Bill sent in about one third bigger than it should be.

All which rather amuses me, on the whole, though I spit out a Word now and then: and indeed am getting a Surveyor to overhaul the Builder: a hopeless Process, I believe all the while.

Meanwhile, I go about in my little Ship, where I do think I have two honest Fellows to deal with. We have just been boarding a Woodbridge Vessel that we met in these Roads, and drinking a Bottle of Blackstrap round with the Crew.

With me just at present is my Brother Peter, for whose Wife (a capital Irishwoman, of the Mrs. O'Dowd Type) my Paper is edged with Black. No one could be a better Husband than he; no one more attentive and anxious during her last Illness, more than a year long; and, now all is over, I never saw him in better Health or Spirits. Men are not inconsolable for elderly Wives; as Sir Walter Scott, who was not given to caustic Aphorisms, observed long ago.

When I was sailing about the Isle of Wight, Dorsetshire, etc., I read my dear old Sophocles again (sometimes omitting the nonsense-verse Choruses) and thought how much I should have liked to have them commented along in one of your Lectures. All that is now over with you: but you will look into the Text now and then. I have now got Munro's Lucretius on board again. Why is it that I never can take up with Horace – so sensible, elegant, agreeable, and sometimes even grand?

143 To Spalding
Groome, 65   Lowestoft. October 7, 1866

Lusia Kerrich was one of FitzGerald's Geldestone nieces. Geldestone was pronounced, and as here sometimes written, 'Gelson'. FitzGerald's letters now begin increasingly to quote Posh Fletcher's picturesque language. Posh was now part-owner of a herring lugger to whose cost FitzGerald had contributed.

. . . I was noticing for several Days how many *Robins* were singing along the 'London Road' here; and (without my speaking of it) Lusia Kerrich told me they had almost a *Plague* of Robins at Gelson: 3 or 4 coming into the Breakfast room every morning; getting under Kerrich's Legs, etc. And yesterday Posh told me that *three* came to his Lugger out at sea; also another very pretty Bird, whose name he didn't know, but which he caught and caged in *the Binnacle*, where it was found dead in due time . . . P.S. Posh (as Cooper, whom I question, tells me) was *over* 12 *miles from Land* when the *four* Robins came aboard: a Bird which he nor Cooper had ever seen to visit a Ship before. The Bird he shut up in the Binnacle he describes as of 'all sorts of Colours' – perhaps a Tomtit! – and I fear it was *roasted* in the Binnacle, when Posh lighted up at night, forgetting his Guest. 'Poor little fallow!'

144 To Robert Hindes Groome

Groome, 33   Lowestoft. December 2, 1866

Groome, Rector of Monk Soham and later Archdeacon of Suffolk, was a very musical friend of FitzGerald's, and often stayed with him at Woodbridge. This letter refers to FitzGerald's eccentric eldest brother John, who had inherited Boulge Hall where – close as it was – FitzGerald never visited him, but John fitfully called on FitzGerald at Woodbridge.

. . . How could you *expect* my Brother 3 times? You, as well as others, should really (for his Benefit, as well as your own) either leave it all to Chance, or appoint *one* Day, and then decline any further Negotiation. This would really spare poor John an immense deal of (in sober Truth) 'taking the Lord's name in vain'. I mean his eternal D.V., which, translated, only means, 'If *I* happen to be in the Humour'. You must know that the feeling of being *bound* to an Engagement is the very thing that makes him wish to break it. Spedding once told me this was rather my case. I believe it, and am therefore shy of ever making an engagement. *O si sic omnia!*

145 To Spalding

Groome, 65–6   Lowestoft. December 4, 1866

I am sorry you can't come, but have no doubt that you are right in *not* coming. You may imagine what I do with myself here: somehow, I do believe the Seaside is more of my Element than elsewhere, and the old Lodging Life suits me best. That, however, I have at Woodbridge; and can be better treated nowhere than there.

I have just seen Posh, who had been shooting his Lines in the Morning: had fallen asleep after his Sunday Dinner, and rose up like a Giant refreshed when I went into his house. His little Wife, however, told him he must go and tidy his Hair, which he was preparing to obey. Oh! these are the People who somehow interest me; and if I were not now too far advanced on the Road to Forgetfulness, I should be sad that my own Life had been such a wretched Concern in comparison. But it is too late, even to lament, now . . .

There is a wedding-party next door: at No. 11; I being in 12; *Becky* having charge of both houses. There is incessant vulgar Giggling and Tittering, and 5 meals a Day, Becky says. Oh! these are not such Gentlefolks as my Friends on the Beach, who have not 5 meals a Day. I wonder how soon I shall quarrel with them, however – I don't mean the Wedding Party . . . At Eight or half-past I go to have a Pipe at Posh's, if he isn't half-drunk with his Friends.

146 To Bernard Quaritch

Quaritch, 10   Woodbridge. 1867

The first edition of FitzGerald's translation of the Rubaiyat of Omar Khayyam, *issued by the bookseller and publisher Bernard Quaritch in 1859, remained unsold and almost unnoticed for two years, till a copy, remaindered at the price of one penny, found its way into the hands of Rossetti, Swinburne and William Morris, and the work gradually became well known in the literary world in England and America. By 1867 a second edition was needed, and FitzGerald agreed with Quaritch to revise his translation; the revised version contained 35 extra stanzas and many alterations, not all for the better.*

Pray don't waste your learned Catalogues on me who now buy nothing but Mudie's Secondhand Memoirs.

One Catalogue you sent me some weeks ago recalled to me what Edward Cowell had told me a year ago; viz. that you had partly sold, partly lost, the copies of Omar Khayyam; and thought a small Edition would sell.

Well – I have done with such things; and I suppose you find that such 'livraisons' even if they do sell, are not worth the trouble of keeping etc.

But as poor Omar is one I have great fellow feeling with, I would rather vamp him up again with a few Alterations and Additions than anything else.

You must tell me, Busy and Great Man as you now are, whether you care to take charge of such a shrimp of a Book if I am silly enough to reprint it . . .

147 To F. Tennyson

L.F., II, 89–91   Woodbridge. January 29, 1867

Tennyson's Lucretius *was privately printed in 1868, the year in which Tennyson began building his house at Aldworth, near Haslemere, to replace the Isle of Wight house, Farringford, where he could no longer enjoy real privacy. Mrs Carlyle died of a heart attack, alone in a carriage after the shock of an accident to her dog, in April 1866. The herring lugger which FitzGerald was having built, in partnership with Posh Fletcher, who was to be its master, was eventually not called after the heroine of Wilkie Collins's* Woman in White, *but* Meum and Tuum *('mine and thine', in honour of the partnership; but known to all Lowestoft fishermen as* Mum and Tum*).*

. . . In answer to my yearly Letter to Alfred and Co. I heard (from Mrs) that they were about to leave Freshwater, frightened away by Hero-worshippers, etc., and were going to a Solitude called Greyshott Hall, Haslemere; which, I am told, is in Hants. Whether they go to settle there I don't know. Lucretius' Death is thought to be too free-spoken for Publication, I believe; not so much in a religious, as an amatory, point of View. I should believe Lucretius more likely to have expedited his Departure because of Weariness of Life and Despair of the System, than because of any Love-philtre. I wrote also my yearly Letter to Carlyle, begging my compliments to his Wife: who, he replies, died, in a very tragical way, last April. I have since heard that the Papers reported all the Circumstances. So, if one lives so much out of the World as I do, it seems better to give up that Ghost altogether . .

I . . . have just, to my great sorrow, finished 'The Woman in White' for the third time, once every last three Winters. I wish Sir Percival Glyde's Death were a little less of the minor Theatre sort; then I would swallow all the rest as a wonderful Caricature, better than so many a sober Portrait. I really think of having a Herring-lugger which I am building named 'Marian Halcombe', the brave Girl in the Story. Yes, a Herring-lugger; which is to pay for the money she costs unless she goes to the Bottom: and which meanwhile amuses me to consult about with my Sea-folks. I go to Lowestoft now and then, by way of salutary Change: and there smoke a Pipe every night with a delightful Chap, who is to be Captain. I have been, up to this time, better than for the last two winters: but feel a Worm in my head now and then, for all that. You will say, only a Maggot. Well; we shall see. When I go to Lowestoft, I take Montaigne with me; very comfortable Company. One of his Consolations for *The Stone* is, that it makes one less unwilling to part with Life. Oh, you think that it didn't need much Wisdom to suggest that? Please yourself, Ma'am. January, just gone! February, only twenty-eight Days: then March with light till six p.m.: then April with a blush of Green on the Whitethorn hedge: then May, Cuckoos, Nightingales, etc.; then June, Ship launched, and nothing but Ship till November, which is only just gone. The Story of our Lives from Year to Year. This is a poor letter: but I won't set The Worm fretting. Let me hear how you are: and don't be two months before you do so.

148 To Donne

L.F., II, 91–3   Woodbridge. February 15, 1867

. . . When your letter was put into my hands, I happened to be reading Montaigne, L. III. Ch. 8, De l'Art de Conferer, where at the end he refers to Tacitus; the only Book, he says, he had read consecutively for an hour together for ten years. He does not say very much: but the Remarks of such a Man are worth many Cartloads of German Theory of Character, I think: their Philology I don't meddle with. I know that Cowell has discovered they are all wrong in their Sanskrit. Montaigne never doubts Tacitus' facts: but doubts his Inferences; well, if I were sure of his Facts, I would leave others to draw their Inferences. I mean, if I were Commentator, certainly: and I think if I were Historian too. Nothing is more wonderful to me than seeing such Men as Spedding, Carlyle, and I suppose Froude, straining Fact to Theory as they do, while a scatter-headed Paddy like myself can keep clear. But then so does the Mob of Readers. Well, but I believe in the Vox Populi of two hundred Years: still more, of two thousand. And, whether we be right or wrong, we prevail: so, however much wiser are the Builders of Theory, their Labour is but lost who build: they can't reason away Richard's Hump, nor Cromwell's Ambition, nor Henry's Love of a new Wife, nor Tiberius' beastliness. Of course, they had all their Gleams of Goodness: but we of the Mob, if we have any Theory at all, have that which all Mankind have seen and felt, and know as surely as Day-light; that Power will tempt and spoil the Best.

Frederick Tennyson. Photograph by Julia Margaret Cameron.
(*Lincolnshire Library Service*)

Well, but what is all this Lecture to you for? Why, I think you rather turn to the re-actionary Party about these old Heroes. So I say, however right you may be, leave us, the many-headed, if not the wise-headed, to go our way, only making the Text of Tacitus as clear for us to flounder about in as you can. That, anyhow, must be the first Thing. Something of the manners and customs of the Times we want also: some Lights from other contemporary Authors also: and then, 'Gentlemen, you will now consider your Verdict, and please yourselves.' . .

149 To Spalding
Groome, 69   Lowestoft. May 18, 1867

Posh is very busy with his Lugger, which will be decked by the middle of next Week. I have just left him: having caught him with a Pot of white paint (some of which was on his Face), and having made him dine on cold Beef in the Suffolk Hotel Bowling-green, washing all down with two Tankards of Bullard's Ale. He was not displeased to dine abroad; as this is Saturday, when he says there are apt to be 'Squalls' at home, because of washing, etc., His little Boy is on the mending hand: safe, indeed, I hope, and believe, unless they let him into Draughts of Air: which I have warned them against.

Yesterday we went to Yarmouth, and bought a Boat for the Lugger, and paraded the Town, and dined at the Star Tavern (*Beefsteak for one*), and looked into the Great Church: where when Posh pulled off his Cap, and stood erect but not irreverent, I thought he looked as good an Image of the Mould that Man was originally cast in, as you may chance to see in the Temple of *The Maker* in these Days.

The Artillery were blazing away on the Denes; and the

little Band-master, who played with his Troop here last summer, joined us as we were walking, and told Posh not to lag behind, for he was not at all ashamed to be seen walking with him. The little well-meaning Ass! . . .

150 To Cowell
L.F., II, 94   Lowestoft. June 17, 1867

. . . I am here in my little Ship – cool and sequestered enough, to be sure – with no Company but my Crew of Two, and my other – Captain of the Lugger now a-building: a Fellow I never tire of studying – If he *should* turn out knave, I shall have done with all Faith in my own Judgment: and if he should go to the Bottom of the Sea in the Lugger – I shan't cry for the Lugger.

Well, but I have other Company too – Don Quixote – the 4th Part: where those Snobs, the Duke and Duchess (how vulgar Great Folks then, as now!) make a Fool and Butt of him. Cervantes should have had more respect for his own Creation: but, I suppose, finding that all the Great Snobs could only *laugh* at the earlier part, he thought he had better humour them . . .

151 To Mrs Browne
Wright, II, 49–50   Lowestoft. August 10, 1867

This letter is evidence that FitzGerald, if he had homosexual tendencies, was not aware of this himself. His description of night-wanderings on the Lowestoft beach, hoping to be accosted by young sailors, sounds to modern ears unmistakably homosexual; but this letter, mentioning that such contacts were sought to replace a lost friend, was addressed to the widow of that very friend. It is unthinkable that FitzGerald should, in full awareness of his own tendencies, have written in this way to this particular person. 'This captain' is of course Posh Fletcher.

In 1859 (the autumn and winter of it) I lived here, and used to wander about the shore at night longing for some fellow to accost me who might give some promise of filling up a very vacant place in my heart, but only some of the more idle and worthless sailors came across me. When I got acquainted with this captain three years ago I asked him why he had never come down to see me at the time I speak of. Well, he had often seen me, but never thought it becoming in him to accost me first, or even to come near me. Yet he was the very man I wanted, with, strangely enough, some resemblance in feature to a portrait of you may guess whom, and much in character also, so that I seem to have jumped back to a regard of near forty years ago, and while I am with him feel young again, and when he goes shall feel old again . . . a man of the finest Saxon type, with a complexion *vif. male et flamboyant*, blue eyes, a nose less than Roman, more than Greek, and strictly auburn hair that any woman might sigh to possess. Further, he was a man of simplicity of soul, justice of thought, tenderness of nature, a gentleman of nature's grandest type . . .

152 To Mowbray Donne

F.F., 89–90   Woodbridge. Oct. 16 (1867?)

Mowbray Donne, son of William Bodham Donne, sometimes stayed with FitzGerald at Lowestoft and went sailing with him. Trollope's Last Chronicle of Barset *was published in 1867.*

I have just come back from our Harbour mouth for two hours (to go back in Ship there) and, finding your Letter, dated Sunday, *will* answer it, in part, at any rate. You conclude from what I have already said that I am not yet shut up for the Winter: I thought I shd. have had to give up the Ghost last week, when the Cold came on like a Giant, & made me shake in my Cabin, under all the Coats, Waistcoats & Breeches I could pile upon me. But *this* week comes a lovely warm S. Wester, & so I keep at our Harbour: cruising about a little by day, & by night walking on the Sands under the Moon. After that, Grog at the small Inn: Sailors jabbering inside. My Captain's Wife is going fast into a Decline: he does all he can for her: and I see thinks much about her. The other day she began to despair of herself: & he told her (in all sincerity and Affection) that, once she despaired, it would 'clew her up in no time' . . . I have been sunning myself with Boccacio's Decameron on board: but all these Immortals – D Quixote – Sophocles – Montaigne etc I somehow keep for Summer & Ship: – when *they* fail me, then Mudie comes in. I fancied I could always read A. Trollope: but his last Barset has made me skip here & there. The Account of old Harding with his Violoncello in Vol. II is – *better* than Sterne – inasmuch as it is more unaffected and true . . .

153 To Joseph Fletcher
Blyth, 55–7   Woodbridge. 1867

The first season's fishing of FitzGerald's and Fletcher's lugger proved unrewarding financially. FitzGerald did not mind about the money, but he had begun to worry about Fletcher's carelessness in keeping accounts, and drinking tendencies, because they conflicted with his idealized picture of his partner. It is understandable that Fletcher, a man in his thirties, should have resented this paternalistic sermon of FitzGerald's, however affectionate and pathetic.

. . . And now, Poshy, I mean to read you a short Sermon, which you can keep till Sunday to read. You know I told you of *one* danger – and I do think the only one – you are liable to – Drink.

I do not the least think you are *given* to it: but you have, and will have, so many friends who will press you to it: perhaps *I* myself have been one. And when you keep so long without *food; could* you do so, Posh, without a Drink – of some of your bad Beer too – now and then? And then, does not the Drink – and of bad Stuff – take away Appetite for the time? And will, if continued, so spoil the stomach that it will not bear anything *but* Drink. And this evil comes upon us gradually, without our knowing how it grows. That is why I warn you, Posh. If I am wrong in thinking you want my warning, you must forgive me, believing that I should not warn at all if I were not much interested in your welfare. I know that you do your best to keep out at sea, and watch on shore, for anything that will bring home something for Wife and Family. But do not do so at any such risk as I talk of.

I say, I tell you all this for your own sake: and something for my own also – not as regards the Lugger – but because, thinking you, as I do, so good a Fellow, and being glad of your Company; and taking *Pleasure* in seeing you prosper; I should now be sorely vext if you went away from what I believe you to be. Only, whether you do well or ill, *show me all above-board*, as I really think you have done; and do not let a poor old, solitary, and sad Man (as I really am, in spite of my Jokes), do not, I say, let me waste my Anxiety in vain.

I thought I had done with new Likings: and I had a more easy Life perhaps on that account: *now* I shall often think of you with uneasiness, for the very reason that I have so much Liking and Interest for you.

There – the Sermon is done, Posh. You *know* I am not against Good Beer while at Work: nor a cheerful Glass after work: only do not let it spoil the stomach or the Head.

154 To Donne

F.F., 85   Woodbridge. Wednesday (1867?)

Spedding had sent to FitzGerald a bust of Tennyson. FitzGerald's house Little Grange was now ready and furnished, with a garden and livestock (as will be seen from Letter 156), and some of his Kerrich nieces stayed there every summer, but he himself was still living in his Woodbridge lodgings, looked after by his landlord Berry and Berry's wife.

I had your letter this morning: and by Noon comes a huge Box – very heavy, my Landlord says – 'Shall he unpack it?' – 'If he likes' – He finds a heap of Sawdust: & by and bye comes up again to tell me he can't make out what is forthcoming – 'Something like the end of a dead Nose' – So I went down: & directly I saw the Address on the Box, knew what it must be. At last we get out A.T. all safe & sound . . . Oddly enough, I had said to Spedding in a Letter a few days ago, that the Reason why I had never sent for his handsome Present, now that I have a house to put it in, is simply – that I dared not have it where my poor Epileptic Niece, who takes great pleasure in coming to my House, might be frightened at it; I am obliged to take down all my dark Italian Faces from the Walls: she would dream of them: and I shall now have to send Tennyson away into a Barn, when she comes next . . .

155 To Pollock

M.L., 88   Woodbridge. November 11, 1867

. . . Are you overrun in London with 'Champagne Charlie is my Name'? A brutal Thing: nearly worthless – the Tune, I mean – but yet not quite – else it would not become so great a Bore. No: I can see, to my Sorrow, that it has some Go – which Mendelssohn had not. But Mozart, Rossini,

'Posh' Fletcher. Photographer unknown.
(*David Craik and Suffolk County Council*)

and Handel had.

I can't help thinking that Opera will have to die for a time: certainly there seems to be no new Blood to keep it alive: and the Old Works of Genius want rest. I have never heard Faust: only Bits – which I suppose were thought the best Bits. They were expressive – musically ingenious, etc. – but the part of Hamlet – the one Divine Soul of Music, Melody – was not there. I think that such a fuss can be made about it only because there is nothing better.

156 To Herman Biddell

M.L., 89   Woodbridge. December 22, 1867

It occurs to me that, when I last saw you, you gave me hopes of finding a *Chanticleer* to replace that aged fellow you saw in my Domains. *He* came from Grundisburgh; and surely you spoke of some such Bird flourishing in Grundisburgh still. I will not hold out for the identical plumage – worthy of an Archangel – I only stipulate for one of the sort: such as are seen in old Story books; and on Church-vanes; with a plume of Tail, a lofty Crest and Walk, and a shrill trumpet-note of Challenge: any splendid colours: black and red; black and Gold; white, and red, and Gold! Only so as he be 'gay', according to old Suffolk speech.

Well, of course, you won't trouble yourself about this: only, don't *forget* it, next time you ride through Grundisburgh. Or if, in the course of any Ride, you should see any such Bird, catch him up at once upon your Saddle-bow, and bring him to the distressed Widows on my Estate . . .

157 To Mowbray Donne

F.F., 93   Lowestoft. December 31, 1867

The second, revised, edition of the Rubaiyat *was to appear two months later, in February 1868.*

... I am really reprinting that old Persian; all the copies of which have gone off, at a steady sale of 2 per annum; the greater portion having, I believe, been lost by Quaritch when he changed house. It is the only one of all my Great Works that has ever been asked for: – I am persuaded, *because* of the Wickedness, which is now at the heart of so much – Goodness! Not that the Persian has anything at all new: but he has dared to *say* it, as Lucretius did: and now it is put into tolerable English Music – That is all ...

158 To Spalding

Groome, 72   Lowestoft. July 13, 1868

The lugger partnership lost money again in 1868, and Fletcher's wife became more and more ailing. FitzGerald again spent the summer at Lowestoft, where Thompson and his wife (whom FitzGerald thoroughly approved of when they finally met) visited him. But most of his time was spent with Fletcher.

... When *are* we to have rain? Last night it lightened to the South, as we sat in the Suffolk Gardens – I, and Posh, and Mrs Posh, and Sparks ... Posh and I had been sauntering in the Churchyard, and reading the Epitaphs: looking at his own little boy's Grave – 'Poor little Fellow! He wouldn't let his Mother go near him – I can't think why – but kept his little Fingers twisted in my Hair, and wouldn't let me go; and when Death strook him, as I may say, halloo'd out Daddy!'

M.L., 94–5   Lowestoft. January 15, 1869

*The tendency of Victorian biographers to whitewash their subjects – like
John Forster in his Oliver Goldsmith or Spedding in the Francis Bacon
edition on which, FitzGerald often complained, his friend was wasting
his life – exasperated FitzGerald as much as the opposite, automatically
debunking, approach of many biographers today exasperates some
readers now.*

. . . Here I have got to read Walpole's Memoirs of the
Reigns of George II and III. I can't read all; but I doubt if
I could any such Diaries of Politics by any other man. One
sees he has his hates and likings (much more of the first
than of the last), and that he likes to write Epigrams. But I
still believe he is right in the main. And what astonishing
pains for a fastidious man who only lived to please himself!
I like Walpole too for his loyalty to his Father: who, I
should fancy, thought but little of a Son so very unlike
himself. Sir Robert always reminds me of Palmerston; and
I declare they seem to me the most genuine English
Premiers, unless one excepts the two Pitts. Horace Walpole
seems to me to understand Burke and Fox well – the Good
and Idle Apprentice as Selwyn called them. Coleridge and
his School try to set up Burke as *the* man of his Time; I
think we Irish folks can see the Irishman in Burke much
better. So with Goldsmith: Forster and Co. try to clear
him of the Blunders and Vanity which such fools as
Johnson, Reynolds, etc., laughed at; but we Paddies know
how a Paddy may write like an Angel and talk like poor
Poll. It astonishes me to see the best English Brains, like
old Spedding's, go the whole Hog so with any Hero they
take up . .

160 To Spalding

Groome, 74–5   Lowestoft. September 4, 1869

Newson was the captain of FitzGerald's yacht Scandal. *FitzGerald's disillusion with Posh Fletcher deepened during 1869, though their lugger partnership did rather better financially. FitzGerald worried over Fletcher's drinking and his unbusinesslike ways, and Fletcher resented what he considered fussy interference and bossiness. FitzGerald's depression was increased by the deterioration of his eyesight from overstrain and an accident with a paraffin lamp. He was now unable to read by artificial light, and had to employ a reader.*

I wish you *were* coming here this Evening, as I have several things to talk over.

I would not meddle with the Regatta – to Newson's sorrow, who certainly *must* have carried off the second £10 prize. And the Day ended by vexing me more than it did him. Posh drove in here the day before to tan his nets: could not help making one with some old friends in a Boat-race on the Monday, and getting very fuddled with them on the Suffolk Green (where I was) at night. After all the pains I have taken, and all the real anxiety I have had. And worst of all, after the repeated promises he had made! I said, there must now be an end of the Confidence between us, so far as *that* was concerned, and I would so far trouble myself about him no more. But when I came to reflect that this was but an outbreak among old friends on an old occasion, after (I do believe) months of sobriety; that there was no concealment about it; and that though obstinate at first as to how little drunk, etc, he was very repentant afterwards – I cannot let this one flaw weigh against the general good of the man. I cannot if I would: what then is the use of trying? But my confidence in *that* respect must be so far shaken, and it vexes me to think that I can never be *sure* of his not being overtaken so. I declare that it makes me feel ashamed to play the Judge on one who stands immeasurably above me in the scale, whose faults are better than so many virtues. Was not this very outbreak that of a great genial Boy among his old Fellows? True, a Promise was broken. Yes: but if the Whole Man be of the Royal Blood of Humanity, and do Justice in the Main, what are *the people* to say? *He* thought, if he thought at all, that he kept his promise in the main. But there is no use talking: unless I part company wholly, I suppose I must take the evil with the good.

Well, Winter will soon be here, and no more 'Suffolk' Bowling-greens. Once more I want you to help in finding me a lad, or boy, or lout, who will help me to get through the long Winter nights – whether by cards or reading – now that my eyes are not so up to their work as they were. I think they are a *little* better: which I attribute to the wearing of these hideous Goggles, which keep out Sun, Sea, Sand, etc. But I must not, if I could, tax them as I have done over books by lamplight until Midnight. Do pray consider this for me, and look about. I thought of a sharp lad – that son of the Broker – if he could read a little decently he would do. Really one has lived quite long enough . . .

161 To Pollock

M.L., 105–6 Woodbridge. November 20, 1869

. . . I am about to write my yearly letter to Carlyle, I suppose he still lives in Chelsea. His Niagara Pamphlet was almost tragic to me: such a helpless outcry from the Prophet who has so long told us what not to do, but never what *to* do. I don't know if he still maintains his Fame at the former height.

There was an absurd article in my old Athenaeum comparing the relative merits of Tennyson and Browning:
awarding the praise of Finish, etc., to A.T., and of origin-
ality to B.! I am not perhaps sufficiently read in the latter:
for I never could read him: and I have reliance on my own
intuition that, such being the case, he is not a rival to A.T.,
whom I judge of by his earlier poems (up to 1842). In
Browning I could see little but Cockney Sublime, Cockney
Energy, etc.; and as you once very wittily said to me that
Miss Brontë was a 'great Mistress of the Disagreeable', so,
if B. has power, I must consider it of that sort. Tennyson
has stocked the English language with lines which once
knowing one can't forgo. Cowell tells me that even at
Oxford and Cambridge Browning is considered the
deepest! But 'this also will pass away'. But not A.T.

162 To Pollock

M.L., 106–9   Woodbridge. December 7, 1869

Tennyson was now established in his new house, Aldworth. FitzGerald's
distinction, in relation to Tennyson, between the kind of wife who makes
a poet happy and the kind who makes him a better poet, shows that anti-
feminist as he was, and preferring the loyally submissive type of woman,
he was open-minded enough to see that she might fail to provide a needed
stimulus. His correspondence with the actress and author Fanny Kemble,
which had started two years earlier, was perhaps giving him some new ideas.

It is very good of you to write to me. You have plenty to
do, and I have nothing to do, or to tell in return. So it is,
however, that only last night, or this morning, as I was
lying awake in bed, I thought to myself that I would write
to you – yes, and have a letter from you once before
Christmas – before New Year 1870, at any rate. And when
I came down this morning with the pleasing prospect of

half-an-hour's walk in the East wind before breakfast, here was your letter anticipating mine.

It is capital, your going to see old Alfred in his lordly Pleasure-house looking over the Weald: I think one misses water in those otherwise fine sweeps of Down and Weald. But then water is the only thing we East Anglians have to show: and dismal cold it shows now. I don't know if the woodlands look better. This time of Year is certainly next door to Death. I half long to be at Rome, which Mrs Kemble, who winters there, tells me about. But then the packing, unpacking, rushing to packets, railways, hotels, etc., with the probable chance of wishing oneself back in one's own dull Woodbridge after all!

Leave well – even 'pretty well' – alone: that is what I learn as I get old. I have only been pretty well myself lately: diminished of Grog and Pipe, which made the happiest hour of the twenty-four, and actually trying some Homeopathic Nux Vomica instead – whether for better or worse I won't say: for, directly one has said it, you know –

Then, my dear Eyes not having quite recovered the paraffin, a lad comes to read at half-past seven till – stumbling at every other word, unless it be some Story that carries him along. So now we are upon the Woman in White: third time of reading in my case: and I can't help getting frightened now . . .

Mrs A.T. is all you say, indeed: a Lady of a Shakespearian type, as I think A.T. once said of her: that is, of the Imogen sort, far more agreeable to me than the sharp-witted Beatrices, Rosalinds, etc. I do not think she has been (on this very account perhaps) so good a helpmate to A.T.'s Poetry as to himself . . .

Now in ten minutes the Mate of a Three-masted Schooner is coming to say Goodbye before he starts to Genoa (they call it) with a cargo of – Red Herring. And then my reader! He is the son of a Cabinet-maker: and last night read 'her future husband' as 'her *furniture* husband'. This is true.

163 To Mrs Thompson

L.F., II, 109–10   Woodbridge. Winter, 1869

In 1867 FitzGerald had started a correspondence with Aldis Wright, Librarian of Trinity College Cambridge, who edited FitzGerald's letters after his death. Aldis Wright wanted copies of FitzGerald's works for Trinity library, and among those sent was a translation of Aeschylus' Agamemnon which FitzGerald published in 1869.

. . . I was rather taken aback by the Master's having discovered my last – yes, and bona-fide my last – translation in the volume I sent to your Library. I thought it would slip in unobserved, and I should have given all my little contributions to my old College, without after-reckoning. Had I known you as the Wife of any but the 'quondam' Greek Professor, I should very likely have sent it to you: since it was meant for those who might wish for some insight into a Play which I must think they can scarcely have been tempted into before by any previous Translation. It remains to be much better done; but if Women of Sense and Taste, and Men of Sense and Taste (who don't know Greek) can read, and be interested in such a glimpse as I give them of the Original, they must be content, and not look the Horse too close in the mouth, till a better comes to hand.

My Lugger has had (along with her neighbours) such a Season hitherto of Winds as no one remembers. We made £450 in the North Sea; and (just for fun) I did wish to realize £5 in my Pocket. But my Captain would take it all to pay Bills. But if he makes another £400 this Home

Voyage! Oh, then we shall have money in our Pockets. I
do wish this. For the anxiety about all these People's lives
has been so much more to me than all the amusement I
have got from the Business, that I think I will draw out of
it if I can see my Captain sufficiently firm on his legs to
carry it on alone. True, there will then be the same risk to
him and his ten men, but they don't care; only I sit here
listening to the Winds in the Chimney, and always thinking
of the Eleven hanging at my own fingers' ends.

This Letter is all desperately about me and mine,
Translations and Ships. And now I am going to walk in
my Garden: and feed *my* Captain's Pony with white
Carrots; and in the Evening have *my* Lad come and read
for an hour and a half (he stumbles at every third word, and
gets dreadfully tired, and so do I; but I renovate him with
Cake and Sweet Wine), and I can't just now smoke the
Pipe nor drink the Grog . . .

164 To Pollock

M.L., 110–11   Woodbridge. December 28, 1869

The second set of Tennyson's Idylls of the King *appeared in 1869; his*
'Northern Farmer' had appeared in the Enoch Arden *volume of 1864.*

. . . I found the new Idylls on the Lowestoft Bookstall: but
I can get no more interested in them than in any of their
Predecessors: except the old Morte d'Arthur. That *that*
was the finest subject in the whole Legend is implied, I
think, by the Poet himself attacking it from the first. The
Story – the Motive – of the others does not interest me in
itself; nor do I think that A.T. has touched the right Key
in treating of it. The whole Legend, and its parts, appear
to me scarce fitted to interest any but the child-like readers
of old knightly days whom they were intended to amuse, I

suppose: not, in the main, *very* much beyond Jack the Giant-killer, etc., and I think such stories are best told in the old simple English of the Romance itself. When elaborated into refined modern verse, the 'opus' and the 'materia' seem to me disproportioned. Something in the same way as Cowper's Miltonic rhythm was quite out of tune with Homer. I may be quite wrong in all these reasons for my indifference to these Poems; I only know I do not like Dr Fell; and have some considerable – perhaps more considerable – reliance on my unreasoning than on my reasoning affections in such matters.

And while Guinevere, Pelleas, and Co. leave me quite unconcerned about them, the Lincolnshire Farmer positively brought tears to my Eyes. There were Humanity, Truth, and Nature come back again; the old Brute becoming quite *tragic* in comparison, just as Justice Shallow does, seen through Shakespeare's Humour . . .

165 To Laurence

L.F., II, 113–14   Woodbridge. January 13, 1870

FitzGerald was beginning to think he had better terminate his partnership with Fletcher, though he still admired the fisherman enough to commission a portrait of him.

. . . If you were down here, I think I should make you take a life-size Oil Sketch of the Head and Shoulders of my Captain of the Lugger. You see by the enclosed that these are neither of them of a bad sort: and the Man's Soul is every way as well proportioned, missing in nothing that may become A Man, as I believe. He and I will, I doubt, part Company; well as he likes me, which is perhaps as well as a sailor cares for any one but Wife and Children: he likes to be, what he is born to be, his own sole Master, of himself, and of other men. So now I have got him a fair start, I think he will carry on the Lugger alone: I shall miss my Hobby, which is no doubt the last I shall ride in this world: but I shall also get eased of some Anxiety about the lives of a Crew for which I now feel responsible. And this last has been a Year of great Anxiety in this respect . . .

166 To Pollock
M.L., 123–4   Woodbridge. July 13, 1870

FitzGerald's musical conservatism was getting more pronounced as he grew older. Earlier he had admired at least one contemporary composer, Mendelssohn, but now in a letter of reminiscences about performances of Rossini's Otello, *which he had seen in the past, he consigned Mendelssohn too, with all the other most celebrated contemporary composers, to perdition.*

. . . I always thought that Rossini's vein was Comic, and the Barber his Masterpiece: but he is always melodious and beautiful, and that will make him live when Meyerbeer, Gounod, Mendelssohn, Wagner and Co. lie howling, by the side of Browning and Co., in some limbo of Dante's first Act of the Comedy. I say the Arts are nothing if not beautiful . . .

167 To Laurence
L.F., II, 116–17   Lowestoft. August 2, 1870

In June 1870 FitzGerald gave Fletcher a mortgage on his share of the lugger and withdrew from the partnership, but their friendship held good for a little longer. The war which FitzGerald tried to disregard was the Franco–Prussian War which had broken out in the previous month.

. . . The Lugger is now preparing in the Harbour beside

me; the Captain here, there, and everywhere; with a word
for no one but on business; the other side of the Man you
saw looking for Birds' Nests; all things in their season. I
am sure the Man is fit to be King of a Kingdom as well as
of a Lugger. To-day he gives the customary Dinner to his
Crew before starting, and my own two men go to it; and
I am asked too: but will not spoil the Fun.

I declare, you and I have seen A Man! Have we not?
Made in the mould of what Humanity should be, Body and
Soul, a poor Fisherman. The proud Fellow had better have
kept me for a Partner in some of his responsibilities. But
no; he must rule alone, as is right he should too.

I date from the Inn where my Letters are addressed; but
I write in the little Ship which I live in. My Nieces are now
here; in the town, I mean; and my friend Cowell and his
Wife; so I have more company than all the rest of the year.
I try to shut my Eyes and Ears against all tidings of this
damnable War, seeing that I can do no good to others by
distressing myself.

168 To Spalding
Groome, 77–9   Lowestoft. September 8, 1870

*The worst disillusion with Posh Fletcher came after another drinking
bout, in breach of a pledge of sobriety. The friendship was not even yet
quite broken, but FitzGerald's obsessive admiration of, and trust in,
Fletcher, which had worried his friends and had made him something of a
laughing-stock in Lowestoft, gradually faded away.*

. . . I had a letter from Posh yesterday, telling me he was
sorry we had not 'parted Friends'. That he had been indeed
'*a little the worse* for Drink' – which means being at a Public-
house half the Day, and having to sleep it off the remainder:
having been duly warned by his Father at Noon that all had

183

been ready for sailing 2 hours before, and all the other Luggers gone. As Posh could *walk*, I suppose he only acknowledged a *little* Drink; but, judging by what followed on that *little* Drink, I wish he had simply acknowledged his Fault. He begs me to write: if I do so, I must speak very plainly to him: that, with all his noble Qualities, I doubt I can never again have Confidence in his Promise to break this one bad Habit, seeing that he has broken it so soon, when there was no occasion or excuse: unless it were the thought of leaving his Wife so ill at home. The Man is so beyond others, as I think, that I have come to feel that I must not condemn him by general rule; nevertheless, if he ask me, I can refer him to no other. I must send him back his own written Promise of Sobriety, signed only a month before he broke it so needlessly: and I must even tell him that I know not yet if he can be left with the Mortgage as we settled it in May . . .

P.S. I enclose Posh's letter, and the answer I propose to give to it. I am sure it makes me sad and ashamed to be setting up for Judge on a much nobler Creature than myself. But I consider this a case in which the outbreak was worse than needless, and such as must almost destroy any Confidence I can feel for the future. I can only excuse it as a sort of Desperation for his Wife's Illness – strange way as he took for improving the occasion. You see it was *not* old Friends not seen for some time, but one or two of the Crew he is always with.

I had thought of returning him *his* written Promise as worthless: desiring back my Direction to my Heirs that he should keep on the lugger in case of my Death. But I will wait for what you say about all this. I am really sorry to trouble you over and over again with the matter. But I am so fearful of blundering, where a Blunder may do so much harm. I think that Posh ought to be made to feel this severely: and, as his Wife is better, I do not mind making him feel it, if I can. On the other hand, I do not wish to drive him, by Despair, into the very fault which I have so tried to cure him of. Pray do consider, and write to me of this, returning the two Papers. His mother did not try to excuse him at all: his Father would not even see him go off. She merely told me parenthetically, 'I tell him he seems to do it when the Governor is here'.

169 To Quaritch

Quaritch, 15–16   Lowestoft. September 20, 1870

This note, written in the form of a telegram on the back of a receipted bill from Quaritch, shows that FitzGerald's sense of fun still survived amid his habitual sadness. His Kerrich nieces as well as the Cowells joined him at Lowestoft this summer, and sailing expeditions in the Scandal *were still enjoyable. Meanwhile Napoleon III and the French Army had just surrendered at Sedan, and the Prussians were demanding the cession of Alsace-Lorraine, and blockading Paris.*

10 a.m.
From on board Ship where Professor Cowell is just going for a Sail with yours truly E. FG.
$10\frac{1}{2}$ a.m.
A Melton Mowbray Pork Pie and a Bottle of Sherry just hoisted on board for the Professor's Luncheon.
11 a.m.
Professor himself just hoisted on board. He begs his Compliments.
$11\frac{1}{2}$ a.m.
Topsail just hoisting in order to get the Professor and the Pork Pie out of Harbour. Wind very light. S.E.

Please to tell Count Bismarck that, if he could batter down Paris, without killing the Parisians, it would do more to keep France quiet for the next 20 years than the cession of Alsace Lorraine.

170 **To Pollock**

L.F., II, 117–18   Woodbridge. November 1, 1870

I must say that my savageness against France goes no further than wishing that the new and gay part of Paris were battered down; not the poor working part, no, nor any of the People destroyed. But I wish ornamental Paris down, because then I think the French would be kept quiet till they had rebuilt it. For what would France be without a splendid Palace? I should not wish any such Catastrophe, however, if Paris were now as I remember it: with a lot of old historic houses in it, old Gardens, etc., which I am told are now made away with. Only Notre Dame, the Tuileries, and perhaps the beautiful gilt Dome of the Invalides do I care for. They are historical and beautiful too.

But I believe it would be a good thing if the rest of Europe would take possession of France itself, and rule it for better or worse, leaving the French themselves to amuse and enlighten the world by their Books, Plays, Songs, Bon Mots, and all the Arts and Sciences which they are so ingenious in. They can do all things but manage themselves and live at peace with others: and they should themselves be glad to have their volatile Spirits kept in order by the Good Sense and Honesty which other Nations certainly abound in more than themselves . . .

171 **To Fanny Kemble**

F.K., 3–5   Woodbridge. July 4, 1871

FitzGerald's correspondence with Fanny Kemble, which had begun three years earlier, was now very regular. She had an odd but inflexible rule to write only in reply to letters received, but always to answer these at once, at the same length as the letter answered. FitzGerald wrote to her once a month, at the full moon. The yacht Scandal *had been sold earlier this year, but FitzGerald kept a small boat for sailing on the river.*

... Well, I have sold my dear little Ship, because I could not employ my Eyes with reading in her Cabin, where I had nothing else to do. I think those Eyes began to get better directly I had written to agree to the Man's proposal. Anyhow, the thing is done; and so now I betake myself to a Boat, whether on this River here, or on the Sea at the Mouth of it.

Books you see I have nothing to say about. The Boy who came to read to me made such blundering Work that I was forced to confine him to a Newspaper, where his Blunders were often as entertaining as the Text which he mistook. We had 'hangarues' in the French Assembly, and, on one occasion, 'ironclad Laughter from the Extreme Left'. Once again, at the conclusion of the London news, 'Consolations closed at 91, ex Div.' – And so on. You know how illiterate People will jump at a Word they don't know, and twist it into some word they are familiar with. I was telling some of these Blunders to a very quiet Clergyman here some while ago, and he assured me that a poor Woman, reading the Bible to his Mother, read off glibly, 'Stand at a Gate and swallow a Candle'. I believe this was no Joke of his: whether it were or not, here you have it for what you may think it worth ...

Now I am going for a Sail on the famous River Deben, to pass by the same fields of green Wheat, Barley, Rye, and Beet-root, and come back to the same Dinner. Positively the only new thing we have in Woodbridge is a Waxen Bust (Lady, of course) at the little Hairdresser's opposite.

She turns slowly round, to our wonder and delight; and I caught the little Barber the other day in the very Act of winding her up to run her daily Stage of Duty. Well; she has not got to answer Letters, as poor Mrs Kemble must do to hers always sincerely

172 To Pollock
L.F., II, 128   Winter, 1871

. . . I have been reading Sir Walter's Pirate again, and am very glad to find how much I like it – that is speaking far below the mark – I may say how I wonder and delight in it. I am rejoiced to find that this is so; and I am quite sure that it is not owing to my old prejudice, but to the intrinsic merit and beauty of the Book itself. With all its faults of detail, often mere carelessness, what a broad Shake-spearean Daylight over it all, and all with no Effort, and – a lot else that one may be contented to feel without having to write an Essay about. They won't beat Sir Walter in a hurry (I mean, of course his earlier, Northern, Novels) and he was such a fine Fellow that I really don't believe any one would wish to cast him in the Shade.

173 To Pollock
M.L., 134–5   Woodbridge. December 9, 1871

The case of Thomas Castro, alias Arthur Orton, who claimed to be the missing heir to the Tichborne estate, lasted till March 1872. 'Indentity' for 'identity' is still one of the commonest of all misprints, seen daily in newspapers.

The Tichborne Trial! I gloat over it every night from 8 to 10, my Boy reading it to me with tolerable fluency. His mistakes amuse me sometimes by showing how errors creep into Print under the Compositor's hands. Yesterday the 'face-smiles' of letters were handed in. We have the honour of contributing one witness from a neighbouring Village to confirm the Claimant's *in*dentity, as the Boy reads it: but he tells me that his Father knows of another who could swear to the contrary . . .

174 **To Pollock**
L.F., II, 131   Woodbridge. December 24, 1871

FitzGerald's failure to appreciate Jane Austen is the oddest quirk of his anti-feminism, as it might have been thought that her dry eighteenth-century irony and elegance would exactly suit his mainly anti-Romantic palate.

. . . Can't you send me your Paper about the Novelists? As to which is the best of all I can't say: that Richardson (with all his twaddle) is better than Fielding, I am quite certain. There is nothing at all comparable to Lovelace in all Fielding, whose Characters are common and vulgar types; of Squires, Ostlers, Lady's maids, etc., very easily drawn. I am equally sure that Miss Austen cannot be third, any more than first or second: I think you were rather drawn away by a fashion when you put her there: and really old Spedding seems to me to have been the Stag whom so many followed in that fashion. She is capital as far as she goes: but she never goes out of the Parlour; if but Magnus Troil, or Jack Bunce, or even one of Fielding's Brutes, would but dash in upon the Gentility and swear a round Oath or two! I must think the 'Woman in White', with her Count Fosco, far beyond all that. Cowell constantly reads Miss Austen at night after his Sanskrit Philology is done: it composes him, like Gruel: or like Paisiello's Music, which Napoleon liked above all other, because he said it didn't interrupt his Thoughts.

175 To Anna Biddell

L.F., II, 134–5   Woodbridge. February 22, 1872

Anna Biddell was a sister of FitzGerald's farmer friend Herman Biddell. Disraeli's novel Lothair *was published in 1870.*

. . . I have lost the Boy who read to me so long and so profitably: and now have another; a much better Scholar, but not half so agreeable or amusing a Reader as his Predecessor. We go through Tichborne without missing a Syllable, and, when Tichborne is not long enough, we take to Lothair! which has entertained me well. So far as I know of the matter, his pictures of the manners of English High Life are good: Lothair himself I do not care for, nor for the more romantic parts, Theodora, etc. Altogether the Book is like a pleasant Magic Lantern: when it is over, I shall forget it: and shall want to return to what I do not forget, some of Thackeray's monumental Figures of 'pauvre et triste Humanité', as old Napoleon called it: Humanity in its Depth, not in its superficial Appearances.

176 To Fanny Kemble

F.K., 10–11   Woodbridge. February 27, 1872

The Thanksgiving described in this letter was for the recovery of the Prince of Wales from typhoid, of which his father the Prince Consort had died eleven years earlier. This letter gives one of FitzGerald's rare reminiscences of his childhood at Bredfield, and of his brilliant and imposing but unloving – and unloved – mother.

. . . I do not think you have been to see the Thanksgiving Procession, for which our Bells are even now ringing – the old Peal which I have known these – sixty years almost – though at that time it reached my Eyes through a Nursery

Window about two miles off. From that window I remember seeing my Father with another Squire passing over the Lawn with their little pack of Harriers – an almost obliterated Slide of the old Magic Lantern. My Mother used to come up sometimes, and we Children were not much comforted. She was a remarkable woman, as you said in a former letter: and as I constantly believe in outward Beauty as an Index of a Beautiful Soul within, I used sometimes to wonder what feature in her fine face betrayed what was not so good in her Character. I think (as usual) the Lips: there was a twist of Mischief about them now and then, like that in – the Tail of a Cat! – otherwise so smooth and amiable . . .

177 To Quaritch

Quaritch, 17–19 Woodbridge. March 31, 1872

FitzGerald's Rubaiyat *had by now at last become famous, in England where* Fraser's Magazine *gave it a very admiring review in 1870, and in America, and the translator's identity (it had been published anonymously) was no longer a secret. Quaritch proposed a third edition to FitzGerald, combining the versions in the first and second editions, each of which had their partisans among readers.*

Easter Sunday my own Birthday (64). I wonder how it is with Omar but I think I know . . .

You must think I have followed Omar underground, not to have answered yours sooner – but I have been looking over him in consequence of your letter, to see what I could make of him. I wonder that, with all your great Business, you care to be troubled again with this little one: but if you really wish to set off old Omar once more to America, I would do what I could for his outfit.

I daresay Edition 1 is better in some respects than 2, but I think not altogether. Surely, several good things were added – perhaps too much of them which also gave Omar's thoughts room to turn in, as also the Day which the Poem occupies. He begins with Dawn pretty sober and contemplative: then as he thinks and drinks, grows savage, blasphemous etc., and then again sobers down into more expansion than the first Edition gave. I daresay Edition 1 best pleased those who read it first: as first Impressions are apt to be strongest.

By the same rule might not those who read the 2nd Edition first go the other way? The Gentleman in Fraser and some others seemed well satisfied.

As to the relative fidelity of the two Versions, there isn't a Pin to choose – not in the opening Stanzas you send.

All this seems making too much fuss about a small thing. But the truth is, that on looking over the two Versions, and ready to adopt your plan of reconciling two in one, I considered that such a scheme, with brackets etc. *would be* making too much of the thing: and you and I might both be laughed at for treating my Omar as if it were some precious fragment of Antiquity.

Besides I doubt if the two Versions could now – as altered – separately dovetail into one another without some fresh alteration – which I have lost heart and even Eyes for.

I doubt therefore that, if Omar be republished, he must go forth in one Shape or another – in his first, or second, suit. And I certainly vote for Version 2, with some whole Stanzas which may be 'de trop' cut out, and some of the old readings replaced . . .

By the by, Cowell wrote me some months ago that Edition 1 had been reprinted by someone in India. So I have lived not in vain, if I have lived to be *Pirated*!

178 To Fanny Kemble

F.K., 15   Woodbridge. June 6, 1872

... I am quite sure of the merit of George Eliot, and (I should have thought) of a kind that would suit me. But I have not as yet found an Appetite for her. I have begun taking the Cornhill that I may read Annie Thackeray – but I have not found appetite for her as yet. Is it that one recoils from making so many new Acquaintances in Novels, and retreats upon one's Old Friends, in Shakespeare, Cervantes, and Sir Walter? Oh, I read the last as you have lately been reading – the Scotch Novels, I mean: I believe I should not care for the Ivanhoes, Kenilworths, etc., any more. But Jeanie Deans, the Antiquary, etc., I shall be theirs as long as I am yours sincerely.

179 To Pollock

L.F., II, 158–9   Woodbridge. 1873

The companionship of characters in books now meant more and more to FitzGerald during his lonely winters in Woodbridge, broken only by occasional short trips to London. In the summers his nieces and friends like the Cowells, the Thompsons, Pollock, Frederick Tennyson, visited him and he took seaside lodgings at Lowestoft or Aldeburgh. But in the winter his chief company was the boys who read to him in the evenings. Trollope's Eustace Diamonds *was published in 1873, in which year the second Tichborne case, the Claimant's trial for perjury, began. In February 1874 he was given a 14-year sentence.*

... This is Sunday Night: 10 p.m. And what is the Evening Service which I have been listening to? The 'Eustace Diamonds': which interest me almost as much as Tichborne. I really give the best proof I can of the Interest I take in Trollope's Novels, by constantly breaking out into

Fanny Kemble. Lithograph by R. J. Lane after Sir Thomas
Lawrence. (*National Portrait Gallery*)

Argument with the Reader (who never replies) about what is said and done by the People in the several Novels. I say 'No, no! She must have known she was lying!' 'He couldn't have been such a Fool! etc.'

180 To Donne
F.F., 106   Woodbridge. March, 1873

After many years solicitation from Nieces, Crabbes, and two or three other old Friends, I got myself Photo'ed at the Beginning of this Year. And I don't like not to send a Copy to you, one of my very oldest and dearest Friends – The Artist always does *three* of every Sitter: but my bad Eyes blinked so (I suppose) in the Full face, turned toward the Machine, that we only took Copies of the two which turn away: and here they are for you to choose from – as also for Mowbray, if he likes. They are so unexpectedly complimentary, that I should not know either was meant for me; but also I must say I should not send them to my Friends if they were not so complimentary. For I think one should only hand over a presentable Likeness of oneself to those who have a Regard for one: and they, as well as I, must *believe* in the Likeness, though they wouldn't know it, inasmuch as Phoebus Apollo struck it off; and he should be the God of Truth . . . I call one *The Statesman*: and the other, *The Philosopher*.

181 To Mrs Browne
Wright, II, 125–6   Woodbridge. 1873

In reply to an often-repeated invitation from Mrs Browne to come and stay at Goldington, FitzGerald finally made the position clear.

. . . I have not been out on a visit *anywhere* since just before my sister Kerrich died in May 1863, ten years ago, not even to my brother's house, two miles off here, though we are very good friends. I do not even call on my old friends when I have to run to London about once a year. I don't state this as if I thought it commendable, quite the contrary; but so it has been, as I say, for ten years, and too late to alter now. I state it to you that you may not think that you are an exception to other old friends . . .

182 To Pollock
L.F., II, 162   Spring, 1873

FitzGerald had been looking over the volume containing his Euphranor *and the* Agamemnon *translation which had been privately printed in 1869. 'Emergency', now a commonplace word, struck FitzGerald as an offensive neologism.*

. . . When I look over the little Prose Dialogue, I see lots that might be weeded. I wonder at one word which is already crossed – *'Emergency'*. 'An Emergency!' I think Blake could have made a Picture of it as he did of the Flea. Something of the same disgusting Shape too . . . Blake seems to me to have fine things: but as by random, like those of a Child, or a Madman, of Genius. Is there one good whole Piece, of ever so few lines? . . .

183 To Fanny Kemble
F.K., 31–3   Woodbridge. Autumn, 1873

FitzGerald here reminisces about his visit to Paris from April to June 1830 (see Letter 1). A month after that visit, an uprising in Paris overthrew Charles X and established the 'July Monarchy' of Louis Philippe. G. G. Gervinus, Professor of History and Literature at Gottingen, was the author of Shakespeare Commentaries *(1849–50) in which, following Goethe in* Wilhelm Meister, *he saw Hamlet as a*

*truth-loving but inert and phlegmatic character, though with a sensitive
excitability which could make him dangerous; by nature one of Shakespeare's humorous characters, though trapped in tragedy. This was a
version of Hamlet with which FitzGerald could identify.*

... When I was in Paris in 1830, just before that Revolution, I stopped one Evening on the Boulevards by the
Madeleine to listen to a Man who was singing to his Barrel-
organ. Several passing 'Blouses' had stopped also: not only
to listen, but to join in the Songs, having bought little
'Libretti' of the words from the Musician. I bought one
too; for, I suppose, the smallest French Coin; and assisted
in the Song which the Man called out beforehand (as they
do Hymns at Church), and of which I enclose you the poor
little Copy. '*Le Bon Pasteur*, s'il vous plait' – I suppose the
Circumstances: the 'beau temps', the pleasant Boulevards,
the then so amiable People, all contributed to the effect this
Song had upon me; anyhow, it has constantly revisited my
memory for these forty-three years; and I was thinking,
the other day, touched me more than any of Béranger's
most beautiful Things. This, however, may be only one of
'Old Fitz's Crotchets', as Tennyson and others would call
them ...

Gervinus's Theory of Hamlet is very striking. Perhaps
Shakespeare himself would have admitted, without ever
having expressly designed, it. I always said, with regard to
the Explanation of Hamlet's Madness or Sanity, that
Shakespeare himself might not have known the Truth any
more than we understand the seeming Discords in People
we know best. Shakespeare intuitively imagined, and
portrayed, the Man without being able to give a reason –
perhaps – I believe in Genius doing this ...

184 To Pollock

L.F., II, 172–3　　　　　　　Woodbridge. July 23, 1874

In 1874 FitzGerald's life composed itself into a more tranquil settled shape for his remaining years. In February he served all remaining business relations with Posh Fletcher, and henceforth saw little of him. Later in the spring he finally moved into his own house, Little Grange, and began to enjoy being surrounded with all his books and possessions, entertaining relations and friends, being well looked after by a married couple, called Howe, and sitting and walking in a brightly-flowered garden. In July he went by sea to Edinburgh, to see Walter Scott's home at Abbotsford. 'Gurlyle' was FitzGerald's nickname for Carlyle. 'Jedburgh Abbey' should be Dryburgh.

. . . I did get to Abbotsford, and was rejoiced to find it was not at all Cockney, not a Castle, but only in the half-castellated style of heaps of other houses in Scotland; the Grounds simply and broadly laid out before the windows, down to a field, down to the Tweed, with the woods which he left so little, now well aloft and flourishing, and I was glad. I could not find my way to Maida's Grave in the Garden, with its false Quantity,

> Ad januam Domini, etc.

which the Whigs and Critics taunted Scott with, and Lockhart had done it. 'You know I don't care a curse about what I write'; nor about what was imputed to him. In this, surely like Shakespeare: as also in other respects. I will worship him, in spite of Gurlyle, who sent me an ugly Autotype of Knox whom I was to worship instead.

Then I went to see Jedburgh Abbey, in a half ruined corner of which he lies entombed – Lockhart beside him – a beautiful place, with his own Tweed still running close by, and his Eildon Hills looking on. The man who drove me about showed me a hill which Sir Walter was very fond of visiting, from which he could see over the Border, etc. This hill is between Abbotsford and Jedburgh: and when his Coach horses, who drew his Hearse, got there, to that hill, they could scarce be got on.

My mission to Scotland was done; but some civil pleasant people, whom I met at Abbotsford, made me go with them (under Cook's guidance) to the Trossachs, Katrine, Lomond, etc., which I did not care at all about; but it only took a day. After which, I came in a day to London, rather glad to be in my old flat land again, with a sight of my old Sea as we came along.

And in London I went to see my dear old Donne, because of wishing to assure myself, with my own eyes, of his condition; and I can safely say he looked better than before his Illness, near two years ago. He had a healthy colour; was erect, alert, and with his old humour, and interest in our old topics . . .

185 To Groome

Groome, 33–4 Lowestoft. February 16, 1875

You may have heard that my Brother Peter is dead, of Bronchitis, at Bournemouth. He was taken seriously ill on Thursday last, and died on Saturday without pain; and I am told that his last murmured words were *my* name – thrice repeated. A more amiable Gentleman did not live, with something *helpless* about him – what the Irish call an 'Innocent man' – which mixed up Compassion with Regard, and made it perhaps stronger . . .

186 To Fanny Kemble

F.K., 68–70   Lowestoft. April 9, 1875

... It has been indeed the Devil of a Winter: and even now – Today as I write – no better than it was three months ago. The Daffodils scarce dare take April, let alone March; and I wait here till a Green Leaf shows itself about Woodbridge.

I have been looking over four of Shakespeare's plays ... Hamlet, Macbeth, Tempest, and Shylock – I heard them talking in my room – all alive about me.

By the by – How did *you* read To-morrow and To-morrow, etc. All the Macbeths I have heard took the opportunity to become melancholy when they came to this: and, no doubt, some such change from Fury and Desperation was a relief to the Actor, and perhaps to the Spectator. But I think it *should* all go in the same Whirlwind of Passion as the rest: Folly! – Stage Play! – Farthing Candle; Idiot, etc. Macready used to drop his Truncheon when he heard of the Queen's Death, and stand with his Mouth open for some while – which didn't become him.

I have not seen his Memoir: only an extract or two in the Papers. He always seemed to me an Actor by Art and Study, with some native Passion to inspire him. But as to Genius – we who have seen Kean!

I don't know if you were acquainted with Sir A. Helps, whose Death (one of this Year's Doing) is much regretted by many. I scarcely knew him except at Cambridge forty years ago: and could never relish his Writings, amiable and sensible as they are. I suppose they will help to swell that substratum of Intellectual *Peat* (Carlyle somewhere calls it) from which one or two living Trees stand out in a Century. So Shakespeare above all that Old Drama which he grew amidst, and which (all represented in him alone) might henceforth be left unexplored, with the exception of a few twigs of Leaves gathered here and there – as in Lamb's Specimens. Is Carlyle himself – with all his Genius – to subside into the Level? Dickens, with all his Genius, but whose Men and Women act and talk already after a more obsolete fashion than Shakespeare's? I think some of Tennyson will survive, and drag the deader part along with it, I suppose. And (I doubt) Thackeray's terrible Humanity.

And I remain yours ever sincerely
A very small Peat-contributor
E.F.G.

187 To Fanny Kemble
F.K., 71–4   Lowestoft. April 19, 1875

. . . Macready's Memoirs . . . I am now reading at Leisure: for it does not interest me enough to devour at once. It is however a very unaffected record of a very conscientious Man, and Artist; conscious (I think) that he has not a great Genius in his Profession, and conscious of his defect of Self-control in his Morals. The Book is almost entirely about *himself, his* Studies, *his* Troubles, *his* Consolations, etc.; not from Egotism, I do think, but as the one thing he had to consider in writing a Memoir and Diary. Of course one expects, and wishes, that the Man's self should be the main subject; but one also wants something of the remarkable people he lived with, and of whom one finds little here but that 'So-and-so came and went' – scarce anything of what they said or did, except on mere business; Macready seeming to have no Humour; no intuition into Character, no Observation of those about him (how could he be a great Actor then?) – Almost the only exception I have yet reached is his Account of Mrs Siddons, whom he worshipped . . . On the whole, I find Macready (so far as I have gone) a just, generous, religious, and affectionate Man; on the whole, humble too! One is well content to assure oneself of this; but it is not worth spending 28s. upon.

Macready would have made a better Scholar – or Divine – than Actor, I think: a Gentleman he would have been in any calling, I believe, in spite of his Temper – which he acknowledges, laments, and apologizes for, on reflection.

Now, here is enough of my small writing for your reading. I have been able to read, and admire, some Corneille lately: as to Racine – 'Ce n'est pas mon homme', as Catherine of Russia said of him. Now I am at Madame de Sévigné's delightful Letters; I should like to send you a Bouquet of Extracts . . .

188 To Annie Thackeray
H. Tennyson, 126–7   Woodbridge. May 18, 1875

The FitzGerald family spent the years 1816–18 in France, at St Germain and then in Paris. FitzGerald was then a boy of eight, so this vivid reminiscence makes it regrettable that he did not use his 'total recall' for more descriptions of the world of his childhood. After Thackeray's death, FitzGerald exchanged letters once a year with his daughter Annie, and often mentioned her novels with an indulgence he did not usually show to women writers.

I suppose you love Paris as your Father did – as I used to do till it was made so other than it was, in the days of Louis XVIII, when I first lived in it. *Then* it was all irregular and picturesque; with shops, hotels, cafés, theatres, etc. inter-mixed all along the Boulevards, all of different sorts and sizes.

Think of my remembering the *then* Royal Family going in several carriages to hunt in the Forest of St. Germain's

– Louis XVIII first, with his Gardes du Corps, in blue and silver: then Monsieur (afterwards Charles X) with *his* Guard in green and gold – French horns blowing – 'tra, tra, tra' (as Madame de Sévigné says), through the lines of chestnuts and limes – in flower. And then *Madame* (of Angouleme) standing up in her carriage, blear-eyed, dressed in white with her waist at her neck – standing up in the carriage at a corner of the wood to curtsey to the English assembled there – my mother among them. This was in 1817. Now *you* would have made a delightful description of all this; you will say *I* have done so but that is not so. And yet I saw, and see, it all . . .

189 To Pollock
L.F., II, 181   Lowestoft. September 22, 1875

. . . I dare say I may have told you what Tennyson said of the Sistine Child, which he then knew only by Engraving. He first thought the Expression of his Face (as also the Attitude) almost too solemn, even for the Christ within. But some time after, when A.T. was married, and had a Son, he told me that Raffaelle was all right: that no Man's face was so solemn as a Child's, full of Wonder. He said one morning that he watched his Babe 'worshipping the Sunbeam on the Bedpost and Curtain' . . .

190 To Laurence
L.F., II, 190   Woodbridge. December 30, 1875

. . . I cannot get on with Books about the Daily Life which I find rather insufferable in practice about me. I never could read Miss Austen, nor (later) the famous George Eliot. Give me People, Places, and Things, which I don't and can't see; Antiquaries, Jeanie Deans, Dalgettys, etc. . . .

As to Thackeray's, they are terrible; I really look at them on the shelf, and am half afraid to touch them. He, you know, could go deeper into the Springs of Common Action than these Ladies: wonderful he is, but not Delightful, which one thirsts for as one gets old and dry.

191 To Charles Eliot Norton

L.F., II, 190–91   Woodbridge. January 23, 1876

The American scholar and critic Charles Eliot Norton, one of the earliest public acclaimers of FitzGerald's Rubaiyat *translation, became a regular correspondent of FitzGerald's from 1873 onwards. Both men were friends of Carlyle.*

. . . I suppose you may see one of the Carlyle Medallions: and you can judge better of the Likeness than I, who have not been to Chelsea, and hardly out of Suffolk, these fifteen years and more. I dare say it is like him: but his Profile is not his best phase. In two notes dictated by him since that Business he has not adverted to it: I think he must be a little ashamed of it, though it would not do to say so in return, I suppose. And yet I think he might have declined the Honours of a Life of 'Heroism'. I have no doubt he would have played a Brave Man's Part if called on; but, meanwhile, he has only sat pretty comfortably at Chelsea, scolding all the world for not being Heroic, and not always very precise in telling them how. He has, however, been so far heroic, as to be always independent, whether of Wealth, Rank, and Coteries of all sorts: nay, apt to fly in the face of some one who courted him. I suppose he is changed, or subdued, at eighty: but up to the last ten years he seemed to me just the same as when I first knew him five and thirty years ago. What a Fortune he might have made by showing himself about as a Lecturer,

as Thackeray and Dickens did; I don't mean they did it for
Vanity: but to make money: and that to spend generously.
Carlyle did indeed lecture near forty years ago before he
was a Lion to be shown, and when he had but few Readers.
I heard his 'Heroes' which now seems to me one of his best
Books. He looked very handsome then, with his black
hair, fine Eyes, and a sort of crucified Expression . . .

192 To Quaritch
Quaritch, 40–41   Woodbridge. January 25, 1876

In 1876 FitzGerald's Agamemnon *translation, which had been
privately printed in 1869, was published by Quaritch. This letter of
FitzGerald's to his publisher shows his exceptional unlikeness to the
ordinary author, who tends to demand more advertisements of his books,
more prominence for his name in reviews; but FitzGerald was always
more afraid of ridicule than hopeful of praise. H. S. Wilson had written
to Quaritch saying that he was about to publish a paper on Omar
Khayyam – should he mention FitzGerald by name as translator? The
other Edward FitzGerald whom Quaritch knew to his cost was a book-
thief. The 'lord of that name' was Lord Edward FitzGerald, who died
in prison in Dublin in 1798 after taking part in an unsuccessful rebellion.*

. . . As for my *Name*. I always told you it would do both of
us more harm than good by appearing on Title page or in
Advertisement. *Good*, it could not; so many E.FG's; no
one of them celebrated but the Lord of that name.

Why, there is one beside myself in this very Woodbridge,
an Ex-policeman; there lately was another, a Parson, in a
neighbouring Village; you knew another to your Cost. In
fact one of us was generally hanged in Ireland once a Year
till the Law was altered –

Shall all these dispute my Glory? . . . So much for Title
pages etc. As to Reviews; as I suppose that *one of us* is
known to be the Culprit by several among the small Circles

of *Omarians*, Mr Wilson will do as he finds most convenient to himself in naming *one of us* as the *understood* Translator, or simply saying 'The Translator' in the Review he kindly proposes, and which of course I shall be glad of.

You can if you choose advertise Agamemnon in your Catalogue as 'by the Translator of Omar' – which will have all the more force *after* Mr Wilson's Review, I hope.

But I am afraid you will only provoke the Jealous Gods by printing me as if I were a Browning. And the Danger more because of so many of The Gods knowing more of Greek than of Persian. But I suppose you make your Calculation.

Thank you – as once before – for your invitation to your pleasant Haverstock. But I scarce ever go to London now; and when I do, only to be back the same Day, without looking up even 50 year-old Friends. But I remain theirs and yours

One of the E.FG's.

193 To Norton
L.F., II, 193–5   Woodbridge. February 7, 1876

Norton had sent FitzGerald a copy of Among My Books *by the American poet and critic James Russell Lowell, who now also became a correspondent of FitzGerald's. Reading Lowell's book sent FitzGerald back to some of the classics on his own bookshelves.*

. . . Dante's face I have not seen these ten years: only his Back on my Book Shelf. What Mr Lowell says of him recalled to me what Tennyson said to me some thirty-five or forty years ago. We were stopping before a shop in Regent Street where were two Figures of Dante and Goethe. I (I suppose) said, 'What is there in old Dante's Face that is missing in Goethe's?' And Tennyson (whose

Profile then had certainly a remarkable likeness to Dante's) said: 'The Divine.' Then Milton; I don't think I've read him these forty years; the whole Scheme of the Poem, and certain Parts of it, looming as grand as anything in my Memory; but I never could read ten lines together without stumbling at some Pedantry that tipped me at once out of Paradise, or even Hell, into the Schoolroom, worse than either. Tennyson again used to say that the two grandest of all Similes were those of the Ships hanging in the Air, and 'the Gunpowder one', which he used slowly and grimly to enact, in the Days that are no more. He certainly then thought Milton the sublimest of all the Gang; his Diction modelled on Virgil, as perhaps Dante's.

Spenser I never could get on with, and (spite of Mr. Lowell's good word) shall still content myself with such delightful Quotations from him as one lights upon here and there: the last from Mr Lowell.

Then, old 'Daddy Wordsworth,' as he was sometimes called, I am afraid from my Christening, he is now, I suppose, passing under the Eclipse consequent on the Glory which followed his obscure Rise. I remember fifty years ago at our Cambridge, when the Battle was fighting for him by the Few against the Many of us who only laughed at 'Louisa in the Shade,' etc. His Brother was then Master of Trinity College; like all Wordsworths (unless the drowned Sailor) pompous and priggish. He used to drawl out the Chapel responses so that we called him the 'Meeserable Sinner' and his brother the 'Meeserable Poet.' Poor fun enough: but I never can forgive the Lakers all who first despised, and then patronized 'Walter Scott,' as they loftily called him: and He, dear, noble, Fellow, thought they were quite justified. Well, your Emerson has done him far more Justice than his own Countryman Carlyle, who wont allow him to be a Hero in any way, but sets up such a cantankerous narrow-minded Bigot as John Knox in his stead. I did go to worship at Abbotsford, as to Stratford on Avon: and saw that it was good to have so done. If you, if Mr Lowell, have not lately read it, pray read Lockhart's account of his Journey to Douglas Dale on (I think) July 18 or 19, 1831. It is a piece of Tragedy, even to the muttering Thunder, like the Lammermuir, which does not look very small beside Peter Bell and Co.

My dear Sir, this is a desperate Letter; and that last Sentence will lead to another dirty little Story about my Daddy: to which you must listen or I should feel like the Fine Lady in one of Vanbrugh's Plays, 'Oh my God, that you won't listen to a Woman of Quality when her Heart is bursting with Malice!' And perhaps you on the other Side of the Great Water may be amused with a little of your old Granny's Gossip.

Well then: about 1826, or 7, Professor Airy (now our Astronomer Royal) and his Brother William called on the Daddy at Rydal. In the course of Conversation Daddy mentioned that sometimes when genteel Parties came to visit him, he contrived to slip out of the room, and down the garden walk to where 'The Party's' travelling Carriage stood. This Carriage he would look into to see what Books they carried with them: and he observed it was generally 'WALTER SCOTT's.' It was Airy's Brother (a very veracious man, and an Admirer of Wordsworth, but, to be sure, more of Sir Walter) who told me this. It is this conceit that diminishes Wordsworth's stature among us, in spite of the mountain Mists he lived among. Also, a little stinginess; not like Sir Walter in that! I remember Hartley Coleridge telling us at Ambleside how Professor Wilson and some one else (H. C. himself perhaps) stole a Leg of Mutton from Wordsworth's Larder for the fun of the Thing.

194 To Fanny Kemble

F.K., 105–6 Lowestoft. April, 1876

FitzGerald could now look back with some objectivity on his terminated relationship with Posh Fletcher, though something of its glamour persisted. In his late years he became much attached to Madame de Sévigné's letters, and often talked of, but never achieved, visiting Brittany to see her country house, Les Rochers, near Vitré.

From Lowestoft still I date: as just ten years ago when I was about building a Lugger, and reading Montaigne. The latter holds his own with me after three hundred years: and the Lugger does not seem much the worse for her ten years' wear, so well did she come bouncing between the Piers here yesterday, under a strong Sou'-Wester. My Great Captain has her no more; he has what they call a 'Scotch Keel' which is come into fashion: her too I see: and see him too steering her, broader and taller than all the rest: fit to be a Leader of Men, Body and Soul; looking now Ulysses-like. Two or three years ago he had a run of constant bad luck; and, being always of a grand convivial turn, treating Everybody, he got deep in Drink, against all his Promises to me, and altogether so lawless, that I brought things to a pass between us. 'He should go on with me if he would take the Tee-total Pledge for one year' – 'No – he had broken his word', he said, 'and he would not pledge it again', much as he wished to go on with me. That, you see, was very fine in him; he is altogether fine – a Great Man, I maintain it: like one of Carlyle's old

Norway Kings, with a wider morality than we use; which is very good and fine (as this Captain said to me) 'for you who are born with a silver spoon in your mouths'. I did not forget what Carlyle too says about Great Faults in Great Men: even in David, the Lord's Anointed. But I thought best to share the Property with him and let him go his way. He had always resented being under any Control, and was very glad to be his own sole Master again: and yet clung to me in a wild and pathetic way. He has not been doing better since: and I fear is sinking into disorder.

This is a long story about one you know nothing about except what little I have told you. But the Man is a very remarkable Man indeed, and you may be interested – you must be – in him.

'Ho! parlons d'autres choses, ma Fille', as my dear Sévigné says. She now occupies Montaigne's place in my room: well – worthily: she herself a Lover of Montaigne, and with a spice of his free thought and speech in her. I am sometimes vext I never made her acquaintance till last year: but perhaps it was as well to have such an acquaintance reserved for one's latter years. The fine Creature! much more alive to me than most Friends – I should like to see her 'Rochers' in Brittany . . .

195 To Norton
L.F., II, 198–9   Woodbridge. June 10, 1876

'Old Hallam' in this letter is Henry Hallam, author of An Introduction to the Literature of Europe During the 15th, 16th and 17th Centuries; *Patmore is P. G. Patmore, author of* My Friends and Acquaintances; *Procter is B. W. Procter, poet and dramatist under the pseudonym of Barry Cornwall.*

. . . Only a week ago I began my dear Don Quixote over again; as welcome and fresh as the Flowers of May. The Second Part is my favourite, in spite of what Lamb and Coleridge (I think) say; when, as old Hallam says, Cervantes has fallen in Love with the Hero whom he began by ridiculing. When this Letter is done I shall get out into my Garden with him, Sunday though it be.

We also have Memoirs of Godwin, very dry, I think; indeed with very little worth reading, except two or three Letters of dear Charles Lamb, 'Saint Charles', as Thackeray once called him, while looking at one of his half-mad Letters, and remembering his Devotion to that quite mad Sister. I must say I think his Letters infinitely better than his Essays; and Patmore says his Conversation, when just enough animated by Gin and Water, was better than either: which I believe too. Procter says he was far beyond the Coleridges, Wordsworths, Southeys, etc. And I am afraid I believe that also . . .

And now for the Garden and the Don: always in a common old Spanish Edition. Their coarse prints always make him look more of the Gentleman than the better Artists of other Countries have hitherto done.

Carlyle, I hear, is pretty well, though somewhat shrunk: scolding away at Darwin, The Turk, etc.

196 To Fanny Kemble
F.K., 113–15   Woodbridge. September 21, 1876

This account of a happy visit by Tennyson to Woodbridge shows that FitzGerald's fear of actually meeting his celebrated friends, lest there should be disappointment and constraint in the meeting, was an idle one which needlessly cut him off from the mental stimulus and enjoyment in which his life was now so deficient.

Have your American Woods begun to hang out their Purple and Gold yet? on this Day of Equinox. Some of ours begin to look rusty, after the Summer Drought; but have not turned Yellow yet. I was talking of this to a Heroine of mine who lives near here, but visits the Highlands of Scotland, which she loves better than Suffolk – and she said of those Highland Trees – 'O, they give themselves no dying Airs, but turn Orange in a Day, and are swept off in a Whirlwind, and Winter is come'.

Now too one's Garden begins to be haunted by that Spirit which Tennyson says is heard talking to himself among the flower-borders. Do you remember him?

And now – Who should send in his card to me last week – but the old Poet himself – he and his elder Son Hallam passing through Woodbridge from a Tour in Norfolk. 'Dear old Fitz', ran the Card in pencil, 'We are passing thro''. I had not seen him for twenty years – he looked much the same, except for his fallen locks; and what really surprised me was, that we fell at once into the old Humour, as if we had only been parted twenty Days instead of so many Years. I suppose this is a Sign of Age – not altogether desirable. But so it was. He stayed two Days, and we went over the same old grounds of Debate, told some of the old Stories, and all was well. I suppose I may never see him again: and so I suppose we both thought as the Rail carried him off: and each returned to his ways as if scarcely diverted from them. Age again! – I liked Hallam much; unaffected, unpretending – no Slang – none of Young England's nonchalance – speaking of his Father as 'Papa' and tending him with great Care, Love, and Discretion . . .

197 To Fanny Kemble

F.K., 116–17   Lowestoft. October 24, 1876

Little – Nothing – as I have to write, I am nevertheless
beginning to write to you, from this old Lodging of mine,
from which I think our Correspondence chiefly began –
ten years ago. I am in the same Room: the same dull Sea
moaning before me: the same Wind screaming through the
Windows: so I take up the same old Story. My Lugger was
then about building: she has passed into other hands now:
I see her from time to time, bouncing into Harbour, with
her '244' on her Bows. Her Captain and I have parted . . .
I saw him, a few days ago, in his house, with Wife and
Children; looking, as always, too big for his house: but
always grand, polite, and unlike anybody else. I was noticing the many Flies in the room – 'Poor things' he said, 'it is
the warmth of our Stove makes them alive'. When Tennyson was with me, whose Portrait hangs in my house in
company with those of Thackeray and this Man (the three
greatest men I have known), I thought that both Tennyson
and Thackeray were inferior to him in respect of Thinking
of Themselves. When Tennyson was telling me of how
The Quarterly abused him (humorously too), and desirous
of knowing why one did not care for his later works, etc.,
I thought that if he had lived an active Life, as Scott and
Shakespeare; or even ridden, shot, drunk, and played the
Devil, as Byron, he would have done much more, and
talked about it much less. 'You know', said Scott to
Lockhart, 'that I don't care a Curse about what I write',
and one sees he did not. I don't believe it was far otherwise
with Shakespeare. Even old Wordsworth, wrapt up in his
Mountain mists, and proud as he was, was above all this
vain Disquietude: proud, not vain, was he: and that a
Great Man (as Dante) has some right to be – but not to
care what the Coteries say . . .

198 To Norton

L.F., II, 214–15   Woodbridge. February 1, 1877

FitzGerald was a propagandist for the poetry of Crabbe, whose Suffolk landscapes were so familiar to him, and whose son and grandson were friends of his. In the late 70s he spent much time on editing Crabbe's Tales of the Hall *and trying to interest his English and American correspondents in the project. The edition was privately printed in 1879 and published in 1882.*

. . . You shall one day see my 'Tales of the Hall', when I can get it decently arranged, and written out (what is to be written), and then you shall judge of what chance it has of success. I want neither any profit, whether of money, or reputation: I only want to have Crabbe read more than he is. Women and young People never will like him, I think: but I believe every thinking man will like him more as he grows older; see if this be not so with yourself and your friends. Your Mother's Recollection of him is, I am sure, the just one: Crabbe never showed himself in Company, unless to a very close and experienced observer: his Company manner was exactly the reverse of his Books: almost, as Moore says, '*doucereux*'; the apologetic politeness of the old School over-done, as by one who was not born to it. But Campbell observed his 'shrewd Vigilance' awake under all his 'politesse', and John Murray said that Crabbe said uncommon things in so common a way that they escaped recognition . . .

199 To Donne

W.B.D.F., 325   Lowestoft. February 14, 1877

The news about which FitzGerald 'kept himself from bothering' was that of the 'Bulgarian atrocities', the Turks' massacre of their Bulgarian subjects which Gladstone passionately denounced, while Disraeli, then Prime Minister, sided with the Turkish Government. 'Thackeray's Lord Hertford' was his Lord Steyne, in Vanity Fair, *based, like Disraeli's Lord Monmouth in* Coningsby, *on the real-life Marquis of Hertford.*

. . . I have really not looked into a Newspaper since Christmas, and so have kept myself from bothering about what I can't help. Gladstone I always looked on as Doctrinaire, but honest, as Politicians can be: D'Israeli as a very clever Quack, whose Statesmanship is as flashy and 'superficial as his Novels'. Indeed I judge the Fellow by his Books. I read 'Coningsby' in the Summer, and find no impression left: *his* 'Lord Hertford' a curious contrast to Thackeray's. And I have been reading Trollope's 'Phineas Redux' here; *infinitely* better than Dizzy in the record of London Society, Clubs, Political Parties, etc., never a *caricature* as Dizzy is . . .

200 **To Allen**
L.F., II, 219–20   Woodbridge. Summer, 1877

FitzGerald was always fascinated by the character of John Wesley (see Letter 136). What he says here about biographers who venture to speculate about 'any other Man's Soul and Motives' must make any of his own biographers tremble; he would have been outraged by the application of modern psycho-analysis to the reticent intricacies of his personality. But see Letters 201 and 202 where he justifies the revelation of Lamb's and Keats's heart-secrets so long as they were not discreditable, and Letter 221 where he admits the reader's enjoyment even of what ought not to have been published of Carlyle's reminiscences.

. . . I think I will send you (when I can lay hand on it) two volumes of some one's Memorials of Wesley's Family: which you can look over, if you do not read, and return to me also. I wonder at your writing to me that I gave you his

Journal so long as thirty years ago. I scarce knew that I was so constant in my Affections: and yet I think I do *not* change in literary cases. Pray read Southey's Life of him again: it does not tell all, I think, which might be told of Wesley's own character from his own Mouth: but then it errs on the right side: it does not presumptuously guess at Qualities and Motives which are not to be found in Wesley: unlike Carlyle and the modern Historians, Southey, I think, cannot be wrong by keeping so much within the bounds of Conjecture: Conjecture about any other Man's Soul and Motives!

201 To Fanny Kemble

F.K., 134–6   Woodbridge. February 22, 1878

Keats's letters to Fanny Brawne were first published in 1878. The 'notes on Catullus' were Criticisms and Elucidations of Catullus *by H. A. J. Munro. The silhouette of Tennyson was done on the way back from an excursion from London to Gravesend in January 1842.*

. . . If you have not already read – *buy* Keats' Love-Letters to Fanny Brawne. One wishes she had another name; and had left some other Likeness of herself than the Silhouette (cut out by Scissors, I fancy) which dashes one's notion of such a Poet's worship. But one knows what misrepresentations such Scissors make. I had – perhaps have – one of Alfred Tennyson, done by an Artist on a Steamboat – some thirty years ago; which, though not inaccurate of outline, gave one the idea of a respectable Apprentice. But Keats' Letters – It happened that, just before they reached me, I had been hammering out some admirable Notes on Catullus – another such fiery Soul who perished about thirty years of age two thousand years ago; and I scarce felt a change from one to other. From Catullus' better parts, I mean; for there is too much of filthy and odious – both of Love and Hate. Oh, my dear Virgil never fell into that: he was fit to be Dante's companion beyond even Purgatory . . .

Snowdrops and Crocuses out: I have not many, for what I had have been buried under an overcoat of Clay, poor little Souls. Thrushes tuning up; and I hope my old Blackbirds have not forsaken me, or fallen a prey to Cats.

202 To Donne

W.B.D.F., 336   Woodbridge. March 14, 1878

FitzGerald sent with this letter a four-page calendar of the events of Charles Lamb's life which he had made to accompany the confusingly-arranged edition of Lamb's letters. The 'terrible year of 1796' was the one in which Lamb's sister Mary killed her mother.

. . . I hesitated at expatiating so on the terrible year 1796, or even mentioning the Drink in 1804: but the first is necessary to show what a Saint and Hero the man was; and only a Noodle would fail to understand the Drink, etc., which never affected Lamb's conduct to those he loved. Bless him! 'Saint Charles!' said Thackeray one day taking up one of his Letters, and putting it to his Forehead . . .

I and my good Reader have made four of Sir Walter's Novels last us over four winter months; only taking him for a last 'Bonne bouche'. Who is the best Novelist I don't know: but I know that Sir Walter is the most *delightful* to me. Much weariness, some even *bad*. But, on the whole, I look back to each with Love; and with sadness to think that I may never read them again. I only speak of the earlier Scott novels . . .

203 To Norton

L.F., II, 241–2   Woodbridge. April 4, 1878

I wish you would not impose on yourself to write me a
Letter; which you say is 'in your head'. You have Literary
work, and a Family to enjoy with you what spare time your
Professional Studies leave you. Whereas I have nothing of
any sort that I am engaged to do: all alone for months
together: taking up such Books as I please; and rather
liking to write Letters to my Friends, whom I now only
communicate with by such means. And very few of my
oldest Friends, here in England, care to answer me, though
I know from no want of Regard: but I know that few
sensible men, who have their own occupations, care to
write Letters unless on some special purpose; and I now
rarely get more than one yearly Letter from each. Seeing
which, indeed, I now rarely trouble them for more. So pray
be at ease in this respect: you have written to me, as I to
you, more than has passed between myself and my fifty
years old Friends for some years past . . .

I am quite content to take History as you do, that is, as
the Squire-Carlyle presents it to us; not looking the Gift
Horse in the Mouth. Also, I am sure you are right about
the Keats' Letters. I hope I should have revolted from the
Book had anything in it detracted from the man: but all
seemed to me in his favour, and therefore I did not feel I
did wrong in having the secret of that heart opened to me.
I hope Mr Lowell will not resent my thinking he might so
far sympathize with me. In fact, could he, could you, resist
taking up, and reading, the Letters, however doubtful
their publication might have seemed to your Conscience? . . .

218

204 To Fanny Kemble

F.K., 136–8   Woodbridge. April 16, 1878

FitzGerald still occasionally read the work of contemporaries like Musset, but he was withdrawing more and more into the company provided him by the writers of his favourite books, by Scott in Guy Mannering, *Richardson in* Clarissa, *and his newly-discovered Madame de Sévigné.*

(Where, by the by, I heard the Nightingale for the first time yesterday Morning. That is, I believe, almost its exact date of return, wind and weather permitting . . .) . . . When my Oracle last night was reading to me of Dandie Dinmont's blessed visit to Bertram in Portanferry Gaol, I said 'I know it's Dandie, and I shouldn't be at all surprised to see him come into this room'. No – no more than – Madame de Sévigné! I suppose it is scarce right to live so among Shadows; but – after near seventy years so passed – 'Que voulez-vous?' . . .

Yesterday the Nightingale; and To-day, a small, still, Rain which we had hoped for, to make 'poindre' the Flower-seeds we put in Earth last Saturday. All Sunday my white Pigeons were employed in confiscating the Sweet Peas we had laid there; so that To-day we have to sow the same anew.

I think a Memoir of Alfred de Musset, by his Brother, well worth reading. I don't say the best, but only to myself the most acceptable of modern French Poets; and, as I judge, a fine fellow – of the moral French type (I suppose some of the Shadow is left out of the Sketch), but of a Soul quite abhorrent from modern French Literature – from V. Hugo (I think) to E. Sue (I am sure). He loves to read – Clarissa! which reminded me of Tennyson, some forty years ago, saying to me à propos of that very book, 'I love those large, *still*, Books' . . .

205 To Charles Merivale

M.L., 210   Woodbridge. December 15, 1878

Merivale, the historian of Rome and Dean of Ely, was a contemporary and friend of FitzGerald at Cambridge.

. . . You in some measure ask me about Mrs Kemble. I did not see much of her acting, nor hear much of her reading, for in truth I did not much admire either. She herself admits she had no liking for the stage, and (in a capital paper in some magazine) that she had not a *Theatrical* gift, though she had, she thinks, a *Dramatic*, a distinction which I leave for herself to explain. In such readings of hers as I heard, she seemed to me to do the men and the soldiers best, such as the warlike lords in King John. I did not hear her Hotspur, which should have been good, as was her brother Jack's at school. I never heard such capital declamation as *his* Hotspur, and Alexander's Feast, when we were at Bury together, he about eighteen, and then with the profile of Alexander himself, as I have seen it on medals, etc. When *you* knew him he had lost, I suppose, his youthful freshness. His sister Fanny, I say, I did not much admire in public: but she was, and is, a noble-hearted and noble-souled woman, however wayward; and no one more loyal, not only to her own, but to her brother's friends and schoolfellows. And does she not write finely too? Sometimes in long sentences too, which spin out without entanglement from her pen . . .

206 To Fanny Kemble

F.K., 142–3   Woodbridge. April 3, 1879

... I am getting my 'Tales of the Hall' printed, and shall one day ask you, and three or four beside, whether it had better be published ... I shall not be in the least disappointed if you tell me to keep it among 'ourselves', so long as 'ourselves' are pleased; for I know well that Publication would not carry it much further abroad; and I am very well content to pay my money for the little work which I have long meditated doing. I shall have done 'my little owl'. Do you know what that means? No. Well then; my Grandfather had several parrots of different sorts and Talents: one of them ('Billy', I think) could only huff up his feathers, in what my Grandfather called an owl fashion; so when Company were praising the more gifted Parrots, he would say – 'You will hurt poor Billy's feelings – Come! Do your little owl, my dear!' – You are to imagine a handsome, hair-powdered, Gentleman doing this – and his Daughter – my Mother – telling of it.

And so it is I do my little owl ...

I looked in at the famous Lyceum Hamlet; and soon had looked, and heard, enough. It was incomparably the worst I had ever witnessed, from Covent Garden down to a Country Barn. I should scarce say this to you, if I thought you had seen it; for you told me you thought Irving might have been even a great Actor, from what you saw of his Louis XI – I think. When he got to 'Something too much of this', I called out from the Pit door where I stood, 'A good deal too much', and not long after returned to my solitary inn.

207 To Fanny Kemble

F.K., 144–6   Woodbridge. April 25, 1879

FitzGerald's eldest brother John died a month after this letter was written, and his sister Andalusia in December.

. . . My Brother keeps waiting – and hoping – for – Death: which will not come: perhaps Providence would have let it come sooner, were he not rich enough to keep a Doctor in the house, to keep him in Misery. I don't know if I told you in my last that he was ill; seized on by a Disease not uncommon to old Men – an 'internal Disorder' it is polite to say; but I shall say to you, disease of the Bladder. I had always supposed he would be found dead one good morning, as my Mother was – as I hope to be – quietly dead of the Heart which he had felt for several Years. But no; it is seen good that he shall be laid on the Rack – which he may feel the more keenly as he never suffered Pain before, and is not of a strong Nerve. I will say no more of this. The funeral Bell, which has been at work, as I never remember before, all this winter, is even now, as I write, tolling from St. Mary's Steeple . . .

Dickens' Copperfield . . . came to an end last night, because I would not let my Reader read the last Chapter. What a touch when Peggotty – the man – at last finds the lost Girl, and – throws a handkerchief over her face when he takes her to his arms – never to leave her! I maintain it – a little Shakespeare – a Cockney Shakespeare, if you will: but as distinct, if not so great, a piece of pure Genius as was born in Stratford. Oh, I am quite sure of that, had I to choose but one of them, I would choose Dickens' hundred delightful Caricatures rather than Thackeray's half-dozen terrible Photographs . . .

You may judge, I suppose, by the N.E. wind in London

what it has been hereabout. Scarce a tinge of Green on the hedgerows; scarce a Bird singing (only once the Nightingale, with broken Voice), and no flowers in the Garden but the brave old Daffydowndilly, and Hyacinth – which I scarcely knew was so hardy. I am quite pleased to find how comfortably they do in my Garden, and look so Chinese gay. Two of my dear Blackbirds have I found dead – of Cold and Hunger, I suppose; but one is even now singing – across that Funeral Bell . . .

208 To James Russell Lowell

L.F., II, 268–71   Woodbridge. June 13, 1879

Lowell was now American Minister in Spain, and made several plans to visit FitzGerald in Woodbridge, but never brought off the visit.

. . . You have told me nothing of yourself, Calderon, and Cervantes, both of whom, I suppose, are fermenting and maturing, in your head. Cowell says he will come to this coast this Summer with Don Quixote that we may read him together: so, if you should come, you will find yourself at home. I have said all I can about your taking any such trouble as coming down here only to shake hands with me, as you talk of. I never make any sort of 'hospitality' to the few who ever do come this way, but just put a fowl in the Pot (as Don Quixote's *ama* might do), and hire a Shandry-dan for a Drive, or a Boat on the river, and 'There you are', as one of Dickens' pleasant young fellows says. But I never can ask any one to come, and out of his way, to see me, a very ancient, and solitary, Bird indeed. But you know all about it. 'Parlons d'autres choses', as Sévigné says . . .

As to Gray – Ah, to think of that little Elegy inscribed among the Stars, while —, — & Co., are blazing away with their Fireworks here below. I always think that there is more Genius in most of the three volume Novels than in Gray: but by the most exquisite Taste, and indefatigable lubrication, he made of his own few thoughts, and many of other men's, a something which we all love to keep ever about us. I do not think his scarcity of work was from Design: he had but a little to say, I believe, and took his time to say it . . .

Only think of old Carlyle, who was very feeble indeed during the winter, having read through all Shakespeare to himself during these latter Spring months. So his Niece writes me. I do not hear of his doing the like by his Goethe.

I had another shot at your Hawthorne, a Man of fifty times Gray's Genius, but I could not take to him. Painfully microscopic and elaborate on dismal subjects, I still thought: but I am quite ready to admit that (as in Goethe's case) the fault lies in me. I think I have a good feeling for such things; but 'non omnia possumus, etc.'; some Screw loose. 'C'est égal'. That is a serviceable word for so much.

Now have I any more that turns up for this wonderful Letter? I should put it in, for I do think it might amuse you in Madrid. But nothing does turn up this Evening. Tea, and a Walk on our River bank, and then, what do you think? An hour's reading (to me) of a very celebrated Murder which I remember just thirty years ago at Norwich: then 'Ten minutes' Refreshment'; and then, Nicholas Nickleby! Then one Pipe: and then to Bed . . .

209 To Norton
L.F., II, 275–6 Lowestoft. September 3, 1879

Cowell, now Professor of Sanskrit at Cambridge, often joined Fitz-Gerald at Lowestoft in the summer.

. . . Now, you would like to be here along with me and my

delightful Cowell, when we read the Second Part of Don Quixote together of a morning. This we have been doing for three weeks; and shall continue to do for some ten days more, I suppose: and then he will be returning to his Cambridge. If we read very continuously we should be almost through the Book by this time: but, as you may imagine we play as well as work; some passage in the dear Book leads Cowell off into Sanskrit, Persian, or Goody Two Shoes, for all comes within the compass of his Memory and Application. Job came in to the help of Sancho a few days ago: and the Duenna Rodriguez' age brought up a story Cowell recollected of an old Lady who persisted in remaining at 50; till being told (by his Mother) that she could not be elected to a Charity because of not being 64, she said 'She thought she could manage it'; and the Professor shakes with Laughter not loud but deep, from the centre . . .

210 To Fanny Kemble

F.K., 164   Woodbridge. November 13, 1879

Benjamin Robert Haydon's picture of The Raising of Lazarus, *now in the Tate Gallery, shows a grimly haggard countenance. The 'Cromwell Hurricane', just before Cromwell's death on 3 September 1658, tore roofs off houses and blew down huge trees. 'My old man' was FitzGerald's gardener Howe.*

. . . 'Clerke Sanders' has been familiar to me these fifty years almost; since Tennyson used to repeat it, and 'Helen of Kirkconnel', at some Cambridge gathering. At that time he looked something like the Hyperion shorn of his Beams in Keats' Poem: with a Pipe in his mouth. Afterwards he got a touch, I used to say, of Haydon's Lazarus. Talking of Keats, do not forget to read Lord Houghton's

Life and Letters of him: in which you will find what you may not have guessed from his Poetry (though almost unfathomably deep in that also) the strong, masculine, Sense and Humour, etc., of the man: more akin to Shakespeare, I am tempted to think, in a perfect circle of Poetic Faculties, than any Poet since.

Well: the Leaves which hung on more bravely than ever I remember are at last whirling away in a Cromwell Hurricane – (not quite that, neither) – and my old Man says he thinks Winter has set in at last. We cannot complain hitherto. Many summer flowers held out in my Garden till a week ago, when we dug up the Beds in order for next year. So now little but the orange Marigold, which I love for its colour (Irish and Spanish) and Courage, in living all Winter through . . .

211 To Fanny Kemble

F.K., 171–2   Woodbridge. February 3, 1880

. . . I only hope my MS. is not very bad; for I am writing by Candle, before my Reader comes. He eat such a Quantity of Cheese and Cake between the Acts that he could scarce even see to read at all after; so I had to remind him that, though he was not quite sixteen, he had much exceeded the years of a Pig. Since which we get on better. I did not at all like to have my Dombey spoiled; especially Captain Cuttle, God bless him, and his Creator, now lying in Westminster Abbey. The intended Pathos is, as usual, missed: but just turn to little Dombey's Funeral, where the Acrobat in the Street suspends his performance till the Funeral has passed, and his Wife wonders if the little Acrobat in her Arms will so far outlive the little Boy in the Hearse as to wear a Ribbon through his hair, following his Father's Calling.

It is in such Side-touches, you know, that Dickens is inspired to Create like a little God Almighty . . .

212 To W. A. Wright

M.L., 235 Woodbridge. February 23, 1880

I have been to London for two days . . . I visited Mrs Kemble every day, or Night rather: and also my poor dear Donne, who is decidedly feebler than I saw him in October. The only Theatre I looked into was that of the Aquarium, on my way from Mrs Kemble: 'As You Like It' being played by Housemaids and Cooks, it seemed to me; a wonder to me, who yet had been apprised of what Shakespeare had fallen to. So that when some Hunting- horns began, and some men to sing, 'What shall he have that killed the Deer?' to the good old Tune, I was fairly overset by the reaction from detestable, and waited for no more . . .

213 To Lord Houghton

L.F., II, 285–6 Woodbridge. May 10, 1880

FitzGerald had known Monckton Milnes, now Lord Houghton, slightly ever since their Cambridge days, and thought him a 'good-natured, unaffected man'. FitzGerald was only just seven at the time of the Waterloo anniversary which he here remembers so vividly.

I think I have sent you a yearly letter of some sort or other for several years, so it has come upon me once again. I have nothing to ask of you except how you are. I should just like to know that, including 'yours' in you. Just a very few words will suffice, and I daresay you have no time for more. I have so much time that it is evident I have nothing to tell, except that I have just entered upon a military career in so far as having become much interested in the battle of

Waterloo, which I just remember a year after it was fought, when a solemn anniversary took place in a neighbouring parish where I was born, and the village carpenter came to my father to borrow a pair of Wellington boots for the lower limbs of a stuffed effigy of Buonaparte, which was hung on a gibbet, and guns and pistols were discharged at him, while we and the parson of the parish sat in a tent where we had beef and plum pudding and loyal toasts. To this hour I remember the smell of the new-cut hay in the meadow as we went in our best summer clothes to the ceremony . . .

214 To Charles Keene

L.F., II, 292   Aldeburgh. July 7, 1880

Keene, an artist best known for his contributions to Punch, *met FitzGerald in 1877 at Dunwich, which FitzGerald had taken to visiting in the summer with another new friend, the artist Edwin Edwards; Edwards and his wife and Keene all stayed several times at Little Grange with FitzGerald. In these years FitzGerald also began again to visit Aldeburgh, where he had spent holidays as a child. Thomas Churchyard was a Woodbridge friend of FitzGerald's, and a 'Sunday' painter whose work is today much sought after.*

. . . I wish you were here, not for your own sake, for it is dull enough. No Sun, no Ship, a perpetual drizzle; and to me the melancholy of another Aldbro' of years gone by. Out of that window there 'le petit' Churchyard sketched Thorpe headland under an angry Sunset of Oct. 55 which heralded a memorable Gale that washed up a poor Woman with a Babe in her arms: and old Mitford had them buried with an inscribed Stone in the old Churchyard, peopled with dead 'Mariners'; and Inscription and Stone are now gone. Yesterday I got out in a Boat, drizzly as it was: but today there is too much Sea to put off. I am to be home by the week's end, if not before. The melancholy of Slaughden last night, with the same Sloops sticking sidelong in the mud as sixty years ago! And I the venerable Remembrancer.

215 To W. W. Goodwin

M.L., 247   Woodbridge. July 26, 1880

William Watson Goodwin was Professor of Greek Literature at Harvard, and a friend of Norton's.

... I know nothing of English Schools now, but I wish the young Gentlemen did not talk slang (as I hear they do), 'Awful – Jolly – beastly', etc. – but leave that to the young Ladies, whom I *hear of* – but do not *hear* – as abounding in that way. Last week's Academy tells me of a not otherwise ill-written Novel in which the Hero talks of having '*Spooned* other womer', though he is only in love with the Lady to whom he thus confides. And when I am told how Ladies (with, I suppose, their Husbands', and Brothers', and Fathers' sanction) prostitute their faces in Photograph among Actresses, etc., in London Shops, I do not think this Country can have long to live, though it may last my time.

216 To Fanny Kemble

F.F., 200–201   Woodbridge. December 6, 1880

In 1880 FitzGerald's translation of Sophocles' Oedipus Tyrannus was privately printed, and he spent a year of more movement than was now usual with him, visiting Lowestoft twice, Aldeburgh, Merton (where Crabbe the Younger was Rector) and in November London, to see Fanny Kemble and Donne, and to have a taste of opera, but this only reminded him of the more glittering stars and audiences of his youth. 'The old Haymarket Opera', in which he remembered the soprano Giuditta Pasta

and the tenor G. B. Rubini singing and the ballerina Marie Taglioni
dancing, was the Italian Opera House, on the site now occupied by Her
Majesty's Theatre. 'The dear Little Haymarket opposite', where he had
once seen the comic actor John Liston and the singer, actress and male
impersonator Madame Vestris, was the present Haymarket Theatre.
Its remodelling by the Bancrofts in the winter of 1879–80, doing away
with the pit and confining the stage within the proscenium arch, had
provoked a first-night riot on 31 January 1880.

. . . I went to the Pit of my dear old Haymarket Opera:
remembering the very corner of the Stage where Pasta
stood when Jason's People came to tell her of his new
Marriage; and (with one hand in her Girdle – a movement
(Mrs Frere said) borrowed from Grassini) she interrupted
them with her 'Cessate – intesi!' – also when Rubini,
feathered hat in hand, began that 'Ah te, oh Cara' – and
Taglioni hovered over the Stage. There was the old
Omnibus Box too where D'Orsay flourished in ample
white Waistcoat and Wristbands: and Lady Blessington's:
and Lady Jersey's on the Pit tier: and my own Mother's,
among the lesser Stars, on the third. In place of all which I
dimly saw a small Company of less distinction in all
respects; and heard an opera (*Carmen*) on the Wagner
model: very beautiful Accompaniments to no Melody: and
all very badly sung except by Trebelli, who, excellent. I ran
out in the middle to the dear Little Haymarket opposite –
where Vestris and Liston once were: and found the
Theatre itself spoilt by being cut up into compartments
which marred the beautiful Horse-shoe shape, once set off
by the flowing pattern of Gold which used to run round
the house.

Enough of these Old Man's fancies – But – Right for all
that! . . .

217 To Thompson

L.F., II, 296–7   Woodbridge. December 15, 1880

FitzGerald was now over seventy; except for poor eyesight, his health had been excellent for much of his life, but in recent years he had been subject to bronchitis most winters, and his heart had suffered. Now he began to feel, without regret, that he had not long to live.

. . . I have myself been somewhat bothered at times for the last three months with pains and heaviness about the Heart: which I knew from a Doctor was unsettled five years ago. I shall not at all complain if it takes the usual course, only wishing to avoid *Angina*, or some such form of the Disease. My Family get on gaily enough till seventy, and then generally founder after turning the corner . . .

218 To Fanny Kemble

L.F., II, 298–9   Woodbridge. March, 1881

Two deaths of friends early in 1881 affected FitzGerald deeply: Carlyle's in February and, still more, that of James Spedding, badly hurt in an accident but still hoped for when this letter was written.

It was very, very good and kind of you to write to me about Spedding. Yes: Aldis Wright had apprised me of the matter just after it happened, he happening to be in London at the time; and but two days after the accident heard that Spedding was quite calm, and even cheerful; only anxious that Wright himself should not be kept waiting for some communication that S. had promised him! Whether to live, or to die, he will be Socrates still.

Directly that I heard from Wright, I wrote to Mowbray Donne to send me just a Post Card daily, if he or his Wife could, with but one or two words on it, 'Better', 'Less well', or whatever it might be. This morning I hear that all is going on even better than could be expected, according to Miss Spedding. But I suppose the Crisis, which you tell me of, is not yet come; and I have always a terror of that French Adage, 'Monsieur se porte mal – Monsieur se porte mieux – Monsieur est –!' Ah, you know, or you guess, the rest.

My dear old Spedding, though I have not seen him these twenty years and more, and probably should never see again; but he lives, his old Self, in my heart of hearts; and all I hear of him does but embellish the recollection of him, if it could be embellished; for he is but the same that he was from a Boy, all that is best in Heart and Head, a man that would be incredible had one not known him . . .

219 To Norton

L.F., II, 301–3   Woodbridge. March 13, 1881

Spedding died on 9 March. Carlyle's literary executor J. A. Froude was much criticized for the speed and frankness with which he published the Reminiscences *in which Carlyle accused himself over the difficulties of his marriage, and commented unflatteringly on contemporaries.*

. . . It seems almost wrong or unreasonable of me to be talking thus of myself and my little Doings, when not only Carlyle has departed from us, but one, not so illustrious in Genius, but certainly not less wise, my dear old Friend of sixty years, James Spedding: whose name you will know as connected with Lord Bacon. To re-edit his Works, which did not want any such re-edition, and to vindicate his Character which could not be cleared, did this Spedding sacrifice forty years which he might well have given to accomplish much greater things; Shakespeare, for one. But Spedding had no sort of Ambition, and liked to be kept at one long work which he knew would not glorify himself.

He was the wisest man I have known: not the less so for plenty of the Boy in him; a great sense of Humour, a Socrates in Life and in Death, which he faced with all Serenity so long as Consciousness lasted. I suppose something of him will reach America, I mean, of his Death, run over by a Cab and dying in St. George's Hospital to which he was taken, and from which he could not be removed home alive. I believe that had Carlyle been alive, and but as well as he was three months ago, he would have insisted on being carried to the Hospital to see his Friend, whom he respected as he did few others. I have just got the Carlyle Reminiscences, which will take me some little time to read, impatient as I may be to read them. What I have read is of a stuff we can scarce find in any other Autobiographer: whether his Editor Froude has done quite well in publishing them as they are, and so soon, is another matter. Carlyle's Niece thinks, not quite. She sent me a Pipe her Uncle had used, for Memorial. I had asked her for the Bowl, and an Inch of stem, of one of the Clay Pipes such as I had smoked with him under that little old Pear Tree in his Chelsea garden many an Evening. But she sent me a small Meerschaum which Lady Ashburton had given him, and which he used when from home.

220 To Laurence

L.F., II, 304   Woodbridge. March 13, 1881

... I began to think my own Eyes, which were blazed away by Paraffin some dozen years ago, were going out of me just before Christmas. So for the two dreary months which followed I could scarce read or write. And as yet I am obliged to use them tenderly: only too glad to find that they are better; and not quite going (as I hope) yet. I think they will light me out of this world with care. On March 31

I shall enter on my seventy-third year: and none of my Family reaches over seventy-five.

When I was in London I was all but tempted to jump into a Cab and just knock at Carlyle's door, and ask after him, and give my card, and – run away . . .

The cold wind will not leave us, and my Crocuses do not like it. Still I manage to sit on one of those Benches you may remember under the lee side of the hedge, and still my seventy-third year approaches.

221 To Fanny Kemble

L.F., II, 305–7   Woodbridge. March 20, 1881

I have let the Full Moon pass because I thought you had written to me so lately, and so kindly, about our lost Spedding, that I would not call on you so soon again. Of him I will say nothing except that his Death has made me recall very many passages in his Life in which I was partly concerned. In particular, staying at his Cumberland Home along with Tennyson in the May of 1835. 'Voilà bien longtemps de ça!' His Father and Mother were both alive: he, a wise man, who mounted his Cob after Breakfast and was at his Farm till Dinner at two; then away again till Tea: after which he sat reading by a shaded lamp: saying very little, but always courteous and quite content with any company his Son might bring to the house, so long as they let him go his way: which indeed he would have gone whether they let him or no. But he had seen enough of Poets not to like them or their Trade: Shelley, for a time living among the Lakes: Coleridge at Southey's (whom perhaps he had a respect for – Southey I mean); and Wordsworth whom I do not think he valued. He was rather jealous of 'Jem', who might have done available service in the world, he thought, giving himself up to such

Dreamers; and sitting up with Tennyson conning over the Morte d'Arthur, Lord of Burleigh, and other things which helped to make up the two volumes of 1842. So I always associate that Arthur Idyll with Basanthwaite Lake, under Skiddaw. Mrs. Spedding was a sensible, motherly Lady, with whom I used to play Chess of a Night. And there was an old Friend of hers, Miss Bristowe, who always reminded me of Miss La Creevy if you know of such a Person in Nickleby.

At the end of May we went to lodge for a week at Windermere, where Wordsworth's new volume of Yarrow Revisited reached us. W. was then at his home: but Tennyson would not go to visit him: and of course I did not: nor even saw him.

You have, I suppose, the Carlyle Reminiscences: of which I will say nothing except that much as we outsiders gain by them, I think that, on the whole, they had better have been kept unpublished, for some while at least.

222 To Fanny Kemble

L.F., II, 310–12   Woodbridge. April, 1881

FitzGerald's comments on the dangers of leaving one's literary executor to decide which of one's privately recorded opinions of one's contemporaries should be published after one's death seem ironical when the fracas caused by the publication of his own comments on Mrs Browning (see Letter 121) is remembered.

Somewhat before my usual time, you see; but Easter comes, and I shall be glad to hear if you keep it in London, or elsewhere. Elsewhere there has been no inducement to go until To-day: when the Wind though yet East has turned to the Southern side of it; one can walk without any wrapper; and I dare to fancy we have turned the corner of

Winter at last . . . As for the Birds, I have nothing but a Robin who seems rather pleased when I sit down on a Bench under an old Ivied Pollard, where I suppose he has a Nest, poor little Fellow. But we have terrible Superstitions about him here; no less than that he always kills his Parents if he can: my young Reader is quite determined on this head: and there lately has been a Paper in some Magazine to the same effect.

My dear old Spedding sent me back to old Wordsworth too, who sings (his best songs I think) about the Mountains and Lakes they were both associated with: and with a quiet feeling he sings that somehow comes home to me more now than ever it did before.

As to Carlyle, I thought on my first reading that he must have been égaré at the time of writing . . . I must think Carlyle's judgments mostly, or mainly, true; but that he must have 'lost his head' if not when he recorded them, yet when he left them in any one's hands to decide on their publication. Especially when not about Public Men, but about their Families. It is slaying the Innocent with the Guilty. But of all this you have doubtless heard in London more than enough. 'Pauvre et triste Humanité!' One's heart opens again to him at the last: sitting alone in the middle of her Room. 'I want to die'. 'I want – a Mother'. 'Ah mamma Letizia!' Napoleon is said to have murmured as he lay. By way of pendant to this recurs to me the story that when Ducis was wretched his Mother would lay his head on her Bosom – 'Ah, mon homme! mon pauvre homme!' . . .

And now I have written more than enough for yourself and me: whose Eyes may be the worse for it to-morrow. I still go about in Blue Glasses, and flinch from Lamp and Candle . . .

223 To Fanny Kemble

F.K., 219–20   Woodbridge. April, 1881

FitzGerald's reference to Mrs Kemble hearing of the cuckoo 'at Mr. W. Shakespeare's' was because she was staying at Leamington, within reach of Stratford-upon-Avon.

... It has been what we call down here 'smurring' rather than raining, all day long: and I think that Flower and Herb already show their gratitude. My Blackbird (I think it is the same I have tried to keep alive during the Winter) seems also to have 'wetted his Whistle', and what they call the 'Cuckoo's mate', with a rather harsh scissor note, announces that his Partner may be on the wing to these Latitudes. You will hear of him at Mr. W. Shakespeare's, it may be. There must be Violets, white and blue, somewhere about where he lies. I think. They are generally found in a Churchyard, where also (the Hunters used to say) a Hare: for the same reason of comparative security, I suppose ...

224 To Fanny Kemble

L.F., II, 320–21   Woodbridge. January, 1882

I see my poor little Aconites – 'New Year's Gifts' – still surviving in the Garden-plot before my window: 'still surviving', I say, because of their having been out for near a month agone. I believe that Messrs. Daffodil, Crocus and Snowdrop are putting in appearance above ground, but (old Coward) I have not put my own old Nose out of doors to look for them. I read (Eyes permitting) the Correspondence between Goethe and Schiller (translated) from 1798 to 1806, extremely interesting to me, though I do not understand, and generally skip, the more purely Aesthetic

Parts: which is the Part of Hamlet, I suppose. But in other respects, two such men so freely discussing together their own, and each other's, works interest me greatly. At night, we have the Fortunes of Nigel; a little of it, and not every night: for the reason that I do not wish to eat my Cake too soon. The last night but one I sent my Reader to see Macbeth played by a little Shakespearian company at a Lecture Hall here. He brought me one new Reading; suggested, I doubt not by himself, from a remembrance of Macbeth's tyrannical ways: 'Hang out our *Gallows* on the outward walls'. Nevertheless, the Boy took great Interest in the Play, and I like to encourage him in Shakespeare rather than in the Negro Melodists.

225 To Fanny Kemble
F.K., 244–6   Aldeburgh. August, 1882

J. A. Froude's Thomas Carlyle: a History of the First Forty Years of His Life *was published in 1882.*

I have let the Full Moon go by, and very well she looked, too – over the Sea by which I am now staying. Not at Lowestoft: but at the old extinguished Borough of Alde-burgh, to which – as to other 'premiers Amours', I revert – where more than sixty years ago I first saw, and first felt, the Sea – where I have lodged in half the houses since; and where I have a sort of traditional acquaintance with half the population. 'Clare Cottage' is where I write from; two little rooms – enough for me – a poor civil Woman pleased to have me in them – oh, yes, – and a little spare Bedroom in which I stow a poor Clerk, with his Legs out of the window from his bed – like a Heron's from his nest – but rather more horizontally. We dash about in Boats whether Sail or Oar – to which latter I leave him for his own good

Exercise. Poor fellow, he would have liked to tug at that, or rough-ride a horse, from Boyhood: but must be made Clerk in a London Lawyer's Office: and so I am glad to get him down for a Holyday when he can get one, poor Fellow!

The Carlyle 'Reminiscences' had long indisposed me from taking up the Biography. But when I began, and as I went on with that, I found it one of the most interesting of Books: and the result is that I not only admire and respect Carlyle more than ever I did: but even love him, which I never thought of before. For he loved his Family, as well as for so long helped to maintain them out of very slender earnings of his own; and, so far as these two Volumes show me, he loved his Wife also, while he put her to the work which he had been used to see his own Mother and Sisters fulfil, and which was suitable to the way of Life which he had been used to. His indifference to her sufferings seems to me rather because of Blindness than Neglect; and I think his Biographer has been even a little too hard upon him on the score of Selfish disregard of her. Indeed Mr Norton wrote to me that he looked on Froude as something of an Iago toward his Hero in respect of all he has done for him. The publication of the Reminiscences is indeed a mystery to me: for I should have thought that, even in a mercantile point of view, it would indispose others, as me it did, to the Biography. But Iago must have bungled in his work so far as I, for one, am concerned, if the result is such as I find it – or unless I am very obtuse indeed . . .

226 To Fanny Kemble

L.F., II, 335   Woodbridge. October 17, 1882

. . . It seems to me (but I believe it seems so every year) that our trees keep their leaves very long; I suppose, because of no severe frosts or winds up to this time. And my garden still shows some Geranium, Salvia, Nasturtium, Great Convolvulus, and that grand African Marigold whose Colour is so comfortable to us Spanish-like Paddies. I have also a dear Oleander which even now has a score of blossoms on it, and touches the top of my little Greenhouse; having been sent me when 'haut comme ça' as Marquis Somebody used to say in the days of Louis XIV. Don't you love the Oleander? So clean in its leaves and stem, as so beautiful in its flower; loving to stand in water which it drinks up so fast. I rather worship mine.

227 To Fanny Kemble

F.K., 252–3   Woodbridge. November, 1882

Mary Lynn, with whom FitzGerald fell in love when he was fifteen and they were both on holiday in Aldeburgh, never married. Of all the women who touched, or may have touched, FitzGerald's heart, this pleasant unfussy old lady sounds like the one who might have suited him best as a wife. Marjorie Fleming, who died when she was eight, was a precocious poet and diarist. Dr John Brown, the Edinburgh physician, described her in an essay.

. . . I have been again – twice or thrice – to Aldeburgh, when my contemporary old Beauty Mary Lynn was staying there; and pleasant Evenings enough we had, talking of other days, and she reading to me some of her Mudie Books, finishing with a nice little Supper, and some hot grog (for me) which I carried back to the fire, and *set on the carpet.* She read me (for one thing) 'Marjorie Fleming' from a Volume of Dr. Brown's Papers – read it as well as she could for laughing – 'idiotically', she said – but all the better to my mind. She had been very dismal all day, she said. Pray get some one to read you 'Marjorie' – which I say, because (as I found) it agrees with one best in that way. If only for dear Sir Walter's sake, who doated on the Child; and would not let his Twelfth Night be celebrated till she came through the Snow in a Sedan Chair, where (once in the warm Hall) he called all his Company down to see her nestling before he carried her upstairs in his arms. A very pretty picture . . .

228 To Laurence

L.F., II, 337–8   Woodbridge. November 8, 1882

FitzGerald had revisited Cambridge in the summer of 1881, for the first time in many years, which had revived memories of his undergraduate days, and in 1882 he had his Cambridge dialogue Euphranor *privately reprinted. A friendship dating from even before his Cambridge days ended when Donne, who had long been ill, died in June 1882.*

. . . My days and years go on one so like another: I see and hear no new thing or person; and to tell you that I go for a month or a week to our barren coast, which is all the travel I have to tell of, you can imagine all that as easily as my stay at home, with the old Pictures about me, and often the old Books to read. I went indeed to London last February for the sole purpose of seeing our Donne: and glad I am to have done so as I heard it gave him a little pleasure. That is a closed Book now. His Death was not unexpected, and even not to be deprecated, as you know; but I certainly never remember a year of such havock among my friends as this: if not by Death itself, by Death's preliminary work and warning . . . I wonder to find myself no worse dealt with than by Bronchitis, bad enough, which came upon me last Christmas, hung upon me all Spring, Summer, and Autumn; and though comparatively dormant for the last three wet weeks (perhaps from repeated doses of Sea Air) gives occasional Signs that it is not dead, but, on the contrary, will revive with Winter. Let me hear at least how you have been, and how are; I shall not grudge your being all well . . .

229 To Pollock
L.F., II, 342–3   Woodbridge. (?) Easter, 1883

C. E. Norton's edition of The Correspondence of Thomas Carlyle and Ralph Waldo Emerson *was published in 1883. Tennyson and Richard Monckton Milnes, now Lord Houghton, were both still alive when this edition containing Carlyle's descriptions of them appeared.*

. . . Professor Norton sent me his Carlyle-Emerson – all to the credit of all parties, I think. I must tell the Professor that in my opinion he should have omitted some personal observations which are all fair in a private letter; as about Tennyson being of a 'gloomy' turn (which you know is not so), Thackeray's 'enormous appetite' ditto; and such mention of Richard Milnes as a 'Robin Redbreast', etc.; which may be less untrue, though not more proper to be published of a clever, useful, and amiable man, now living.

230 To Hallam Tennyson
H. Tennyson, *Alfred Lord Tennyson*, II, 276   April 19,
1883

The blank verse line mentioned in this letter was an old joke between FitzGerald and Tennyson, who called it 'the weakest line ever enunciated' when FitzGerald brought it out unintentionally on one of the evenings he shared with Tennyson in his Charlotte Street London lodgings in their youth. 'The paltry poet' was a nickname for Tennyson that FitzGerald often used.

. . . which reminds me of a crow . . . I have to pick with your father. For Wright had heard from someone that he, the Laureate, had added to his wreath one of the very grandest lines in all blank verse,

'A Mister Wilkinson, a clergyman' –

of which I was the author while speaking of my brother-in-law, but which the paltry poet took up as it fell from my inspired lips and has adopted for his own.

You see that bronchitis, ever flourishing his dart over me, fails to make me graver, that is at least while referring to my dear old comrade, whom I should call 'master', and with whom (in spite, perhaps *because*, of his being rather a gloomy soul sometimes, as Carlyle wrote to Emerson) I always did talk more nonsense than to anyone, I believe . . .

231 To Fanny Kemble
F.K., 260   Woodbridge. May, 1883

. . . At last some feeling of Spring – a month before Midsummer. And next week I am expecting my grave Friend Charles Keene of Punch, to come here for a week – bringing with him his Bagpipes, and an ancient Viol, and a Book of Strathspeys and Madrigals; and our Archdeacon will come to meet him, and to talk over ancient Music and Books: and we shall all three drive out past the green hedges, and heaths with their furze in blossom – and I wish – yes, I do – that you were of the Party . . .

232 To Laurence
L.F., II, 346–7   Woodbridge. June 12, 1883

This is FitzGerald's last letter. Next day he went to stay with Crabbe at Merton, and died in his sleep on the night of his arrival.

It is very kind of you to remember one who does so little to remind you of himself . . . If I do not write, it is because I have absolutely nothing to tell you that you have not known for the last twenty years. Here I live still, reading, and being read to, part of my time: walking abroad three or four times a day, or night, in spite of wakening a Bronchitis, which has lodged like the household 'Brownie' within; pottering about my Garden (as I have just been doing) and snipping off dead Roses like Miss Tox; and now and then a visit to the neighbouring Seaside, and a splash to Sea in one of the Boats. I never see a new Picture, nor hear a note of Music except when I drum out some old Tune in Winter on an Organ, which might almost be carried about the Streets with a handle to turn, and a Monkey on the top of it. So I go on, living a life far too comfortable as compared with that of better, and wiser men: but ever expecting a reverse in health such as my seventy-five years are subject to . . .

Tomorrow I am going (for my one annual Visit) to G. Crabbe's, where I am to meet his Sisters, and talk over old Bredfield Vicarage days. Two of my eight Nieces are now with me here in my house, for a two months' visit, I suppose and hope. And I think this is all I have to tell you of

Yours ever sincerely
E.F.G.

Index